THE PREFECTS AND PROVINCIAL FRANCE

by the same author
INTRODUCTION TO
FRENCH LOCAL GOVERNMENT

The Prefects
and
Provincial France

BRIAN CHAPMAN
M.A., D.PHIL.
Lecturer in Government
University of Manchester

George Allen & Unwin Ltd
RUSKIN HOUSE · MUSEUM STREET · LONDON

FIRST PUBLISHED IN 1955

This book is copyright under the Berne Convention. Apart from any fair dealing for the purposes of private study, research, criticism or review, as permitted under the Copyright Act 1911, *no portion may be reproduced by any process without written permission. Enquiry should be made to the publisher.*

© *George Allen & Unwin*

PRINTED IN GREAT BRITAIN
in 12 *point Fournier type*
BY SIMSON SHAND LTD
LONDON, HERTFORD AND HARLOW

To
J.M.C.

Introduction

THIS BOOK is doubly presumptuous. It is written by an Englishman about an institution peculiarly French, and by a layman about problems comprehensible only within a framework of administrative law. My excuse is that the subject is one of first-rate importance, and that no attempt has yet been made by any French scholar to treat it as a whole. There are text books on administrative law by eminent jurists, there are some memoires and biographies of past and present members of the Prefectoral Corps, and there are some detailed technical studies (mainly legal theses) on specific aspects of the work of Prefectures. This material is, however, for the most part either fragmentary or legalistic. No clear picture of the Prefectoral Corps at work, with its administrative and political preoccupations, and its clashes of interests and personalities, emerges even from a detailed examination of the published material. This has had to be supplemented by interviews and discussions with men belonging to or connected with the Corps.

This study does not claim to be authoritative. However, until someone who has actively participated in prefectoral administration distils for the public the essence of a prefectoral career, we shall be forced to rely on the observations of outsiders and on technical essays on minor points.

This book is divided into five chapters each dealing with a particular aspect of prefectoral administration. The first chapter is a resumé of the part the Corps has played in history; the second is a general background to the political and administrative structure within which the Corps works today. The remaining three chapters are concerned with the *chefs de cabinet*, the Sub Prefects and the Prefects. I have not given any technical exposition of French administrative law; this would have made the study too long, and my main concern has been to study the Corps in the general context of French government. The Corps also has a wider political importance, and it is at times necessary to refer to this. Some of these digressions may be a little illogical, but I believe they are necessary for a full appreciation of what the Prefectoral Corps means in France.

It will be evident how much I am indebted to the many members of the Prefectoral Corps, the scholars, the politicians, and the officials of other state services who devoted time and attention to providing me with information. Unfortunately it would be unfair as well as invidious to single out those to whom I owe a special debt. Mr D. N. Chester, Warden of Nuffield College, Oxford, helped me greatly with his acute criticism and advice. I am most indebted to two other people: Professor W. J. M. Mackenzie on whose judgement, encouragement and friendship I have so often relied; and my wife who has been my loyal collaborator and constant companion.

Manchester B.C.
January, 1954

Contents

INTRODUCTION — page 7

I THE PREFECTORAL CORPS IN HISTORY — 11
1. *The Ancien Régime*
2. *The Napoleonic Prefects*
3. *Agents of the Government*
4. *The Third Republic*
5. *Vichy and the Liberation*

II THE ADMINISTRATIVE BACKGROUND — 65
1. *The Theory of Administration*
2. *The Ministries*
3. *The Prefect's Position*
4. *The Local Authorities*
5. *The Officials*
6. *Prefectoral Administration*

III THE CHEF DE CABINET — 76
1. *Recruitment*
2. *The Cabinet*
3. *The Role of the Chef de Cabinet*

IV THE SUB PREFECT — 91
1. *Posts and Numbers*
2. *The Sub Prefect in the Arrondissement*
3. *The Secretary General of the Prefecture*
4. *The Secretary General of Police*

V THE PREFECT — 144
1. *Numbers and Status*
2. *Appointment*
3. *The Prefect's Powers*
4. *The Prefect's Government*
5. *Public Opinion and the Prefect*

APPENDIX A — 234
APPENDIX B — 235
BIBLIOGRAPHY — 239
INDEX — 243

CHAPTER ONE

The Prefectoral Corps in History

THE PREFECTORAL CORPS has been so intimately connected with French internal politics since its foundation in 1800, that a proper 'history' of the Corps would run into several volumes.

There are, however, significant periods in the life of the Corps which have left behind a substantial body of prefectoral mythology. The purpose of this preliminary chapter is to bring forward those elements in prefectoral history which (at the present day) still condition the behaviour of Prefects, and, more particularly, public opinion about prefects.

Throughout the nineteenth century the Prefectoral Corps was a political organization, and to some extent this is still so. Each new political régime endowed the Corps with some of its own characteristics. For the sake of clarity this chapter is divided into five parts: the system under the *ancien régime*, Napoleon's reforms and the creation of the Prefectoral Corps (1800–1815), the life of the Prefects under the autocratic governments of the nineteenth century (1816–1879), the Third Republic (1879–1940), the Corps during the Vichy régime and the Liberation (1940–1950).

1. *The Ancien Régime*

The predecessors of the Prefects were the civil administrators of the provinces of France, the Intendants, whose official title was *intendants de justice, police, et finances, et commissaires départis dans les généralités du Royaume pour l'exécution des ordres du Roi*.[1] They were nominated by the King usually from the ranks of the

[1] Fr. Olivier-Martin: *Précis d'Histoire du Droit français*. Paris, 1945. p. 350–1.

King's *maîtres des requêtes* and were responsible only to him. They had no security of tenure in office, their warrants of appointment were individual and differed one from the other, they were paid directly from the royal Exchequer, but they were lodged at the expense of the province in which they served.

The office of the Intendant took shape under Louis XIII as part of Richelieu's policy of centralization; it was temporarily abolished in 1648 at the instigation of the *parlement* of Paris, but was re-introduced in 1654. Thereafter, Intendants gradually absorbed many functions previously shared between various traditional office holders, as well as those previously performed by itinerant royal inspectors.

At the time of the French Revolution in 1789 there were thirty-two Intendants serving in France, and some others in the colonies overseas.[1] In France their area of government—the *généralité*—covered four or five modern Departments, and it is probably more accurate to consider the Intendant as the forerunner of the regional Prefect than of the Prefect. A *généralité* was normally subdivided into several small areas to which were appointed *sub délégués:* these officials, and the areas in which they served, have much in common with the present Sub Prefects and the *arrondissements*.

But comparison with modern France is unreal, for the *généralités* of the Intendants frequently included more ancient areas of government, and traditional administrative and judicial bodies. The *généralité* of Gascogne and Béarn, for instance, included three *parlements*. Further, the powers of the Intendants were wider than those of the modern Prefect, and were to a large extent uncodified.

An Intendant had the power to issue *ordonnances* throughout the *généralité* for purposes of administration and for the execution of the laws. He had authority to issue orders to the police authorities in his area—Mayors, Consuls, Echevins, and Jurats, and he attended the sessions of the *états provinciaux*. He also sat

[1] E. Perrot: *Les institutions publiques et privées de l'Ancienne France jusqu'en 1789*. Paris, 1935. p. 493.

with the principal judicial body in the province, the *parlement*, and enforced royal edicts and the orders of the Chancellor of France. He was responsible for repressing certain crimes, with authority to hang criminals or send them to the royal galleys. He was the supreme financial authority in the province, responsible for drawing up the tax schedules and for auditing the Treasurer's accounts.

His influence extended into many other fields—trade, agriculture, communications, public works, and the development of local industry. He sometimes took the field in military expeditions, and was responsible for recruiting, transporting and victualling troops. In several cases he acted as the secular arm of the militant Church against Protestants and heretics.[1]

In all, the influence of the Intendant depended to a great extent upon his personality, and it was limited only by the trust of the King. In the ancient formula, he was *le Roi présent dans la province*.[2]

The French Revolution was in part a reaction against the centralization of power in the hands of the King and his agents. The Constituent Assembly of 1789 therefore undertook, as part of its reform of the constitutional framework of the Kingdom, to establish a system of local government based on more democratic principles. The office of Intendant was abolished, but it was found that this merely gave rise to pressure for self-government in the old provinces. Such large territorial areas fortified by powerful local assemblies would gravely threaten the supremacy of the Assembly; indeed, the claims of some provinces were so extravagant that they would have amounted to transforming France into a federation.[3]

[1] The crusade against the Camisards earned for the Intendant of Languedoc, Lamoignon de Basville, the title of 'Tyrant of Languedoc'.

[2] For an able and sympathetic study of an Intendant see E. Pelletier: *L'Intendant Mégret d'Etigny*. Imprimerie préfectorale. Toulouse 1951. M. Pelletier as Prefect of the Haute Garonne and IGAME of the 5th Region is the direct administrative successor of Mégret d'Etigny.

[3] Talleyrand wrote, for instance, 'les pays d'états ne trouvaient plus dans leurs contrats de réunion à la France, que les moyens d'opposition á toutes les

The discussions in the Constituent Assembly went far to confirm these fears, for the representatives of the provinces, and the provincial assemblies themselves, demanded an extreme form of self-government, their own institutions, and the maintenance of individual privileges and rights. But if there was one benefit which the *ancien régime* had bestowed on France, it was her unity. The pretensions of the provinces therefore were hotly contested both by those concerned with the integrity of the French State, and by those inspired by the abstract principles of government of the eighteenth century philosophers.

The supporters of the provinces were defeated, and federalism was outlawed as a crime. On August 11, 1789, the Constituent Assembly ruled that 'a national constitution and public liberty are more advantageous to the provinces than the privileges which some of them now enjoy, and whose sacrifice is now necessary for the intimate union of all parts of the Empire. It is therefore decreed that all the particular privileges of the provinces, principalities, cities, corps, and communities, be they financial advantages or of any other kind, are henceforth abolished, and are merged in the common law of all the French.'

This motion was followed by the creation of a committee of eight, comprising four Parisians and four provincials, whose task was to draw up an alternative territorial basis of local government. This committee first met on September 13, 1789, and its dominant members were Thouret and Siéyès. The committee reported on September 29, and on November 11 its report was discussed. The committee proposed to divide France into between seventy-five and eighty-five Departments,[1] taking cognisance of historical and geographical affinities; each Department should be further

[1] The anglicized version of the French *département* will be used throughout this book. When there is any possibility of ambiguity, e.g. 'a government department', the word 'division' will be used to describe the bureaucratic sub-division.

---

mesures générales que le gouvernement proposait'. He cited Brittany as an extreme example. *Mémoires du Prince de Talleyrand:* edited by the Duc de Broglie. Paris 1891. Vol. I, p. 110.

divided into districts, varying in number from Department to Department, and these districts should have some affinity with the old *pays*.

The Constituent Assembly then set up a boundary committee to draw up a list of the Departments and districts, and to define their borders. By December 22, 1789, this committee, although harassed by several conflicting projects, presented a new administrative map of France, containing eighty-three Departments.[1] In order to emphasize the break with the past the names of these Departments were not taken from the principal town or from the provinces, but from prominent natural features, such as rivers (Department of the Isère (Grenoble)), mountains (Department of the Jura (Lons-le-Saunier)), or coastal areas (Department of Côtes-du-Nord (St. Brieuc)).

A further law of January 8, 1790, described the new administrative machinery to be set up in the Departments and the districts. Each Department was to have an elected assembly of thirty-six councillors, which nominated from its own number an executive council of eight members. The executive council was responsible for administration, tax assessments, tax-collection, and for preparing the departmental budget. Departmental administration was subject to central inspection by itinerant officers of the King. An elected *procureur général syndic* could attend the meetings of the departmental assembly and of the executive council with a right to be heard; his principal duty was to supervise the way decisions were carried out.

Each district had an organization similar to that of the Department, but its powers were more restricted than those of the departmental bodies.

It soon became apparent that this rapid decentralization was too much for the integrity and ability of local people. In the absence of strong central direction, the departmental assemblies soon slipped into particularism and bland ignorance of national

[1] For a map showing these administrative divisions superimposed on the old provinces, see J. Godechot, *Les Institutions de la France sous la Révolution et l'Empire*. Paris, 1951. p. 96.

affairs. Some executive councils became the instruments of local interests, and others were very corrupt. After the dissolution of the Monarchy and the execution of the King in 1791, the Revolution entered a violent stage in which departmental assemblies became instruments of the various political factions; royalists, girondists and moderates used their influence to foment discontent against the Jacobins, and the Jacobins retaliated with revolutionary violence. The revolutionary Assembly came to rely more and more upon its own *commissaires*, sent out from Paris to stifle anti-revolutionary movements in the provinces. These *commissaires* appointed by the Committee of Public Safety assumed in the name of the people dictatorial powers in the areas to which they were sent on mission. Fouché, as a *commissaire*, could even contemplate the total destruction of Lyons, the second largest city of France.

The wars and uprisings between 1791 and 1799 brought confusion, anarchy and corruption to the Departments. Brigandage was rife, deserters from the army thronged the highways, and monarchist uprisings swept the West. The Directory, after 1795, had only a feeble grasp on the situation; it had no real knowledge of the country's resources, no machinery for acting promptly and simultaneously throughout the country, and no effective instruments for enforcing its orders.[1]

This confusion and inefficiency resulted in Napoleon's coup d'état of 1799, and his appointment as First Consul. It created the greatest suspicion of all local elected authorities. Experience had shown that such bodies could not be relied upon either to administer themselves efficiently or to assist the Government in times of crisis. They bred inefficiency, corruption, tyranny, and anti-state activities. If they were efficient they defied the Government, if they were inefficient they endangered the safety of the State.

---

[1] Madelin terms these local administrations 'ces flasques administrations', which were uncontrolled except by the 'tyrannie haletante' of Paris. Madelin: *Histoire générale du consulat et de l'Empire*. Vol. III. *De Brumaire à Marengo*. Paris, 1937. p. 142.

2. *The Napoleonic Prefects* 1800-1815

The grave conditions of the country could not but cause concern to Napoleon on his accession to power. His military victories had endowed him with the prestige of saviour of the country; he defined his objects as 'to make the Republic dear to its citizens, respected by foreigners, feared by its enemies'. For this purpose a contented well-ordered country was the first essential. His immediate collaborators were therefore instructed to devise a system of local administration which would stem the tendency towards disintegration and prevent its recurrence.

As in many of his other reforms, Napoleon turned to the past for a model. In local government he took the precedent of the Intendants. Through them the pre-revolutionary Government had been able to enforce its will, and the Government controlled its agents by making them subject to instant dismissal when they ceased to keep the trust of the Crown. The powers of the Intendants had, however, been too great, sometimes allowing them to act the petty prince unknown to, or uncontrolled by, the Government. Furthermore, the simple re-creation of the Intendants would have raised public doubts about Napoleon's attitude to the Revolution, for it had been one of the most typical institutions of the ancien régime.

Napoleon needed an organization which would, first, be a real and effective authority in all local affairs; and, second, which would remain an instrument completely under his own control. He needed one official, appointed by himself and subject to instant recall, to reside in each Department. The official was to perform the First Consul's will; when no orders were given he was to interpret by his own sense of the nation's interests, what Napoleon would wish in the circumstances. The same official had to be more than an administrator; he had to govern in Napoleon's name. He had to have unrivalled local prestige, and a personal authority defined later by Napoleon as that of an *'empereur au petit pied'*.

Napoleon's solution was contained in the law of February 17,

1800, 'concerning the division of the Territory of the Republic, and of its Administration'. It was to fill in the details of local government not covered in the new Constitution. Casting back into history, Consul Lebrun had discovered the Roman Prefect, and on his recommendation, Napoleon adopted this new title for his supreme departmental representative.[1]

The general organization of the country was laid down in the 'short and obscure' Constitution drawn up on Napoleon's instruction in 1799 after his coup d'état by two legislative commissions directed by Siéyès, Daunou and Napoleon himself. A detailed analysis of this Constitution would obviously transcend the limits of this study, but two points need emphasis. The first is that in the new hierarchy of government, the supreme power was vested in the First Consul, Napoleon, who was seconded by the two other Consuls, Lebrun and Cambacérès. The Ministers of the various departments were appointed individually to their posts, held no joint meetings. and were subordinate and responsible to the First Consul. Two of these Ministers were partly responsible

---

[1] Madelin says about this name 'le mot sonna antique; Siéyès l'avait prononcé; Bonaparte l'adopta, peut-être parce que, chez lui, le roman était toujours porté à ressusciter les souvenirs des bords du Tibre; sous l'Empire de Rome de l'Illyrie à l'Afrique, des Gaules aux provinces d'Asie, il y avait eu des préfets. Le mot—*praefectus*—l'homme placé à la tête—était d'ailleurs caractéristique. Au fond si l'on se rappelle quel était le pouvoir des Intendants de l'ancien régime, on est amené à constater qu'on les ressuscitait plus encore que les préfets de Dioclétien; mais le mot Intendant sonnait subalterne; préfet avait quelque chose de plus fier et de plus impérieux; et puis en réinstituant bien des choses de l'ancien régime, le Premier Consul entendait sauver les apparences et, ressuscitant les choses, ne pas ressusciter les mots'. Op. cit. p. 144.

However, more recent research seems to show that it was Consul Lebrun and not Siéyès who first suggested the term to Bonaparte: see M. Dupuy, *La fonction préfectorale sous le Consulat et l'Empire*. Revue Administrative, January 1950. There had also been *préfets nationaux* in Switzerland and *préfets consulaires* in the Rome Republic under the constitutions of 1796–99, and they would also serve as a guide, for their functions had something in common with the Prefects Napoleon created in France. Godechot: op. cit. p. 476.

for internal affairs; the Minister of the Interior, Lucien Bonaparte, who was responsible for all internal affairs except the police, and the Minister of Police, Fouché, whose network of police agents and officials covered the entire country, and at one time included the Gendarmerie. This meant that the Prefects when they were appointed had to deal with two Ministers. During the following century there were occasions when this pattern was followed; at other times the Minister of the Interior controlled the police as well. From the Third Republic onwards the Minister of the Interior has always maintained a monopoly over internal affairs.

The second point in the Constitution was that the ninety-eight Departments which existed after the conquests of the Revolution, were retained as the main basis of administrative organization. A new area of administration was also created to act as the subdivision of the Department, the *arrondissement*, which was based partly on the districts of 1790, but more exactly on the existing judicial areas of the *tribunaux de police correctionnelle*. With the newly strengthened municipalities, this made three active areas of local administration, the Communes, the *arrondissements*, the Departments. In each of these one man alone was responsible for administration and execution; the Prefect in the Department, the Sub Prefect in the *arrondissement*, the Mayor in the Commune.

The Commune was the basic area of administration, the lowest echelon in the territorial hierarchy. The Mayor was responsible for communal administration, for carrying out the instructions of the Prefect and Sub Prefect, and for making and enforcing local police regulations. There was a *conseil municipal* which had very few powers, and which could not interfere with administration. In Communes with under 5,000 inhabitants the Mayor was appointed by the Prefect; in larger Communes the Mayor was appointed by the Government on the advice of the Prefect. The Mayor could be suspended by the Prefect and dismissed by the Government.

There were on an average four *arrondissements* to a Department; the executive of an *arrondissement* was the Sub Prefect who was a member of the Prefectoral Corps, was appointed by the

Government, and was the agent in his area of the Prefect. It was through him that the Prefect was supposed to 'procure' action from the municipalities. The Sub Prefects distinguished themselves chiefly in the fields of public assistance, police and highways. They were supported by a nominated *conseil d'arrondissement*, whose principal function was to meet every year to divide up the burden of direct taxation between the Communes in the area.

The Department was the largest area of local government. The salient article of the law on local organization was terse: 'the Prefect alone is responsible for its administration'. (Article three.) This allowed no other state or local official to claim precedence or even equality. The Prefect had no security of tenure in office but was appointed and removable by Napoleon.

He reigned over his Department from the Prefecture, a building provided by the Department, which was both the administrative headquarters and the Prefect's official residence. For administrative assistance he had at his elbow the Secretary General of the Prefecture, a member of the Prefectoral Corps especially charged with supervising administrative work. This work was done by bureaux in the Prefecture, and their number varied from Department to Department. In the Côtes-du-Nord there were five bureaux employing thirty-two officials, while at Dijon there were only two bureaux with twenty officials. The Secretary General replaced the Prefect of right when the Prefect was absent from the Prefecture, but apart from the official signature of documents this was virtually his only formal power. Should the Prefect die, however, it was the senior *conseiller de préfecture* who temporarily took charge.

The Prefect was assisted in the Department by two councils, the *conseil général* and the *conseil de préfecture*.

The *conseil général* was composed of sixteen, twenty or twenty-four councillors, according to the size of the Department, and they were chosen from a list by the Government. They were chosen from amongst the notables of the Department; many were men who had previously served as administrators in the Department under the Revolution, but there was a substantial number of large land owners and royalists. The *conseil général* met once a year for a maximum of two weeks. Its powers were limited; they were concerned with dividing up the burden of taxation between the *arrondissements* and with claims for reductions of tax burdens by *arrondissements*. The *conseil général* also voted additional taxes for use by the Department and heard the Prefect's report upon the employment of such taxes in the previous year. They could also pass general motions, but these had no binding effect.

In the first years the *conseils généraux* were treated with great respect, and Prefects were anxious to obtain the services of the best men. But gradually the Prefects followed Napoleon's declining interest in elected bodies and adopted a summary attitude to them, so that from 1806 onwards the *conseils généraux* had very little significance.

The *conseil de préfecture*, the other body in the Department, fared little better. It was essentially an administrative tribunal to judge litigation arising between the public and the Administration; tax appeals by ordinary citizens, claims for damages caused by administrative acts and compensation claims for expropriation. It met rarely, and was presided over by the Prefect. The councillors were recruited largely from the local administrators of former régimes, with a sprinkling of ex-deputies, royalists, and large land lords. Each *conseil de préfecture* had three, four, or five councillors, and they were nominated by the Government and could always be dismissed.

The *conseil général* and the *conseil de préfecture* did not seriously affect or control the Prefect's actions, and this at the beginning bothered the Tribunate, the body formally responsible for passing legislation. The law was introduced to the Tribunate by Roederer for discussion. He made a clear and formal distinction in the rationalist tradition between the responsibility of the Prefect, which was to administer, that of the *conseil général* which was to divide up the burden of taxation, and that of the *conseil de préfecture* which was to act as the administrative tribunal. The doctrine of the separation of powers was invoked, though it was obvious that this was a fiction.

Two fundamental objections were raised in the Tribunate to the creation of the Prefectoral Corps in the way proposed; objections which recurred throughout the century. The first of these was that the Prefect would inevitably become inimical to local freedom. One questioner, Ganilh, demanded, 'will the Prefects and Sub Prefects not produce all the abuses, all the vexations, all the calamities which afflicted France for so long under the Intendants and the *sub délégués*, if they remain exempt from local supervision?'

The official answer was given by Daunou, who acted as *rapporteur* for the bill. 'How would a Prefect be so forgetful of his duty and of his true interests as to dare to become a petty tyrant? Does he not have a numerous council at his side responsible for dividing up taxation, which can watch his actions, can denounce his conduct to the Minister, and can put at the head of its demands for the Department that of a change of administrator? Is he not flanked by a *conseil de préfecture* to which the law gives authority to judge conflicts with private interests?'

But the Tribunate seems to have remained rather sceptical despite these assurances.

The second objection was that the Prefect might be inefficient, that he might be unable to protect the interests of the Department against other administrations. Chaptal, speaking for the Government, defined good administration as 'that which ensures at one and the same time the forceful and prompt execution of the laws, and smoothness, justice and economy for the administered'. The Prefect would alone be responsible; the Minister would treat only with him, and would be in a position to demand these standards; far more so than under other systems where responsibility was diffused. The Prefect, he reiterated, would have no arbitrary power. He would not be able to discuss the rights and wrongs of a measure. A law would be sent to him, and he would have to apply it, and see that it was generally obeyed.

The assurances given by the Government to meet the Tribunate's objections seem to be somewhat contradictory; but that body, although in many ways uneasy, did not feel themselves able to resist Napoleon's demands, and the law was passed on February 17, 1800.

While the bill was being discussed, Napoleon ordered a list to be prepared of possible candidates for posts in the new Prefectoral Corps: Prefects, Sub Prefects, Secretaries General.[1]

There is controversy as to how the first appointments were made; it seems that Napoleon originally asked Consul Lebrun to draw up a list of candidates, but that Lucien Bonaparte intervened, considering that he as Minister of the Interior should be responsible. Other prominent persons also claimed the right to be heard, and the final list presented by Lucien Bonaparte to Napoleon contained ten columns. The Departments were listed in alphabetical order, with their populations and capital towns, and then against each Department were placed the suggestions of Lucien Bonaparte, Cambacérès, Lebrun, Talleyrand, General Clarke, and 'Others'. A final space was left blank for Napoleon to make the final choice of Prefect. This document proves at least the importance that politicians from the beginning attached to the Prefectoral Corps and their keenness to press the claims of their supporters.

To guide his collaborators in their choice Napoleon simply said, 'I shall use anyone who has the capacity and the will to march forward with me ... These posts are open to Frenchmen of all shades of opinion, provided they are enlightened, and that they have capacity and integrity'. The schism in French life and thought had to be healed, and the Prefects were to be the doctors. They were therefore to come from all schools of thought and from all classes. For this reason Napoleon rejected his original idea that the honour of serving the Government should serve as compensation, and instead he proposed to grant the Prefects a salary that would enable them to live each in his Department at the same

[1] One Prefect and one Secretary General for each Department, one Sub Prefect for each *arrondissement*, except the *arrondissement* in which the departmental capital was situated, which came directly under the Prefect. For some time under Napoleon the Prefect was assisted by a specially appointed *auditeur* of the *Conseil d'Etat*.

standard as the wealthiest inhabitants. They should bring with them the moral advantage of being Napoleon's personal representatives, and also sufficient funds to put them beyond local temptation.

The invitation to serve France, combined with the offer of princely salaries, brought to the doors of the Ministry of the Interior all types and conditions of men. As the *Moniteur* of December 24, 1799, maliciously remarked, no doubt at Napoleon's instigation, 'How many men on the move, how many well-known faces trying to be seen, how many forgotten names stir once again in the dust of the Revolution; how many proud Republicans humble themselves in order to meet face to face the man in authority who can find them a place!'

Finally, on March 2, 1800, Napoleon issued the list of the first prefectoral appointments; sixty-five of the ninety posts were filled by those proposed by Lucien Bonaparte. As he had promised, Napoleon did not hesitate to use any person prepared to follow him. His appointments included former Deputies of the Third Estate, members of the clergy and the nobility, royalists, moderates, Jacobins from the Convention, Deputies and Senators from the Cinq Cent and the *Conseil des Anciens*, ambassadors, émigrés, ex-Ministers, jurists, generals and terrorists.[1] They were chosen with care. Some were recruited to serve in Departments which they knew well, others in Departments to which their particular aptitudes fitted them. To the Moselle, a Department known for its republican sympathies, Napoleon sent a man reputed for his moderate views. In the German speaking Departments of the Rhine valley, he sent Prefects who could speak the language, and had experience of such frontier problems as espionage and contraband.

Napoleon's Prefects were relatively young. Seventy-nine of the first Prefects were in their early forties. Later, he recruited into

[1] There is a valuable estimate of the Prefects and Sub Prefects then appointed as well as a list in: *Tableau contenant des Renseignements sur l'esprit public*, compiled by Fouché in 1801. In *L'Etat de la France en l'An VIII et en l'An IX:* ed. F-A. Aulard. Paris 1897.

the Corps the most brilliant of his young men, to be formed by the daily practice of prefectoral administration as the future leaders of the whole Empire. For instance, Molé, son of an old family, was sent from the *Conseil d'Etat* to Dijon as Prefect of the Côte d'Or at the age of twenty-six, and in three years made a great reputation. He was then appointed director general of *ponts et chaussées* for the whole Empire in 1809.

The new Sub Prefects and Secretaries General also included several members of the old legislative bodies, but in view of the local nature of most of their work, Napoleon called upon many local notables, many of whom had served in the previous local assemblies; he also found a place for Carey, the opera singer.[1]

The wide variety of experience and political background possessed by the first Prefects had the desired effect. It made quite clear that Napoleon considered that the time of national division and internecine warfare had passed. It also pacified the fears of the provinces of France, who still associated the title and work of an emissary of the Government with the excesses and terror of the *commissaires* of the revolutionary Assembly.

The new Prefectoral Corps set out from Paris during the months of March and April, 1800, after receiving their instructions from Napoleon. On their arrival many were welcomed by triumphal processions to their new capitals in the Department, and were fêted as the personal representative of the man who had saved France. Some Prefects were met with situations which required tact and rapid thinking. Méchin, Prefect of the Landes, reached the borders of his Department to be confronted with two rival reception committees, both wishing to escort him in triumph to his capital, Dax. The two columns were nearly at blows, so Méchin received spokesmen from both, parleyed and pacified, and then, mounting an improvised tribune, he harangued the whole assembly on the virtues of unity, harmony and peace. He exhorted them all to remember the higher interests of France. He

[1] For these and several other personal incidents regarding nineteenth century Prefects in this chapter, I am indebted to Pierre-Henry: *Histoire des Préfets*. Paris, 1950.

entered Dax triumphantly, accompanied by a single, united cortège.[1]

Other Prefectures experienced the inconveniencies of a succession of rapid and futile appointments, not a rare occurrence in later decades. Four Prefects succeeded one another within a month in the Prefecture at Besançon.

Besides the territorial Prefects sent to each Department, four others were nominated to be Prefects of Police in Paris, Lyons, Marseilles, and Bordeaux, the four largest cities, where they were to assume responsibility for public order, public morality, and public hygiene, leaving the departmental Prefects responsibility for all the rest of departmental administration. Only the Prefect of Police in Paris survived in office for more than a few months, the remainder becoming *commissaires généraux de police*, subject (in theory) to the authority of the territorial Prefect. The post in Paris has survived as the only main prefectoral post solely concerned with police affairs. The importance and the turbulence of the capital has always needed special attention, and the post ranks still as one of the two highest in the Corps.

The first ministerial instruction received by the Prefects was a statement of principle rather than a memorandum of policy. On March 11, 1800, Lucien Bonaparte ordered them to construct a new France in which all divisions between Frenchmen would be abolished. They were to show that 'the Revolution is finished, that a profound gulf separates for ever what has been from what is'. They were to take no heed of party, intrigue or influence, and their jurisdiction covered everything which could aid the public interest, help national prosperity, and ease the lives of their fellow citizens.

During the next year a succession of more prosaic and workmanlike circulars reached them from Paris. These defined the personal position of the Prefectoral Corps, suggested forms of administrative organization, made arrangements to house the Prefects and Sub Prefects in appropriate quarters, formulated

---

[1] E. Pisani: *La fonction préfectorale.* In *Encyclopédie permanente de l'Administration française.* Paris, 1951. p. 1121.

methods of correspondence between individual Prefects and the Ministry. Their wide and uncertain powers had to be defined in some way in order to clarify their personal status. In one circular they were described as 'hommes du gouvernement', organs of the law and instruments of its execution. They were forbidden to express their own opinions or to impose their individual will in place of the Government's. They were simply to publish the laws and take steps to render policy effective. On no account were they to issue proclamations.

Thus, two sides to the Prefectoral Corps were evident from the start. In the Department, they were supreme; none could challenge their title. Their powers were largely uncodified, and their prestige that of personal delegate of the Government. But in their relations with the centre they were to be efficient agents of execution and to subordinate their wills, policies and ideals to the Government's purpose. They were subject to instant dismissal without cause or explanation. Their great local powers were counterbalanced by strict obedience to the centre.

In practice, the work of the Prefectoral Corps rapidly extended into every sphere of French life, and it provided the firm basis of government in France which permitted Napoleon to undertake his campaigns across the face of Europe. The Prefects were a motive force in the social, political and economic fields. The archives of the Departments still contain projects and plans prepared by the Prefects for hospitals, schools, bridges, barracks, prisons, irrigation systems, town-planning and industries. Some Prefects undertook the arduous task of compiling lists of the agricultural, industrial, commercial and demographic resources in their Departments. Later this index of productive resources was made compulsory throughout France, and these surveys provided the Government (and future Governments) with a hitherto unattainable picture of French resources. On the basis of this knowledge the Prefects were able to intervene effectively in restoring French economic and social life.

On the political side, the Prefects were naturally active in establishing the new departmental assemblies, the *conseils généraux*, and in developing the councils of the Communes and *arrondissements*. This task called for much tact and political acumen, for one of the purposes behind the reorganization was to obtain co-operation both from the supporters of the Revolution and from the moderates and royalists. Local notables of all sides had to be persuaded to work together, and the choice of Mayors in particular required an acute sense of personality and local affairs. In several Departments it was extremely difficult to find men of sufficient ability and character. For example, in the Côte d'Or, a Mayor was found guilty of improper practices, but he was not removed as the Prefect thought it impossible to find any one of sufficient standing to replace him.[1] In the Meurthe the Prefect reported that Mayors would not attempt to repress criminal activities as it would make them unpopular, and in the Aube, the Prefect was unable to obtain replies to the letters he sent to the Mayors who did not know how to answer.[1]

The Prefectoral Corps by its example and by its inherent prestige as representative of the Government did much to raise the morale of the Departments, which had been sadly lowered by the violence of the preceding years and by the elimination of much of the old local élites. By discreetly attending local *salons* and arranging receptions, the Prefect became a new patron of local social life, and helped to establish a more normal standard of moral and social conduct.

As the police authority in the Department, the Prefectoral Corps had to contend with bold and well-organized brigandage which challenged internal security, as well as to put down subversive movements. In the North there were the *chauffeurs* who burnt the feet of their victims to discover where money was hidden, in the West the Chouans who were an unholy mixture of monarchist supporters, escaped criminals and deserters from the Army; and in the South, small but virulent groups such as the *chevaliers du soleil*. The highways were infested by the remains of Armies, foreign mercenaries, escaped convicts, and political refugees. To bring some degree of safety to the public highways

[1] Godechot: op. cit. p. 518.

was a big job, requiring patience and ruthlessness.[1]

Another important task was to pacify the clergy. The excesses of the worshippers of reason, the abolition of the feudal privileges of the Church, the creation of an official church, and the murder of many clerics, had thrown the Church into permanent and violent opposition. Napoleon's Concordat with Rome, and the new relations which it established between Church and State meant that the Prefects had to help with the new church organization, and the new pattern of social life which it introduced in the countryside. Many Prefects had, in the course of executing this policy of rapprochement, to renounce or ignore the opinions and policies they had followed, sometimes violently, in the past.

The Prefectoral Corps, and especially the Sub Prefects, took an active part in setting up welfare centres, hospitals and work houses, and in fostering attention to the many aspects of public assistance. Communes were made responsible for succouring their sick and destitute. Administrative machinery had to be created for regulating entry to public assistance institutions and for providing outdoor relief.

Industry was stimulated by breaking down old customs barriers, agricultural production was helped by schemes of land-drainage and the encouragement of local markets, highways were constructed, the old systems of taxation were overhauled and a new and more equitable distribution of burdens was devised.

For Napoleon, posting across Europe with his armies, the internal stability of France and his immediate rear was imperative. As he advanced and conquered, the new territories were rapidly transformed into Departments of France each endowed with a prefectoral administration. At the height of the Empire in 1810, 130 Prefects stretched across Europe from Rome (the Prefecture of the Tiber), through Mainz (Prefecture of Mont-Tonnerre), to Hamburg (Prefecture of the Bouches-de-l'Elbe). And although

[1] For a description of the conditions in 1800, see the *Bulletin de la Police Générale de la République*, and the *Rapport sur la situation de la République depuis le 18 brumaire, An VIII*, both presented by Fouché. In *L'Etat de la France* ed. Aulard. cit.

these Departments and their Prefects later disappeared, the Prefectoral Corps had in the meantime introduced the principles of French administration, its judicial codes, its financial system, and its conceptions of administrative law, with lasting results.

In return for their devotion, and efficiency, Napoleon gave the Corps power, prestige and influence. After the creation of the *légion d'honneur* in 1804 many members of the Corps received the distinction, and when four years later Napoleon instituted titles, Prefects and Sub Prefects in increasing numbers became Barons and Counts of the Empire.[1]

He raised the Corps to a status little short of that of his military commanders, and on occasions supported them in rejecting the pretensions of the military. General Junot, who arrested the Prefect of Parma, received from the Emperor a letter which still blisters.[2] One of the most notable Prefects of the time remarked, 'they were always sure of being supported, of being listened to, of having a reply and a solution to their queries, and they were never paralysed in their efforts by the fear that they would be left to their own devices and subsequently sacrificed to excuse the Minister's mistakes'.[3]

But, naturally, the faults of the Government were reflected in the Corps, its philosophy in their demeanour, its demands in their administration. From Napoleon, the Corps inherited a taste for dictatorship: with an elaborate police apparatus, munificent public works, strict control of education and ruthless methods of conscription. The Prefectoral Corps took the

[1] J. Regnier: *Les Préfets du Consulat et de l'Empire*. Paris, 1913.

[2] Quoted in Henry, op. cit. p. 38. 'Vous avez traité un préfet comme vous auriez pu faire à un caporal de votre garnison. Il y a là un défaut de tact et un oubli de vous-même qui me paraît inconcevable; ce que vous avez fait est sans exemple. Je n'ai qu'un mot à vous dire: si tout s'arrange à la satisfaction du préfet, je l'oublierai; sinon je ne vous emploierai de ma vie; tout ce que vous pourrez me dire ne fera rien sur mon opinion. Vous avez eu tort, tort que je trouve d'autant plus injuste que le préfet a envoyé des pétitions pour demander un duché pour vous'.

[3] Pisani: loc. cit.

Emperor Napoleon as its model and served him faithfully in his own image. They, like him, lifted France from the chaos of the Revolution and established a firm administrative basis for the future. The work that lasted was the establishment of a new civil society, not the glories and excursions of military adventures.

In meeting the Emperor's demands for men and money the Prefectoral Corps were towards the end of the Empire compelled to neglect their work of civil construction. With misgiving they raised forced levies, collected grain, and rounded up conscripts; they were met with hoarding, mutinies, the storming of gaols and barracks, the destruction by mobs of municipal conscription rolls, sometimes with the connivance of local officials. But unlike Prefects of later generations when faced with unwelcome and tyrannous demands by the Government, some dared boldly to protest. The Count of Castellane, Prefect of the Basses-Pyrénées (Pau), bitterly remarked to Napoleon, 'It is true, Sire, that the Prefects make people pay their taxes, that they provide you with the men with which you carry on your wars, while they maintain peace inside the country. In a word, the Prefects are the scullery boys of your glory; they prepare the dishes: your generals eat them'.[1]

Like the rest of the country, the majority of the Prefectoral Corps were too weary to react strongly when Napoleon fell. Many stayed in their posts when Louis XVIII came to the throne in 1815, and during the Hundred Days, when Napoleon made his last desperate bid to return to power, only a handful of Prefects joined him. The attractions of peace and stability were too great.

But despite this attitude at the last, the Emperor continued to regard the Corps as one of his finest creations.[2] To the Corps he had attracted men of the highest distinction, like de la Tour du Pin, Molé, de Cossé-Brissac, and from it he had obtained some of his most able young men. Writing on St. Helena, Napoleon

[1] D. Jouany: *L'Administration telle qu'elle est*. Revue Administrative, 1951–52. p. 17.

[2] Le Comte de las Cases: *Le Mémorial de Sainte-Hélène*. Pléiade ed. Paris, 1948. Vol. II. p. 466.

marvelled at the dexterity of the institution by which the same impulse could be transmitted throughout the country by one man acting through his Prefects. He considered it as one of the stanchions of his régime and as one of the causes of the greatness of the France he had left.

In France, Louis XVIII for some time kept many of the Imperial Prefects in office, and some lasted through both his reign and that of Charles X. But by then the proud Napoleonic Prefects had become something rather different, which they were to remain for more than half a century.

3. *The Prefects, Agents of the Government* 1816-1879

The Prefectoral Corps unavoidably bears the stamp of the government of the day. When Napoleon at its birth established the principle that its members should be liable to revocation *ad nutum*, he intended them to be great but obedient. Governments of less stature required their Prefects merely to keep the reigning house in power. They then became less administrators than electoral agents and chiefs of police. This was equally true for Louis XVIII (1815–1825), Charles X (1825–1830), Louis-Philippe (1830–1848), the Second Republic (1848–1852), and Napoleon III (1852–1870). The tradition was so strong that it was carried over into the Third Republic (1870–1879).

At the beginning of each new régime, the prefectoral posts, sometimes Sub Prefects as well, were filled by supporters; in part this was to recompense them for services rendered, in part to ensure that the instruments of government under the Prefects' control were used to favour and consolidate the new régimes.

The Left, from its own bitter experiences, regarded the Corps as an abomination, and in 1848, at the beginning of the Second Republic, the republican Minister of the Interior, Ledru Rollin, abolished the Corps in name, and substituted for Prefects, *commissaires de la République*, each governing several Departments. This change only lasted from February 1848 to May 1848, when the Prefectoral Corps was restored. It was too useful an instrument for any government to abolish it.

Under the Third Republic, the doctrine that each Government had the right to control the political sympathies of the Prefectoral Corps led to the chaotic practice of 'massacring' the Corps at each change of Ministry. In the later years of the Third Republic, the Corps achieved some stability, but the first nine years carried on the monarchical tradition of regarding the Corps as the political agent of the Government, entirely subservient to its political preoccupations.

The work of the Corps during this half century, then, was chiefly to bolster up the existing government by electoral management and repressive police actions. In several fields, however, their influence was constructive, and precedents were established which were later to re-fashion the Corps into a creative administrative machine. But since its political rôle is best known, this question will be dealt with first.

Successive governments made the Prefectoral Corps responsible for ensuring the return of government supporters to Parliament.[1] The Prefects used the administrative machinery at their disposal for these ends. The long list of offices filled by the Government and by the Prefects can be found in the *Almanach Royal et National*. There were 667,000 salaried officials, employed as clerks, workmen, and local officials. This was the 'machine' which made the elections.

These official posts were used to bribe the faithful to vote the right way, while indiscreet political activity or lukewarmness at election times was followed by dismissal. In addition, this administrative machine was responsible for the technical and legal arrangements for elections, and by a judicious use of administrative devices the local electorate could often be limited to pro-government supporters. Artificial difficulties were created to prevent opponents being inscribed in the electoral registers, legal technicalities were invoked which required interminable litigation before the administrative courts, and registration was frequently disallowed on the most dubious grounds. On the other hand ineligible electors who served the government were added to the

[1] Prefects and Sub Prefects often sat in one of the houses of Parliament.

registers; the dead were known to vote.

It was also difficult to obtain redress, for the local administrative tribunal was presided over by the Prefect himself, and the election would be past before judgement was given.

Bribes were offered to electors, ballot papers were marked to identify voters, opposition candidates were denied campaign rooms, paper, public meetings, and voting cards. The administrative staff and the facilities of town halls, Sub Prefectures and Prefectures were used in the campaign and government expenditure on public works was often inspired by electoral considerations. Those who worked for opposition candidates were often victimized by their employers or by the State, and some printing firms refused to accept orders from the government's opponents lest their printing licence be withdrawn.[1]

When, *in extremis*, a Prefect found that the election might still go against his candidate, he resorted to heroic measures. M. Lorois, Prefect of Morbihan, and his Sub Prefect, Fromant, at Plöermel discovered to their consternation, while preparing the elections of 1837, that M. Hello, their 'reliable' candidate, was not in fact eligible since he had not resided in the Department for the statutory six months. They of course continued to uphold his candidacy, until three days before the election the opposition candidate discovered the truth and placarded the information round the town. The electoral registers were stored in the Sub Prefecture. Messieurs Lorois and Fromant therefore burnt it down. By return of post the Minister of the Interior agreed that it would be quite improper to hold an election without proper registers, and the election was consequently postponed. When the new register was completed, M. Hello had been a resident in the Department for the statutory six months.[2]

[1] French nineteenth century literature contains several accounts of 'managed' elections and prefectoral pressure. One of the most vivid accounts is by Stendhal: *Lucien Leuwen: Le chasseur vert;* and another by the author of 'The Member of Paris': *French Pictures in English Chalk*, London, Smith, Elder, 1876.

[2] S. Kent: *Electoral Procedure under Louis Philippe*. Yale University Press, 1937, p. 114.

Prefects and Sub Prefects were also expected to act as agents for local politicians. They publicized the grants made by the Government for schools, churches, hospitals, roads, bridges and town halls in the Department and assured the population that they had been the direct result of the good offices of their Deputy. As election day approached the Prefectoral Corps would tour their area and bluntly advise the electorate which way to vote for their own good.

The Ministry came to rely upon the shrewdness and penetration of the Corps. Circulars and questionnaires were sent from Paris requiring information about the mood of the electorate and analyses of past electoral behaviour. Statistics were compiled in the Ministry and elections timed according to prognostications. The choice of candidate suitable for a particular constituency was often referred to the local Prefect.

The Prefects themselves were convoked to Paris for 'inspection' of their private lives and opinions. There grew up a tradition that all the Prefects and the Minister should meet on the eve of an election when electoral strategy was laid down. The ministerial, prefectoral and subprefectoral circulars, memoranda, and proclamations exchanged during these years provide a *vade mecum* of electoral management. Throughout the whole period cynically direct instructions were issued to the Prefects. In 1831, Casimir Périer informed his Prefects that 'the Government will not be neutral in the elections, nor does it desire the administration to be so. The Government insists, however, that the electoral law be executed with the most rigorous impartiality. At the same time, the Government wishes it to be known that the distance between administrative impartiality and administrative indifference is infinite. The Government is convinced that its continuance in office is vital to the interests of the Nation.'[1]

Again, in 1852, Persigny, Minister of the Interior, summarized baldly the whole philosophy of administrative practice. 'The public good can only be assured on condition that the legislative

---
[1] Quoted in Georges Denis Weill: *Les élections législatives depuis 1789*. Paris, 1895. p. 155.

body is in perfect harmony of ideas with the Head of the State. Consequently, M. le Préfet, by the intermediacy of the various agents of the Administration, and by any and every means you consider to be consistent with the feeling of your area (and if necessary by proclamations in the Communes) take all steps necessary to bring to the attention of the electors of your Department those candidates that the Government of Louis Napoleon judges to be the most useful in helping him in his work of reconstruction.'[1]

The administrative literature between 1816 and 1879 is full of similar sentiments and similar instructions. The inevitable result of deforming the political process in this way was to force the opposition into revolutionary and extra-parliamentary channels. To cope with these, Prefects relied upon the extensive and barely defined police powers with which they were endowed.

Extreme movements are recurrent in French history throughout the nineteenth century. The White Terror, under Louis XVIII in the South, Carbonarism, the Congregation, the moral excesses of the Jesuits when they returned to France, the early Socialists, the followers of Louis Blanc, the Paris mob and its history of violent outbursts, and secret anarchist and revolutionary clubs all agitated France. As each change in régime brought to power men with scores to pay, so it gave scope for outrage and revenge. Police protection and investigation would in any case have absorbed much of the Prefects' time.

But the Government often identified with the really violent parties moderate groups whose principal crime was political opposition to the régime, and amongst these, of course, were the moderate Republicans.

The first and predestined casualty was the Press. Prefects and State Advocates vied for the honour of ruining the non-official provincial press by applying ruthless press laws, by vexatious prosecutions, and by withdrawing licences from newsagents. Many local papers were ruined by enormous penalties for breaches of the law, by excessive damages in libel suits, and by

[1] Jouany: loc. cit.

fines for *lèse majesté*. Printers were subjected to continual interference, advertisements were withheld from all but the safe press, and the private lives of editors and their staffs were made miserable. For a brief period in 1848 the republican press had some respite, but Napoleon III's accession to power began a new prefectoral and police campaign against freedom of expression.[1]

The Prefectoral Corps maintained, through the local police, a careful watch on local notables to detect any sign of opposition. Mayors and officials were summarily dismissed for anti-dynastic ideas. Officials in prominent posts who might have political influence were liable to victimization. The *instituteurs* were already showing that attachment to republican ideas and to anti-clerical philosophy which later was to wean part of the countryside away from the *curé* towards the Republic. Discriminatory laws were frequently used to force them to teach the official lessons, and in 1850 the Prefect of the Corrèze advised the Mayors to enforce discipline rigorously and to dismiss any suspected *instituteur*. He lamented that 'education, which was put in their (the *institueurs*') hands to be used as a kindly light to illuminate the countryside, has instead become a torch to set it alight'.[2]

The local monopoly of local information that the Prefects obtained through the local police, was used for political ends. While Louis Napoleon was preparing his *coup d'état* during 1852, to alter his status from President of the Republic to Emperor, the Prefectoral Corps quietly and deliberately created 'la peur de 1852', by their disquieting and alarmist reports on conditions in the Departments, their gloomy forecasts of sudden outrage, and hints of hidden and violent movements. Every small agitation was noted as a potential spark. The Red Spectre of 1852 was largely the work of the Prefectoral Corps, and the bourgeoisie was duly paralysed with fear.

After the *coup d'état* the reaction in the provinces was con-

[1] Weill: op. cit. p. 268 seq.

[2] G. Weill: *Histoire du Parti Républicain en France (1814–1870)*. Paris, 1928. p. 257.

sequently very limited, and all the main centres were quite easily held in check by the Prefects. Prefects were thereupon called to serve on the infamous *commissions mixtes*, composed in each Department of themselves, the local State Advocate and the Army Commandant. These summary tribunals were empowered to cleanse the countryside of noxious and revolutionary elements by deportation, expulsion, the withdrawal of residence permits, internment in a specified place, and police supervision. It is estimated that some 26,000 persons were dealt with by these tribunals.

There are many contemporary instances of the arbitrary nature of the Prefect's police powers, and the Government's willingness to abuse them. In 1858, for example, after Orsini's attempt on Napoleon's life, each Prefect was ordered to find between four and twenty persons in his Department guilty of criminal propensities, communication with exiles abroad, or illegal activities. Some six hundred men were arrested. In an effort to reach his quota the Prefect of the Charente pulled in an innocuous local character simply on the grounds that he was an unfrocked priest and unpopular with his neighbours.[1]

While all the Prefects of this era were prepared to use their police powers for political ends, the Prefects of the Empire stand out as the greatest exponents of the art. They have become a legend in France as the *préfets à poigne*. Haughty, authoritarian, unscrupulous and ruthless, they dominated the internal life of France for nearly twenty years. They were loaded with honours and prestige by Napoleon III, and their social and political eminence was only a little less than that of the general officers of the Army Staff.

The traditions built up under Napoleon III were slow to pass away. Politicians of the early Third Republic thought it quite natural to use the Corps as a political instrument. Thiers, for example, bitterly opposed the law of 1871 on departmental administration, which devolved many powers of decision in the Department to the *conseils généraux*, on the grounds that it

[1] G. Weill: op. cit. p. 324.

would weaken the Prefect's influence, and therefore the power of the Government.[1]

After 1871 the Corps was subject no longer to a permanent head of the state, but to continually changing Ministers of the Interior, who lacked continuity of purpose. Whatever the vices of the Corps under the monarchical régimes at least they had unity of direction and continuity of policy.

In March 1876 Dufaure's Government dismissed all the existing Prefects and the great majority of the Sub Prefects, and replaced them by Republican supporters. In May, 1877, De Fourtou, De Broglie's Minister of the Interior, ejected these in turn and appointed upholders of '*l'ordre moral*'. Dufaure returned to office in December, 1877, threw out De Fourtou's Prefects and re-installed his own supporters. Each batch of Prefects went to their Departments with the traditional instructions concerning elections and when, and in whose favour, to use their police powers. Not until a republican majority was more firmly established in 1879 and tension had lessened, did the Prefectoral Corps gradually settle down to a more stable rôle in the administrative life of the country.

This black picture of repression, cynical manipulation, and the political abuse of police and administrative powers, is not of course complete. The period between 1816 and 1879 is in some ways a high point in French history, and the Prefectoral Corps played a notable and enduring part, although this side of their record is less well-known.

The greatest feats of civil administration performed by the Prefectoral Corps were the work of Prefects of the Seine; a post which, from the first, carried particular eminence and responsibility. The Marquis de Rambuteau, Prefect from 1833 to 1848, and Baron Haussmann, Prefect from 1853 to 1870, transformed Paris from what was in many respects a mediaeval city, into the modern, fascinating and brilliant capital of Europe. Rambuteau's

[1] An appendix in F. H. Brabant: The beginning of the Third Republic in France, London, 1940, gives the proceedings of the committee on the law of 1871, and Thiers' objections. pp. 515–521.

era saw the construction of more than 4,000 houses, four hospitals, eight new bridges, squares, town halls, churches and monuments. He also began clearing the slums that infested the centre of the city and in parts resembled fortresses of vice and crime. He took the first energetic measures to improve public health by constructing public conveniences, drains and pavements, and by street-cleaning.

He became legendary in his own time as the *père des ouvriers*, and at the time of the revolution in 1848, although his Prefecture was stormed, he was quietly escorted by Victor Hugo through the mob to safety.

His successor in the Second Empire was Haussmann, whose town planning record far exceeds even that of Rambuteau. Public works on an immense scale were undertaken, and often entailed the demolition of whole quarters of the city. The main routes through Paris—the Boulevard Sébastopol, the Boulevard St. Michel, the Boulevard St. Germain; many of the quais, the extension of the rue de Rivoli, the Boulevard Haussmann, the most notable pieces of town architecture—the Etoile, the Opéra, the Avenue de l'Opéra, the Place de la République, the Place St. Michel; innumerable other streets; the development of the quartiers of Chaillot and Passy; the development of the suburban Communes; the annexation to the city of Paris of all the area within the old fortifications; the immense and extremely important system of sewers; the provision of fresh water from the Loire Valley and from Brie; as well as the construction of many churches, town halls, the Bois de Boulogne, the Parks of Vincennes and Monceau; all were begun and in great part completed during the years 1852–1870.[1]

At the height of his power Haussmann was effectively Minister for Paris. He was probably the brightest star, political or administrative, of Napoleon III's epoch. He was a masterful man who made many enemies, and his record as a Prefect in his earlier

---

[1] I have attempted to describe Haussmann's work in some detail in: *Baron Haussmann and the Planning of Paris*. Town Planning Review. October 1953, pp. 177–192.

posts in Bordeaux and in the Var was no better than that of his colleagues, especially in his handling of elections and politics. His method of financing the development of Paris was, at the least, unorthodox, and was the immediate cause of his dismissal in 1870. He had many of the vices of his age, including a head-strong taste for authority, but his work was perhaps the best justification for the concentration of authority in the hands of the Prefectoral Corps in a period more notable for abuses than for constructive work.

Napoleon had intended the Prefectoral Corps to be civil leaders in the Provinces, and there were several examples of devotion to duty and a high sense of responsibility. In an emergency the Corps provided leadership and a focal point of authority for administering relief. In more normal times it could produce men with the dynamism and practical vision required for a more sustained effort towards improving local conditions than could be expected from the average provincial Frenchman. Some Prefects and Sub Prefects died, and several were decorated for their gallantry in organizing their areas against natural calamities, particularly the scourge of cholera. There were also many examples of leadership in developing local industry and wealth. The Sub Prefect of Marennes, La Terme, is commemorated by a statue in the town for the part he played in draining the local marshes.

In a third important field the Prefectoral Corps followed precedents laid down by Napoleon. He had used his Prefects as the governors of the lands he conquered; the French expansion of the nineteenth century in the Mediterranean was also followed by the despatch of Prefects to build up civil administration in North Africa, Nice and Savoy.

Four years after the capture of Algiers in 1830, the Prefect of Finisterre was appointed to the capital as *Intendant Civil*, assuming responsibility for purely civilian affairs which had hitherto been under the control of the military commander.

Prefects continued to fill this post, sometimes under different titles, until 1848, when the Constituent Assembly formed after the revolution affirmed that henceforth Algeria was to be a part of metropolitan France. In December, 1848, a prefectoral administration, with Departments and *arrondissements*, was set up.[1]

The Prefects in Algeria were not, however, responsible to the Minister of the Interior, but to the Minister of War. Napoleon III created a special Minister for Algeria, and the Governorship (always a military appointment) was for some time abolished. It was re-created in 1860. The prefectoral administration in Algeria during the nineteenth century was peculiar, therefore, in that it was under the supervision of military men.

The Prefectoral Corps also implemented the French policy of assimilation in the provinces of Nice and Savoy, acquired from Piedmont as the price of helping against the Austrians in 1859. The Prefect of the Haute-Saône, M. Dieu, was sent to these provinces, furnished with a special Imperial warrant to prepare them for annexation. The immediate introduction of French officials and electoral laws ensured the speedy conclusion of the operation. The Department of the Alpes Maritimes was modified to absorb Nice, and Savoy was made into two Departments, with their capitals at Annécy and Chambéry.

Finally, the Corps was always a forcing ground for future leaders of the country. Unlike Napoleon, later governments sometimes regarded appointment to the Corps as a method of rewarding the worthy but mediocre, especially after a successful revolution. Nevertheless, some of the most eminent statesmen and officials of France during the nineteenth century served their apprenticeship in the Corps. Under the July Monarchy alone the Corps provided seven Ministers, one President of the Council of Ministers, two Presidents of one of the Chambers of Parliament, and three Ambassadors. In the early years of the Third Republic Jules Ferry, Léon Bourgeois and the Cambons served as Prefects. Many other members of the Corps became Directors of Ministries, *conseillers d'Etat*, and *conseillers* of the *Cour des Comptes*. At some periods several Prefects and Sub Prefects were Deputies and

---

[1] M. Le Beau: '*L'Administration préfectorale hors du Territoire Métropolitain*'. In *Les Préfets dans l'Histoire*, Paris, 1950.

Senators while still holding their administrative posts, a practice which disappeared under the Third Republic. Members of the Prefectoral Corps are, however, still used for other administrative and government duties, and the French administration as a whole has benefited from the interchange. The converse is also true. The Prefectoral Corps is always open to receive new blood from outside its own ranks, and has been the better for it, except when the new entrants have been appointed purely as a personal political favour.

The period between 1816 and 1879 then, saw established as firm tradition many of Napoleon's guiding rules. The Prefectoral Corps was to be constructive in civil affairs, to provide leadership in the provinces, to train the highest advisers of the Government, to execute faithfully the will of the Government, to ensure the safety of the country, and to protect and further the interests of France. The distortion of these ideals, notably in police repression and political machinations, was the impulse and will of the politicians, for only the political leaders of a country can set the moral tone of its political and administrative life.

4. *The Third Republic*

Until 1870 drastic changes in the composition of the Corps had been made only after the successful overturn of a régime. There were many instances of Prefects and Sub Prefects surviving these changes, frequently by moving from one post to another and sometimes even continuing in the same place. Jessaint remained Prefect of the Marne from 1800 when he was appointed by Napoleon until 1838 when he retired under Louis Philippe. Baron Haussmann was appointed by Guizot as a Sub Prefect after the revolution of 1830, remained in office under the Second Republic, and achieved his greatest fame under Napoleon III.

The first years of the Third Republic, however, seemed to mark the high point of prefectoral instability. In the first nine years there were unprecedented 'massacres' of Prefects.

Then after 1879 and the firmer establishment of Republican

Government, the Prefectoral Corps as well as the politicians benefited from the increased stability. An orthodox prefectoral career could now be envisaged, comparable in many ways with that in other high administrative services, but in order to establish this situation a *modus vivendi* had to be found between the politicians and the administrators. The curious relations between the two branches of government will require some further discussion, but first it is necessary to trace the extent to which the Prefectoral Corps was by now concerned with administration. Although, during the greater part of the nineteenth century the Corps was regarded in law as part of the administrative machine much of its time was occupied with political matters. Until the balance went the other way, and the Corps was in a position to protest that its main interest was to administer on behalf of the government and not to act as a political machine, there was little hope that it would escape interference from the politicians.

The formulation of administrative law and practice was a lengthy process, starting with the first laws passed by Napoleon in 1800. The Prefects retained wide discretionary powers simply because many parts of the law relating to local government were not codified. By the law of June 22, 1833, the *conseils généraux* began to be elected by a restricted suffrage, and a law of May 10, 1838, extended their powers of decision. In practice this did not seriously affect the powers of the Prefect. The next major law on departmental administration was that of March 25, 1852, and it greatly increased the Prefect's authority, for it listed an extensive range of subjects which until that time had been decided by the Minister but which were now 'deconcentrated' to the Prefect.

Successive legislation in many other fields—public works, highways, water, railways, game, hospitals, local finance, communal affairs—added to the already extensive powers of the Prefects. From the point of view of the public and the councils of the local authorities, their powers appeared arbitrary. In practice matters of importance frequently involved ministerial approval, and the Prefect simply acted as the local agent of the Minister. But the appearance of absolute power combined with his known intervention in elections and control of the police apparatus, were sufficient to cause suspicion of prefectoral 'administration' as such.

Two things were necessary to mitigate this state of affairs. First, that local elected bodies should have sufficient authority to balance arbitrary administrative practices. Second, that the Prefects should give less importance to their 'political' (electoral and police) functions and more to purely administrative duties (highways, hospitals, public works, etc).

The Third Republic saw both these things happen. In the first place the basic laws on local government passed in its early years protected local authorities from direct prefectoral pressure. The law on departmental administration of August 10, 1871, while firmly maintaining the Prefect as the executive head of the Department, at the same time granted to the *conseil général* wide powers of control and initiative in all matters of departmental concern. The *conseil* alone could pass the departmental budget, agree to spend money from departmental funds (except when the law made such expenditure universally compulsory), pass contracts, and dispose of departmental property. Those powers devolved to the Prefect as state representative (for example, police and the tutelage of the Communes) remained outside the *conseil's* control; but when he acted for the Department he was liable to examination and control by the *conseil général*. This considerably curtailed his previous powers.

The law of March 28, 1882, provided for the Mayors of the Communes to be elected from the *conseil municipal*, whereas previously they had been nominated by the Minister on the advice of the Prefect. This was followed by the law of April 5, 1884, on municipal administration, which set up a really decentralized system of local administration in which the *conseils municipaux* were responsible for all matters of communal concern, subject only to a strictly defined system of tutelage by the Prefect. In all matters, the *conseil municipal* acted through the Mayor.

These measures lessened the possibility of using local affairs for political ends. A clearer division was established between administration and politics, and by losing those powers styled 'administrative' in law but essentially political in practice, the Prefectoral Corps in fact benefited, since it became less profitable for politicians to interfere with their work. But it was not until the 1914–18 War that the Prefect's administrative functions really took precedence.

Throughout the Third Republic there was, in addition, a great expansion in social and national services, the administration of which was, for reasons of democracy, economy and efficiency, devolved to local authorities. The Prefectoral Corps received its share of extra responsibility; the elected authorities were often called upon to take the decisions to create or organize new services, but the administration of those services was the task of the Prefectures. For example, the laws on public assistance passed between 1890 and 1906 gave wide powers of decision to the *conseils généraux* in matters relating to welfare, hospitals, finance, indoor and outdoor relief, and social service establishments. Their decisions were executed by the Prefectures, and the Prefect was responsible for the general supervision of public assistance in the field.

The Prefects were made locally responsible for supervising or inspecting many other services, For example, communal authorities had to provide primary schools and accommodate the *instituteur*, while a departmental educational body, presided over by the Prefect, was responsible for the discipline of teachers and for the organization of the departmental teachers' training college.

The Prefect continued to nominate many minor officials, and as the local services increased so this power extended—clerks, highway *cantonniers*, officials in hospitals, local policemen, *instituteurs*, and many others.

Decentralization in France during this period from 1870 to 1914 did not, therefore, benefit only the local elected authorities. As their powers of decision increased and the scope of their activities widened, so did the administrative functions of the Prefect expand. As his administrative functions grew in importance so the purely political side of his work retreated into the background. His energies were more absorbed by the increasing burden. The very wide powers which he still possessed could still be turned to political ends if he chose; for example, the appointment of *instituteurs* allowed considerable scope for discrimination, and this was used.

The first World War slowed down the tendency towards decentralization; and although it was continued for a short time after 1920, the economic depression and the ominous trend of world affairs led to a change in policy. Instead of decentralization, a policy of deconcentration was pursued; powers of decision were granted not to elected authorities but to local administrative officers. New economic and social legislation empowered the Prefects to intervene in many fields of industrial and social life. Measures concerning the development of agriculture, the electrification of the countryside, the provision of workers' dwellings, public works, and industrial disputes, all made use of the administrative services of the Prefectures to stimulate, co-ordinate and control local action.

The Prefectures became more than ever the hub of local affairs, staffs increased, and bureaux multiplied. This process was accentuated by the expansion of the local offices of central Ministries. Some Ministries had to cover new specialized fields of work. For example, the Ministry of Agriculture created a new service to control the application of laws concerning agricultural social services. These new services rapidly established their own areas of local administration with the Department as the basic area, and their local offices came under the Prefect. He had supremacy over all state officials in the Department, and he alone was the personal and direct representative of all the Ministers; he alone could authorize expenditure from state funds. State officials under the Third Republic loyally accepted this doctrine, not least because it protected them from publicity and political interference.

These administrations depended upon the local Prefect for accommodation, local information, the appointment of subordinate personnel, and equipment; and from their expansion the Prefects drew a new source of influence, again essentially administrative in character.

Once again the Prefectoral Corps was the instrument for assimilating new territories. In 1918 France recovered from Germany the lost provinces of Alsace-Lorraine; and on November 15 of that year three *commissaires de la République* were despatched to take over the civil administration. In October of the following year these *commissaires* were replaced by ordinary Prefects, under the general control of a *haut commissaire*, M. Alapetite.

The territorial organization of Alsace-Lorraine which the French had handed over to the Germans in 1871 had been somewhat modified. In 1919 the French did not attempt to revert to the pre-1870 local government boundaries in the Departments of Bas-Rhin, Haut-Rhin, the Vosges and Moselle. They adopted the more numerous German areas, and as a result of this the three Departments of Bas-Rhin, Haut-Rhin and Moselle, have today a higher number of *arrondissements* and Sub Prefects than any other Department in France.[1]

The French also retained the rectifications they had been forced to make in 1871 to the boundaries of the Department of Meurthe-et-Moselle as a result of the German annexation. The Térritoire de Belfort, which had been made from the rump of the Department of the Haut-Rhin, was kept; and in 1924 the Térritoire, while keeping its name, was granted the status of a Department and its *administrateur* was replaced by a Prefect.

The history of Alsace-Lorraine was unhappy from its recovery by the French in 1918 till it was lost again in 1940. It had been noted for its particularist sentiments and its own local brand of self-government. On political grounds the French Government tried to assimilate the region into the rest of France as quickly as possible, and thereby alienated a great part of the population. A

---

[1] Moselle now has 7 *arrondissements*, Bas-Rhin 7, Haut-Rhin 6; a total of 20 *arrondissements*. In 1871, there had only been 8 between the three Departments.

strong autonomist movement grew up in protest against the centralization in Paris of affairs previously dealt with locally. On religious and educational matters French governments showed a complete lack of tact and understanding, and attempted to force on Alsace-Lorraine administrative measures and organization less liberal than the system they were to replace. The result was violence on both sides, repression by the French army and police and anti-French political feeling which continued right up to 1940. This is not a chapter in the history of the Corps about which it can be very proud.

As the history of Alsace-Lorraine showed, the Prefects of the Third Republic could not escape the direction of the Government any more than their predecessors. They could only try to apply governmental policy in a humane rather than a brutal way. When Paul Cambon, as Prefect of the Nord in 1880, was told to expel Catholic teaching orders, he put in a letter to his wife the classic dilemma of the Corps, and indeed of all high administrators. 'En nous retirant aujourd'hui nous devons renoncer à la vie publique pour plusieurs années. Or nous ne pouvons exercer une action utile et profitable qu'en n'abondonnant pas la partie.' He was consoled by the thought: 'vivre dans l'avenir plus que dans le présent, et juger ainsi les faits à leur juste mesure'.[1]

Under the Third Republic, the Prefects sometimes found it difficult to reconcile multiplying demands on their allegiance. In previous régimes there had been a single Head of the State, round whom both the political and administrative structure of the country was organized. But under a democratic régime the Minister depended upon the support of political parties and the electorate. The Department was not only an area of local administration, but also a constituency wherein Deputies and Senators contended for the political support of the electorate. The Minister did not wish his administration to conflict with the interests of the local parliamentarians since he depended upon

---

[1] Paul Cambon: *Correspondance 1870-1924* ed. H. Cambon. Paris, 1940. Letter of October 28, 1880. Vol. I. p. 127.

their support to keep him in office. It fell to the Prefect to interpret administrative directives and to use his powers to preserve harmony. In the absence of strong national parties the Deputies and Senators were dependent in their turn on personal local support. Consequently parliamentarians of different shades of opinion competed for the local patronage possessed by the Prefect; state grants to local authorities, the appointment of many local officials, and the control of police powers, were matters which could be turned to considerable advantage by experienced politicians.

A Minister had to seek support where he could find it. If a prominent member of a political group made his support conditional on the appointment of his nominee as Prefect in his Department, or if he demanded the dismissal of an unco-operative Prefect, it was difficult for a Minister to refuse. When Waldeck Rousseau, as Minister of the Interior in the *Grand Ministère*, sent a circular to the Prefects instructing them to ignore attempts by parliamentarians to intervene in administrative matters, Gambetta remarked with some asperity, 'avec ça, mon petit, nous vivrons trois mois ou trois ans'. The Ministry was overturned within six weeks.

Fortunately for the Corps the wishes of one Deputy in the Department were sometimes counter-balanced by those of another. Many parliamentarians had more important favours to ask of a Minister than the removal of a Prefect. A few had public spirit enough to wish not to hamper the administration; others discovered that if one Minister appointed their protégé as Prefect, a future Minister from a different party might deliberately send an enemy. The best Ministers developed a strong administrative conscience and exacted complete loyalty for themselves personally.

The pretensions of some parliamentarians were very great. The following letter was written by Clemenceau to a Deputy whose demands did not concern a Prefect, but a relatively minor Sub Prefect. The letter is dated August 10, 1907.

Mon cher député,

Je reçois une lettre du Directeur du Personnel au Ministère de l'Intérieur, dans laquelle j'aime à penser qu'il me rapporte inexactement l'entretien que vous avez eu avec lui. D'après M. d'Auriac, vous auriez demandé qu'il fût sursis indéfiniment au remplacement de M. L. . . . . dont vous ne contestez d'ailleurs pas que le cerveau soit dérangé. La raison que vous en donneriez c'est que les ennemis de M. L. . . . . sont les ennemis de la République et les vôtres. Il me semble au contraire, que les ennemis de la République et les vôtres devraient avoir tout intérêt à ce que l'Arrondissement que vous représentez reste le plus longtemps possible sous la direction administrative d'un fonctionnaire déséquilibré.

Selon M. d'Auriac vous auriez encore ajouté que s'il n'était pas fait droit à votre requête, vous voteriez contre le gouvernement. Si vous me connaissiez, mon cher député, vous sauriez que les menaces sont sans effet sur moi. Vous voterez comme il vous conviendra, en expliquant à vos électeurs la signification que peuvent avoir vos votes dans votre pensée. Mais, pour moi-même, si je tenais à rester au gouvernement, ce qui n'est pas, je remplirais malgré tout mon devoir strict en cette circonstance, dût votre caprice n'y pas trouver satisfaction.

Je donne donc l'ordre à M. d'Auriac de publier au Journal Officiel le mouvement qui est préparé depuis plusieurs semaines, et je le prie d'inviter selon l'usage, M. le sous-préfet de G . . . . qui va remplacer M. L . . . . à aller vous faire visite pour inaugurer avec vous des relations qui, je l'espère, seront telles que vous pouvez le désirer.

Bien cordialement,
G. Clemenceau.[1]

Ministers of Clemenceau's stature furnished the Prefectoral Corps with a solid basis of support but occasioned additional embarrassment. Freed from the embrace of the local Deputy, the Prefects were nearly hugged to death by the Minister. Of all the strong Ministers of the Interior, Clemenceau stands supreme as the 'tyrant'.

He mercilessly used the Corps as an agent of his own policies, requiring them to enforce government wishes with the greatest energy and dispatch. During the Church and State struggles the Corps was the surest ally of the anti-clerical government. With a completely hostile Army, an uneasy judiciary, and an unsympathetic financial administration the Minister relied upon the Corps to enforce his policy. For a time the Corps was nearly as

[1] Quoted in G. Suarez: Clemenceau. Paris, 1932. Vol. II. pp. 110–111.

unpopular as in the middle of the nineteenth century.

Clemenceau found many occasions to exercise his mordant, black humour on the Corps, which suffered as much as the Ministry of the Interior from his caprices, his political management, and his legendary furies. He threatened one Prefect with instant dismissal for having left his Department without instructions, even though it had been to call on the Minister himself. He recommended the appointment of a half caste Sub Prefect to the *arrondissement* of Blanc; he wanted to nominate M. Gapais to the *arrondissement* of Gap simply for the sake of euphony. He once dismissed from a discussion the name of M. Alapetite (later *haut commissaire* of Alsace-Lorraine) protesting, 'ce n'est pas un préfet, c'est un toast'.[1]

In his own fashion, however, Clemenceau was very loyal to the Corps and rewarded it handsomely for its services. Apart from decorations and individual nominations to high posts, he promulgated on June 16, 1907, a decree fixing the formal etiquette and protocol to be observed between the various branches of government and the Corps. The precedence and honours accorded to the Prefectoral Corps were so great that the Army General Staff and the Judiciary registered indignant but fruitless protests against what they considered a slight on their status.

He always firmly backed his Prefects when they had taken vigorous measures to forestall civil disasters, or had acted energetically in solving them, even when such measures were in some ways ill-conceived, or caused local protest. But he had little sympathy for a member of the Prefectoral Corps who acted halfheartedly: the Corps was a *corps d'autorité*, and must accept the responsibility of leadership. During floods in the south west of France, Clemenceau dismissed the Prefect of the Haute Garonne for failing to take sufficiently energetic steps; but the Prefect's *chef de cabinet* was awarded the *légion d'honneur* for civil courage and initiative.

The pressure of politicians and Ministers inevitably left its mark on the Prefectoral Corps. The first decades of the Third

[1] Henry: op. cit. p. 256.

Republic were those of politicians' revenge on the Corps for its earlier behaviour. The autocratic, masterful and authoritarian Barons and Counts of the Second Empire gave place to cautious, prudent and discreet administrators. A Prefect who wished to make a career in the Corps had to please not only the politicians of the hour but the politicians who were yet to arrive. Thus was formed the agile and diplomatic Prefect upon whom much wit was expended. He was compared to a cat, more attached to the house than the master. Anatole France caused Worms-Clavelin to say, 'le régime est encore assez fort, Dieu merci, pour que je le soutienne'.[1]

At the lowest level Prefects became the tools of the local politicians. It was sometimes usual for the parliamentarians of the Department to require the Prefect, when first appointed, to wait upon them in Paris, a summons which only the boldest Prefect refused.[2] Professor Barthélémy, writing of the pre-1914 era, perhaps also with an eye to the early 1920's, remarked that there were Departments in which no citizen who wanted a warrant, a licence, or a favour, would think of approaching the Prefecture without first passing through his Deputy's office and collecting his *placet*. The Prefect's compliance was then guaranteed. Indeed even in 1923 the Minister of the Interior had to instruct Prefects not to hang around the corridors of the Chamber of Deputies.

But there was a persistent trend towards change. The brutal massacres of Prefects with every change of Ministry gave place to the 'waltz' of Prefects. A new Government involved very few dismissals, but there were some transfers from one Department to another. Only the holders of very senior posts were seriously threatened. The last massacre of the old type during the Third Republic was in 1924 when M. Herriot's Radical Ministry and the *cartel des gauches* eliminated those Prefects who had distinguished themselves too much in the service of the *bloc national*. Even when

[1] In *Histoire contemporaine: IV. 'Monsieur Bergeret à Paris'*.

[2] Jules Cambon had such an experience when appointed to the Rhône in 1887, and refused; but only with the explicit support of the Minister, M. Constans. G. Tabouis: *Life of J. Cambon*. London, 1938. p. 44.

M. Blum's Popular Front government came to office in 1936, involving a real change of political direction, there were few dismissals. A number of transfers gave the appearance of change, but only the most outspoken right-wing Prefects in high posts disappeared. Even Angelo Chiappe, who was closely linked with the extreme militant Right, was only transferred. A great impetus to this process had been given by the social demands upon the State which increased the importance of good administration, as well as by the need to ensure some internal harmony between the social classes, and some pacification of industrial strife in order to face the new international struggles of the 1930's. By 1939 the Prefectoral Corps had its own recognized career firmly based on precedent, in which administrative merit was a qualification as good as, if not better than, political favour. It was bound by its own terms of reference to act politically, yet it had come to regard impartiality as a criterion for action.

5. *Vichy and the Liberation* 1940-1950

When the war of 1939 began the Prefectoral Corps once again assumed the burden of civil administration in time of crisis. More fortunate than those of 1914, the Prefects had had four years in which to prepare their administrative machines for the coming emergency. They had received substantial new powers after 1934 empowering them to intervene in the economic field, and the officials under them were more experienced and competent than their predecessors of the other wars.

Even so, when the war broke out they were faced with complex problems of rationing, production, public order, transport, ARP, evacuation, and industrial relations. The Prefects had to cope with a Right which considered that an agreement with Hitler might be a better bargain than a new Popular Front, and with a Left convinced by the Spanish Civil War that rearmament was a weapon soon to be turned against themselves.

In the spring and summer of 1940 military preparations were even less advanced than those of the civil administration. The great sweep of the German armies across France temporarily destroyed the administrative and political unity of the country. Prefects left entirely to themselves had to treat with the German army, while others had to improvise emergency feeding, housing and air raid services for the mass of refugees who fled into the inner Departments. The Departments in the front line had to cope with major devastations. Some Prefects showed high civil valour, and faced the occupying power with pride and a real care for the populations under their control. Other Prefects disregarded their duties, fled in the face of the enemy, and left a gap that could not be filled unaided by municipal authorities. The Minister of the Interior savagely dismissed them as their names came in.

In June, 1940, the Armistice was signed with Germany; Marshal Pétain's new régime took office, suspended the Constitution of the Third Republic, and started on its authoritarian way. One of its first moves was to examine the high administrative corps in order to eliminate those unfavourable to the régime or too closely connected with the politicians of the Third Republic. The Universities and the Prefectoral Corps were marked bodies. But the Prefectoral Corps was now performing functions which could not be handled by the first political nominee who might turn up. History had shown that its political functions could be carried out by any political nominee, but its administrative duties, which in the conditions of France were of the highest importance, required more substantial qualities.

The Vichy government therefore began with a more subtle policy than its authoritarian predecessors. It removed those high-ranking Prefects who were closely attached to the Third Republic; dismissing some without more ado, transferring others to non-political posts, for instance as directors of hospitals. Their places were taken by men with some previous experience of administration: *conseillers d'Etat*, ministerial directors, some naval and military officers, ex-deputies and senators, and local officials. A number of Sub Prefects and Secretaries General of the Prefecture were promoted to Prefect to maintain administrative continuity. This policy ended in failure, for as the war went on the number of Prefects passing through the Corps increased rapidly, and, by the end, over two hundred Prefects had been swallowed up; the administrative experiment failed.

This was the result of the authoritarian politics of the new régime. Towards the end of 1940 the elected local authorities were reduced to silence by the Government, and the Mayors were put under the strict direct control of the Prefects. The Prefect's powers were brusquely increased. He appointed and suspended Mayors of the smallest Communes, while the Minister appointed those of the largest Communes. He took over all the powers of the *conseil général*. The prefectoral administration was now the centre of all local government, and the idea of decentralization had been completely abandoned.

War-time France was largely governed from the Prefectures; nevertheless the Prefect's authority was from some points of view curtailed. The first cause of this was the nature and philosophy of the Vichy régime. Mandatory instructions were issued to the Prefects which left them little scope for fitting policy to local circumstances. There was a great increase in centralization, and several technical Ministries gave their local representatives powers which challenged the Prefect's claim to supremacy in the Department. Other specially created Vichy organizations like the Militia and the local delegates of the Ministry of Information concerned themselves with supervising the Prefect's political beliefs, and kept check on his policy in order to report back to the Government. The unfortunate Prefects in Departments in the Occupied Zone had, in addition, to contend with the demands and depredations of the German army authorities. As the war went on Prefects who opposed these demands or attempted to save the population from the worst abuses of forced labour and food requisitioning were summarily removed from office. Prefects died in concentration camps as a result of their activities on behalf of the Resistance; some were deported but survived. One of the first organizers of the national resistance movement was Jean Moulin, Prefect of Eure et Loir, who was murdered by the Germans after being caught in a trap near Lyons.

The regionalist theories of the Vichy government seriously threatened the Corps. In April 1941 Vichy regionalized two of the most important branches of prefectoral administration; the police and economic affairs. One of these reforms created eighteen Regional Prefects, each of whom was to take up residence in a specified regional capital: six in unoccupied, twelve in occupied France. The Regional Prefect was also the departmental Prefect for the Department in which the regional capital was situated. He was supported by two immediate collaborators, an Intendant of Police and an Intendant for Economic Affairs. The regional heads of the technical services in the region were to help him as advisory experts. A Prefect-delegate was appointed to assist him in the administration of his own Department.

But the Regional Prefect lacked the essential means for success. Although he assumed some of their powers, the Regional Prefect was not given formal superiority over the departmental Prefects in his region. A major obstacle was that the Minister granted him no powers devolved from the centre, but merely transferred to him some of the powers of the ordinary Prefects. This did not help to solve the problem of over-centralization, but instead aroused the stubborn hostility of the ordinary Prefects. The Regional Prefect was called to deal directly with the Minister and to take back with him from their monthly meetings instructions for the entire region. But this political supremacy merely provoked the departmental Prefects, who saw in the Regional Prefect only a brash political upstart—which he sometimes was.

Only for the first two years could the Regional Prefect be regarded in any sense as an effective authority. After 1943 the decline of the German armed force led to an increasing number of political nominees being appointed as Regional Prefects, and many of them lacked the necessary authority and administrative capacity. The Intendant of Police, who was also appointed by the Government on political grounds, soon began to perform his duties independently of the Regional Prefect. The Intendant himself was often handicapped by the actions of other security forces which carried out their raids and policies without informing him. The Intendant for Economic Affairs was faced with an almost impossible task in face of the rapid decline in the economic situation of the country under war conditions. Finally, no attempt was made to force the other Ministries to adapt their service regions to the new pattern, and they remained entirely uncoordinated.

The result of the Vichy experiment in regional government was to bring the whole idea into disrepute. The new politicians of the Liberation frowned upon the region, since they saw in it an area of government too large to handle by the traditional political processes, and a new field of power and influence outside their own control. The region came to be branded as an authoritarian device.

Nevertheless, for the first two years of the Liberation, from 1944 to 1946, regional administration continued under *commissaires de la République*. Before the Normandy landings De Gaulle issued the absolute rule that every Prefect in office was automatically to be suspended. De Gaulle, in collaboration with the internal Resistance, nominated new Prefects for all the Departments, and *commissaires de la République* to take over from the Regional Prefects.[1]

The *commissaires de la République* all came from outside the Prefectoral Corps; there were four lawyers, three university professors, two journalists, two ex-parliamentarians, two councillors of the *Cour des Comptes*, a senior *ingénieur des ponts et chaussées*, an official of the Ministry of Finance, a doctor, a trade union leader, and an industrialist. Some of the Prefects had been Prefects under the Third Republic, who had either been dismissed by Vichy or had fled the country; others came from other administrative services, several were professors and teachers, and many had been officials in the police, the Post Office, colonial administration, the magistracy and the Navy. Several *rédacteurs de préfecture*, the junior administrators in the Prefectures, were promoted into the Prefectoral Corps in many cases with good

[1] M. Debré: *Un grand mouvement préfectoral: épisode de la Résistance.* Cahiers politiques. February–March, 1946.

results, and men from local administrations became Sub Prefects and Secretaries General. There were, however, several men appointed at this time whose only asset was the support of the local resistance groups, and who had neither administrative experience nor capacity to learn.

Conditions at the time of the Liberation were exacting. Some Vichy Prefects, for instance the Prefect-delegate at Montpellier, were summarily executed by the resistance forces; others managed to hand over their office and slip away; yet others were arrested by their successors and held for trial. Many Sub Prefects, on the other hand, were left alone.

General conditions were very bad in places; the battle still continued in parts of France, the police consisted largely of armed resistance groups, transport was completely dislocated, communications with Paris were cut, there were acute food and housing shortages, and in some parts a virtual breakdown in civil administration. The Prefectoral Corps itself was for a time very unstable. Only twenty Prefects who assumed office at the time of the Liberation were still in the same Prefecture in 1947, although normally this would have been a very short tour of duty. Of course some of the Prefects who moved went to bolster up the administration in very difficult places where a succession of inexperienced Prefects had led to widespread disorder. In the Loire Inférieure (Nantes) there were six Prefects in the space of three years, until a pre-war Prefect who had returned from a concentration camp in Germany assumed control. Some Prefects virtually abdicated their office in favour of the local committees of Liberation, others showed the grossest partisanship, others succumbed to political pressure. In these Departments it took the strongest Prefects, many of whom were experienced men from the Third Republic, to restore some prestige to the Prefectoral Corps. The Liberation showed conclusively that in the modern world it is impossible to improvise a new Corps without solid administrative foundations.

But for all the shortcomings of some of the men thrown for the first time into the job, the Corps, and especially the *commissaires de la République*, showed a sturdiness and a resilience that played a major part in France's return to normal in the next two years.

The *commissaires* were granted extraordinary powers to act in their regions with ministerial authority.[1] They were appointed by an ordinance of January 10, 1944, which empowered them to suspend all laws and regulations then in force, to take all necessary steps to ensure the maintenance of public order and the proper functioning of the administrative services, to suspend any official or elected representative in any public service and replace them with their own nominees, to suspend any legal judgement and criminal sentences, to block all bank accounts, search premises, arrest without warrant and bring to trial any person suspected of activities prejudicial to the safety of the State or the security of the allied armies. They could also requisition men and materials as needed in the public interest and to further the war effort.

These immense powers were exercised in most cases with moderation and discretion, and the *commissaires de la République* as a body stand high for their energy, their standard of duty, and their imagination.

Meanwhile a Purge Committee was set up by De Gaulle's Minister of the Interior to examine the records of members of the Prefectoral Corps who had served under Vichy. Its chairman came from outside the Corps. About sixty men were dismissed, some with, some without, pension, others were placed *en disponibilité*, others were cleared. The Prefects of course fared much worse than the Sub Prefects and the *chefs de cabinet*. Several Prefects who were not compromised but had no positive achievements to their credit went for a time into business, into other branches of administration, into the French military government in Germany, or returned to private life. Some of these Prefects have since come back to office.

Several of the 'parachuted' Prefects, and many named locally by the Resistance, were gradually weeded out by successive

---

[1] M-H. Fabre: *Les pouvoirs du commissaire régional de la République. Etude théorique et pratique de l'Ordonnance du 10 janvier, 1944.* In *Annales faculté de droit, Aix.* 1944. No. 38.

Ministers of the Interior between 1945 and 1947. They had been appointed provisionally in 1944, and their service after the Liberation was on probation until their abilities and capacity as members of the Corps could be tested. By the beginning of 1947 only thirty-eight of the Prefects who had entered the Corps at the Liberation remained in office.

By May 1946, France had recovered so far that the emergency powers of the *commissaires de la République* were no longer necessary. For a time it appeared as if the *commissaires* might remain a permanent part of the administration with the duty of controlling, co-ordinating, and stimulating the activity of the Prefects in their area. But they had aroused the political envy and spite of the National Assembly, and it refused to allow credits for their salaries in the budget of the Minister of the Interior. In May 1946, the post was abolished. During the following year the regional administration which had grown up, and which had served a very useful purpose, was gradually dismantled, and the departmental Prefects resumed their old duties and powers. No one was left to carry on the *commissaires'* work of co-ordination and control, and this was especially dangerous where public security was concerned. All but the identity sections of the regional police offices were returned either to the Prefect or the *Sûreté Nationale*, with effects which became evident when large scale insurrectionary strikes broke out in November and December 1947. The situation was tense and for a time parts of the country were almost controlled by the insurrectionaries. Order was finally restored by the combined efforts of police, military, and other security forces, but the danger had been so great that the Minister of the Interior, M. Moch, decided to take energetic measures to strengthen the country's internal security. In April 1948 he persuaded Parliament to approve a project for the creation of eight *inspecteurs généraux de l'administration en mission extraordinaire*. They were to serve in each military region. Each was given personally a Letter of Service from the Government which he was to use in cases of emergency, and which empowered him to act with ministerial authority over all civil and military organizations in his region. The police were once again put on a regional footing under the over-all control of the IGAME, and a special Secretary General of Police was appointed to his staff to be in charge of the administration, finance and technical services of the police. Operational control of the police remained with the ordinary Prefects except when the IGAME used his Letter of Service.

Some of the first IGAME were appointed from outside the Prefectoral Corps; the others were the Prefects who were serving in the regional capitals. The latter doubled the rôle of departmental Prefect and IGAME. The Government soon decided that a non-resident IGAME without a personal staff or daily administrative duties was unsatisfactory, for he lacked personal authority and the means to act. By 1950 all the IGAME were also resident Prefects in the regional capitals. Their posts can now be regarded as the highest in the Prefectoral Corps, except for those of the Prefects of the Seine and of Police.

The new Secretaries General of Police were chosen from senior Sub Prefects, and the post is now an integral part of prefectoral administration. It is dealt with in some detail in a later chapter.[1]

There were two important legal events which affected the Corps in the period between 1945 and 1950. The first of these was the Constitution itself, which was passed in 1946 and which for a time appeared to threaten the Prefect with a serious decline in importance. The issues raised by the Constitution will be dealt with in the section on the Prefects and their rôle in the Department.[2]

The second event which greatly affected the Corps arose from two ordinances of October 1945, which laid down new lines for the recruitment, training and organization of the whole French Administration. A *corps des administrateurs civils* was formed comprising the highest cadre of officials in all the senior branches of the service, that is to say the *Conseil d'Etat*, the *Cour des Comptes*, the inspectorates general, the foreign service, the

[1] See page 133 seq.
[2] See below page 174.

Prefectoral Corps and the senior posts in the Ministries, protectorates and colonies.

In addition, instead of each service and Ministry deciding on its own standards of entry and holding its own examinations, a special graduate school, the *Ecole nationale d'administration*, was set up. It superseded the old *Ecole libre des sciences politiques*, an unofficial organization which before the war had trained a very high proportion of the senior state officials.

There was much discussion as to whether members of the Prefectoral Corps should also take the rank and prerogatives granted to *administrateurs civils* in the same way as officials in the Ministries. The traditional view[1] was that the real supremacy of the Corps over all other officials in the Department came from its having no guaranteed career, no safeguards and no fixed rules. Their strength was that they alone could claim to be the representatives of the Government, and therefore, by that token, must be subject to dismissal at will. Insecurity was the very essence of their prestige; it was the source of their authority over all other officials. To become *administrateurs civils* like any official in a Ministry would be incompatible with that authority and with the personal nature of their responsibility.

The opposite point of view[2] was that members of the Prefectoral Corps would look like poor relations if they did not have the same status as other officials. Moreover the status of *administrateur civil* would grant them a minimum of security. Although they could be dismissed at will in the interests of the service, they would be legally entitled to a job in another branch of the administration, instead of depending for this on the Minister's favour.

During the discussions that followed, the Prefects as a body rejected security, and the Sub Prefects favoured it. This led to more discussion through 1948 and 1949. Finally the Corps obtained from the Minister the following solution. The Prefectoral Corps should have its own Statute, distinct from that granted to

[1] Expounded best by M. Billecard in the *Bulletin de l'Association des fonctionnaires du Ministère de l'Intérieur*. 1947. No. 2. p. 160.

[2] Held by M. Phalempin.

other state officials. This would allow for inter-change between the *administrateurs civils* of the Ministry of the Interior and the members of the Prefectoral Corps, and those who entered the Ministry from the Corps should be granted a comparable grade as an *administrateur civil*. The remainder of the Statute was to fix the methods of recruitment, promotion, and discipline in the Prefectoral Corps. The Statute was promulgated as the decree of June 19, 1950, and is now the basis of service in the Prefectoral Corps.

CHAPTER TWO

The Administrative Background

THE VARIOUS PHASES of the Prefectoral Corps' history have been marked by definite characteristics: energy and panache under Napoleon, ruthlessness and unscrupulousness under the Second Empire, cunning and pliability in the formative period of the Third Republic. Public opinion has endowed the Corps with a corporate personality, so that the man in the Prefecture is loaded with the vices and virtues of his forebears. A modern Prefect is seen as the descendant of the Prefects of the past, and some citizens are more prepared to pardon the Corps for its adventures and excesses than for its civic virtues.

The prefectoral 'myth' is a part of the French political tradition, which it would be beyond the scope of this study to unravel. Indeed, such things cannot be explained by direct description; the object of this study is to explain in outline the law and practice of the prefectoral system as it now exists, and perhaps this description may illustrate the character of the Corps and the part which its tradition plays in French life.

It seems best to proceed from the bottom rung of the prefectoral hierarchy (the *chefs de cabinet*), through the middle ranks (the Sub Prefects) to the work of the Prefects themselves, at each stage explaining the powers, duties, and daily life of each type of official. The advantages of proceeding in this way are that it takes the reader through the career of a Prefect in the same way as it is experienced by the Prefect himself; and that it gives some idea of the nature of the administrative machine which the Prefect controls before considering what it is that he does with it. But the Prefect himself is the central figure of this study, and the general scope of the system does not become plain until his powers and functions have been described. The object of the present chapter is to do this briefly and formally, and to explain the relation of the Prefectoral Corps to other parts of the central and local administration.

1. *The Theory of Administration*

French jurists classify the activities of the State under three heads. First, it controls those activities which affect the general interest of the State and the totality of its citizens; for example, defence and public safety. Second, it can assist private persons to undertake tasks which are in the general interest, but which the State itself does not wish to perform; for example, technical aid to farmers. Third, the State may itself provide services directly, either in the form of monopoly (e.g. the railways, the post office), or in collaboration with or competition with other organizations (e.g. the health services and hospitals).

To be effective, the State like any other institution must be able to formulate and express its will in a positive form and in a way intelligible to its citizens. In France the origin of this will resides in the people, and its expression and formulation is concentrated into the hands of the representatives of the people. These representatives form Parliament, and the decisions of this body, when issued in the appropriate way, are the laws of the land.

To enforce these laws it is necessary to have a body of men responsible for their execution, and this body is the Executive. The Executive is subordinate in time to the legislature, since its field of action can ultimately be determined by law. Nevertheless, the Executive possesses some autonomy of action. The daily work and organization of the administrative services created by Parliament in themselves require some degree of autonomous action. Besides, the legislator has sometimes given statutory powers to certain members of the Executive to deal promptly with emergencies or with recurring problems the resolution of which demands discretion. Sometimes Parliament has granted to subordinate territorial bodies like the Commune a limited freedom to organize and run their own affairs. Sometimes it lays down the principles of laws and then leaves the technical detail and methods of application to be decided by the Executive. Finally, French jurisprudence recognizes a general need for autonomous action by the Executive apart from statutory authority; the execution of the law, for example, which is its principal function, must in practice involve autonomous regulation and decision.

But the Executive's powers are circumscribed.[1] It must obey and apply the law; it is not authorized to interpret the meaning of the law. It is bound not only by detailed prescriptions in the Constitution but also by the general precepts of conduct which that document contains. It is bound by the principles of natural law as currently applied by the courts; for instance, none of its regulations may have retrospective effect.

To sum up: the activities, powers, duties and responsibilities of the persons who form the Executive—the *fonctionnaires*—are fixed by law or by regulations having the force of law.

2. *The Ministries*

The head of the Executive is the President of the Council of Ministers. Ministers—except those without Portfolio—are each individually responsible for one of the main administrative services organized by the Executive. Besides the Ministries there are special statutory bodies set up for a particular purpose; for instance, the *Cour des Comptes* which acts as the supreme board of audit for all pubic accounts, and the *Conseil d'Etat* which is the supreme administrative court for litigation involving public authorities.

Each Ministry is divided into two parts, the central administration and the exterior services. The central administration of a Ministry consists of offices in Paris with nation-wide responsibility and competence. It is expected to make general policy, co-ordinate services, and control and stimulate its own officials in the execution of their duties. The central administration is divided into several parts. First, there is the Minister's cabinet, which is his

[1] M. Waline: *Traité élémentaire de Droit Administratif.* Paris, 1951. p. 41.

personal office with a staff directly appointed by him. Next come the directorates of the Ministry each of which deals with a major section of the administrative services organized by the Ministry; for example, the Directorate of the *Sûreté Nationale* in the Ministry of the Interior, or the Directorate of the Budget in the Ministry of Finance. In most Ministries there are also 'attached services' which are agencies specializing in a technical aspect of the Ministry's work, such as a laboratory or research organization. Finally, some Ministries have statutory supervision, but not detailed control, of special autonomous public bodies created by Parliament, such as the Tobacco Monopoly and the French National Railways.

Most Ministries also have exterior services. These are composed of officials posted by the Ministry to all parts of France and the French Union to run the services provided by the Ministry. Thus, the Ministry of Finance has in each Department a *trésorier payeur général* who is responsible for the management of public funds; the Ministry of Defence has General Officers Commanding in the nine military regions in France; the Ministry of Public Works has *inspecteurs des ponts et chaussées* in each Department; the Ministry of Education has in each of the seventeen university regions a high administrative and academic authority, the *recteur d'académie*, and in each Department an *inspecteur d'académie* responsible for educational administration and inspection.[1]

These exterior services are staffed by state officials[2] and are responsible for the work of their Ministry in their area. Most Ministries use the Department as the effective area of local administration, but this may be determined by each Ministry to suit its own convenience, and many Ministries group Departments into regions for purposes of inspection and technical co-operation.

[1] A complete list of the services in a Department is contained in Appendix A, and in a region in Appendix B.

[2] Clerical staffs and local experts may be recruited locally, but locally recruited officials of the State are to be distinguished from officials employed by local authorities.

3. *The Prefect's position*

The Prefect's legal position is a result of several factors. In the first place, if we revert for a moment to the juridical concept of the State, it is clear that for practical reasons certain members of the Executive must be legally entitled to act in the name of the State. It is also clear that the State has a permanent interest in good government, in the security of its frontiers, in the stability of society, in the health and welfare of the population. These permanent interests are liable to injury by men or by natural forces, and some members of the Executive have the responsibility and the power to take precautions against such dangers, and in emergency to act rapidly to overcome them.

In the Departments it is the Prefect alone who is legally the permanent representative and incarnation of the State. He alone is entitled to act in the name of the State in legal affairs, and he must protect the population against civil and natural calamities. The Constitution states that the Prefect 'is the representative of the national interest', and this is the first major source of the Prefect's authority.

In the second place we must consider the position of the Prefect with regard to the exterior services of the Ministries.

The officials of each exterior service specialize in one branch of work, and are responsible only to one Minister. The French call them 'technical' officials. It may be best in English to call them 'specialists', in that they are experts qualified in one branch of administration which need not be in the English sense 'technological'. The term and its meaning are important in this context, for the French distinguish between the Prefects and the other state officials in the Department by the fact that Prefects are not 'technical' officials: they are *polyvalent*, that is, 'exerçant leurs fonctions sous l'autorité de plusieurs Ministres et pour assurer la gestion de services dépendant de plusieurs départements ministériels'.[1]

This situation arises because the Minister of the Interior has a

[1] Waline: op. cit. p. 192.

general competence for the internal affairs of France, Algeria, and the Overseas Departments. There is a lengthy historical process behind this. The Ministry of the Interior was created by a law of August 7, 1790, and its original powers are contained in the law of May 25, 1791. The Minister was then charged to maintain the organization of the Kingdom: he was to ensure the liberty, tranquillity, and public prosperity of the country, and he was to control elections, local authorities, education, religious bodies, public security and public safety, mines, highways, public works, rivers, hospitals, agriculture, fisheries, industry and commerce, patents and inventions. His charter, in brief, was to administer all things except war, foreign affairs, justice and finance.

From about 1830 onwards there was a tendency for important bureaux of the Ministry of the Interior to rise first to the status of Directorate, and eventually to break away and become separate Ministries. Thus, the Ministry of Public Education was created in 1828, the Ministry of Public Works in 1830, the Ministry of Agriculture in 1853, the Ministry of Labour in 1906, and the various economic Ministries after the 1914 war. These are the 'technical' Ministries, and although their activity is now beyond the jurisdiction of the Minister of the Interior, he remains generally responsible for the safety, stability and tranquillity of the population. There is a broad sense in which the Minister of the Interior is still responsible for internal government.

The Prefect is the direct subordinate of the Minister of the Interior, and consequently he possesses by delegation part of this general power of internal government. It will be remembered that when Napoleon originally created the Corps the law explicitly charged the Prefect alone with the administration of the Department. In French terminology this means that the Prefect is 'l'administrateur du droit commun'.[1] The grant of powers to local elected assemblies like the *conseils généraux* and the *conseils municipaux*, and the delegation of some powers by the technical

---

[1] R. Bonnaud Delamare: *Attributions juridiques des préfets et sous-préfets*. Editions du Livre, Monte Carlo, 1951. p. 3.

Ministries to their own officials in the Department has not altered the basic legal conception. The Prefect remains the general administrator of the Department with a general responsibility for 'government'.

In order that the Prefect should have sufficient powers to direct, co-ordinate and control the work of the officials of the technical services, the Prefect is not only the delegate of the Minister of the Interior but the personal representative of every other Minister as well, and the delegate of the Government as a whole. 'The Prefect is appointed by a Decree of the Council of Ministers,' says the law, 'and he assures, under the authority of the competent Ministers, the general direction of all the activities of the state officials in the Department.' He alone is 'the representative and the delegate of the Government'. Ministers deal with their own officials on technical matters, but with the Prefect on matters of policy, co-ordination of services, and the supervision of administration. When Ministers delegate powers of decision to lower administrative authorities they are expected to grant them to the Prefect and not to their own officials. Thus the Prefect can control and initiate general policy in the Department, and act as the leader of its government.

4. *The Local Authorities*

The third aspect of the Prefect's position in law is that he is the *tuteur* of the Communes in the Department. The legal basis for this is as follows.

The State recognizes that there are groups of citizens within itself who have common interests. They may be groups of men who wish to form a fishing club. Or they may wish to pool their resources for financial gain or security, such as a mutual benefit society, an industrial company or a trade union. There are yet other groups which have an intrinsic corporate interest because they live together in the same locality; these are the local communities, or *collectivités locales*.

The legislature may impose various conditions on the legal recognition of different types of association. It may allow local sports clubs to acquire legal personality simply by registration; it may insist that the financial arrangements of mutual societies conform to certain rules, in order to prevent fraud; it may insist on special requirements before private businesses can obtain the status of public companies. As the rôle of these corporations more closely resembles and impinges upon the duties and responsibilities of the State itself, so state control becomes more rigorous. Therefore, when the legislature allows local communities a corporate status, it subjects their decisions and their activities to much closer scrutiny than it considers necessary for a football club. It not only requires local authorities to conform to the law (as all persons must); in addition, certain of their acts must obtain the approval of a state authority before they can be regarded as legally valid. The state authority who exercises this supervision over the Communes of a Department is the Prefect.

The other important type of local community is the Department, and it is the Minister of the Interior, and not the Prefect, who is the *tuteur* of the Departments. The Prefect is, however, the head of the Department's executive, responsible for administering its affairs under the control of the *conseil général*, the Department's elected assembly. The Constitution of 1946 introduced the idea that the chairman of the *conseil général* should become the chief executive officer of the Department as the Mayor is of the Commune. But the Constitution postponed the enactment of this principle to later laws which have never been passed. The Prefect remains, as in Napoleon's day, the executive head of the Department.

5. *The Officials*

The Prefect is thus the representative of the State in the Department, the delegate of the Government, the agent of all the Ministers, the *tuteur* of the Communes, and the executive head of the Department. This means that he deals with three levels of officials.

First, there are the state officials serving in the exterior services of their Ministries, who are responsible to their own Ministers, and whose competence is restricted to their specialized work. There is also a special category of state officials, those recruited by the Minister of the Interior for service in the administration of the Prefectures. The two most important grades are the *chefs de division* of the Prefecture and the *attachés* of the Prefecture. They are under the disciplinary control of the Prefect, but major disciplinary measures can be taken only by the Minister. They are responsible, under the supervision of the Prefect, for the efficient administration of the Prefecture. They are liable to transfer from one Prefecture to another, but in practice most of them are firmly established in one place and expect to end their careers in the Prefecture in which they started.

Second, there are the officials employed and recruited by the Departments, the departmental officials. These are the official subordinates of the Prefect in his capacity as chief executive officer of the Department. Most departmental officials are recruited by examination held under the supervision of the Prefect, and they are appointed to office by him. They administer the services set up and financed by the Department; some of them are professional experts such as architects, doctors, and veterinary surgeons, and some of these may give part-time service under contract.

Finally, there are the communal officials. These are recruited and paid by the Communes, but their recruitment is subject to some degree of state supervision. Their pay must not exceed that of comparable officials in state employment and generally they are recruited by an examination which is subject to ministerial or prefectoral approval. Some communal officials—for instance, the *garde champêtre*—can only take office after the appointment has been approved by the Prefect or Sub Prefect, and can only be dismissed with their approval.

6. *Prefectoral Administration*

This sketch of the administrative background needs to complete it some reference to the formal framework of prefectoral administration. This will be much amplified later.

The Prefectoral Corps is based upon the territorial divisions of France. There are ninety Departments in France, three Departments in Algeria, and four Overseas Departments—Martinique, Guiana, Réunion and Guadeloupe. In the capital of each Department there is a Prefecture.

The Department has three sub-divisions. The first, the primordial unit of French local government, is the Commune, of which there are almost 38,000 in France, an average of 426 for each Department. Next, there is the *canton* grouping about thirty Communes, and used mainly for electoral, judicial, and administrative purposes. The third sub-division is the *arrondissement* which consists of about five or six *cantons*, or between one hundred and one hundred and fifty Communes. In the capital of each *arrondissement* is a Sub Prefecture, which is the personal residence of the Sub Prefect and the administrative headquarters of the *arrondissement*.

The Prefecture is likewise the official residence of the Prefect and the general administrative headquarters of the Department. The offices are divided for administrative purposes into divisions and bureaux; some deal with police, some with the tutelage of the Communes, some with departmental affairs, some with state services. In principle, the Prefecture is supposed to relieve the technical services of other Ministries of their administrative burden. An agricultural economist of the Ministry of Agriculture should not be expected to supervise the office routine of sending out forms, collating statistics, or typing circulars to Mayors and farmers. In practice each specialized service acquires a small administrative staff of its own. Since the war they have tended to duplicate the work of the Prefecture. Periodic purges are necessary, and in 1953 and 1954 energetic measures were being taken to centralize routine administrative work into the bureaux and divisions of the Prefecture.[1]

The Prefect is assisted in the organization and administration of the Prefecture by two members of the Prefectoral Corps. One

---

[1] For the growth of this tendency and the problems it has created, see below p. 166 seq.

is the Secretary General of the Prefecture, who is his second in command. The other is his personal assistant who is called either his *chef de cabinet* or his *directeur du cabinet*. The *chef de cabinet* is the lowest ranking member of the prefectoral hierarchy, serving his apprenticeship in the service. In Prefectures where the burden of work and responsibility is so great that it would be unwise to expect the Prefect to rely on an unseasoned and inexperienced novice, a Sub Prefect of some seniority is appointed to act as personal assistant, and he takes the more important title of *directeur du cabinet*.

The prefectoral career thus runs through the grades of *chef de cabinet*, Sub Prefect, Prefect. All grades have certain rights and duties common to all members of the Prefectoral Corps.

They are entitled to free furnished accommodation at the Department's expense. They all have a dress uniform with gold or silk badges of rank which is worn on official occasions. Prefects and Sub Prefects have an expense account, an entertainment allowance and pension rights, and they are entitled to free transport. Prefects take precedence over other state officials. On state visits the Prefect officially receives the President of the Republic at the boundary of his Department, and the Sub Prefect at the boundary of his *arrondissement*. They also officially receive Ministers and Vice-Ministers when they visit.

Prefects are entitled to military honours from all officers and other ranks, and Sub Prefects from all ranks and officers below field rank. If a Prefect dies in office he is buried with full military and civil honours; a Sub Prefect with full civil honours. When a Prefect or Sub Prefect first takes up his post the local civil and military authorities are expected formally to receive him.

The Corps has other prerogatives which will be described later, but these are mentioned here to indicate the special position which is given even to its junior members.

CHAPTER THREE

The Chef de Cabinet

THE *chef de cabinet* is the most junior member of the Prefectoral Corps; he possesses no statutory powers but is nevertheless an integral part of the service.

1. *Recruitment*

This has not always been true. During much of the nineteenth century the *chef de cabinet* was not officially recognized, had little personal status and very little hope of promotion. He was the Prefect's private secretary and was for a long time known as his *secrétaire particulier*. Consequently his appointment was entirely a matter for the individual Prefect to decide, and the Ministry did not try to control his qualifications.

Gradually, as the Prefectoral Corps developed a ladder of promotion, the *chef de cabinet* came to be accepted as a permanent part of the Corps, and it was quite common for him to be promoted to Sub Prefect after a certain time. By the 1880's the post of *chef de cabinet* was regarded as an honourable post for a young man of ambition, with good prospects for promotion to the highest posts in the Corps.

But though the Ministry now accepted him as part of the Corps, it made no attempt to control conditions of entry. This was partly because the post was a useful piece of patronage: Prefects chose young men with good connections; the sons, nephews and friends of Deputies, Senators, Ministers and other Prefects. It was also due to the widely held conviction that the Prefectoral Corps required qualities of political intelligence, social *savoir-faire*, and an understanding of affairs which were not subject to any formal tests. The Prefect himself was, then, the best judge of the most likely young man, for he could select him for his real qualities, unfettered by formal considerations. In 1907, a writer in the Annuaire of the Prefectoral Corps put the general feeling on the subject: 'Pas de noviciat, pas de stage, pas de concours. On n'exige plus à l'entrée de la carrière aucun grade universitaire; ceux qui sont investis de cette sorte de fonctions devant, avant tout, posséder certaines qualités d'esprit et de caractère qui ne peuvent ni s'acquérir dans une école, ni être constatées par des diplômes ou des examens.

'Ces qualités d'esprit et de caractère, une fois réunies, rien n'empêche que le fonctionnaire soit instruit, bon administrateur, rompu au maniement des affaires publiques, et montre dans l'accomplissement de ses devoirs que la bonne administration est un des résultats de la bonne politique.'

It was the classic justification for nepotism.

In the first three decades of this century *chefs de cabinet* entered by various methods. Many entered before or after taking a degree by joining the staff of a Prefect to whom they had been introduced. Some were noticed by a Prefect among the staff of the Prefecture. Others served first as *rédacteurs* in the Ministry of the Interior, where they were well placed to come under the eye of the Director of Personnel, from whom Prefects with a vacancy might seek suggestions.

Several passed through the *Ecole libre des sciences politiques*, a private establishment with official backing, which gave an intensive training at an advanced level to those ambitious for high official posts. It enjoyed a special relation with the Ministries and the *grands corps*, which greatly facilitated direct entry for those possessing its diploma. Many of its students went to serve as supernumerary *chefs de cabinet* on the staffs of important Prefects like those at Strasburg and Marseilles. Others with political connections managed to join the personal staff of some Minister and, as a reward, to enter the Corps later.

But after the 1914 War it became increasingly obvious that the Prefectoral Corps offered a career in which the administrative element was becoming more important than the political. The public and many politicians regarded nepotism as an improper method of entry to administrative posts; people concerned with administration were worried lest the Corps should fall below the necessary standards of administrative ability. After much pressure, a decree of October 12, 1933, enacted that henceforth all *chefs de cabinet* were to be recruited by a special examination held by the Ministry of the Interior.

The first of these examinations was held in the following year. Entry to the examination was restricted to those who already possessed a degree. The first part was a written test, and the most successful candidates were selected for interview. The interview was very important, for it was at this stage that the special qualities required in a prefectoral official were sought out. The most highly placed candidates after the interview were then inscribed in a *liste d'aptitude*, subject to the express right of the Minister of the Interior to reject any person, no matter what his marks, if he considered that his entry to the Corps was contrary to the public interest. To be inscribed on the *liste d'aptitude* did not mean a job. It meant that any Prefect who wanted a *chef de cabinet* must choose him from the list. But there were more names on the list than there were places vacant, and the Prefect could interview as many as he wished before deciding on his new *chef de cabinet*. If at the end of the year a candidate had not been chosen, he had to resit the examination.

The examinations held in these years produced a crop of extremely good candidates. At one time the Ministry tried to raise the qualifications to include a doctorate; but this was found to limit the field too much. Several of the new entrants came from among the junior officials of Prefectures; some came from other administrations such as tax departments, the Post Office, and other Ministries. There were a few teachers, newly qualified barristers and architects, and one or two journalists. These examinations introduced into the Corps many first class men who have since risen to high office.

Examinations were suspended for a time at the beginning of the

War, and a new series was not started until September, 1941. One significant change now was that the examinations for *chef de cabinet* were formally linked with those for *rédacteurs* at the Ministry of the Interior, thus easing transfer between branches and emphasizing their inter-relation.

The last of the wartime examinations was held in April, 1944. For the next two years entry as *chef de cabinet*, as to all other branches of the Prefectoral Corps, became a very haphazard matter. Departments were cut off from Paris, resistance groups sometimes forced their nominations on Prefects and sometimes 'appointed' the Prefect himself. But the *chefs de cabinet* as a body were not so severely treated as the senior branches of the Corps. Those who entered at this time were police officers, a naval officer, an *inspecteur du génie rural*, an official of the Paris Transport Administration, and so on; they were, in many cases, capable officials well able to fill the post, and many of these *chefs de cabinet* were better qualified for their jobs than were their Prefects for theirs.

As soon as possible after the Liberation there was great activity for the reform of the French Administration: in 1945 and 1946 a General Statute for officials was promulgated, a provisional statute for the Prefectoral Corps was drafted, and the *Ecole nationale d'administration* (ENA) was opened to train the new *corps des administrateurs civils*. Under the provisional statute for the Prefectoral Corps, those *chefs de cabinet* who had entered at the Liberation were required to possess a degree before they could become permanently established, and Prefects' nominations to the post had to receive the placet of the Minister of the Interior.

It was decided at this time that in principle the *chefs de cabinet* should be graduates of the ENA, but as an interim measure until the flow of graduates started, the pre-war system of direct entry by examination held under the auspices of the Minister of the Interior should be used to fill vacant posts.

The Statute of the Prefectoral Corps still allows for two types of entry for *chefs de cabinet*: direct entry and graduation through the ENA. At least ten of the posts of *chef de cabinet*, says the Statute, are reserved to graduates of the ENA. The remainder can be chosen from a *liste d'aptitude* compiled after the examination by the Ministry of the Interior. To enter for this examination candidates must now possess one of the diplomas or degrees required by candidates who enter for the ENA. On an average there are 200 candidates, of whom eighteen are put on the *liste d'aptitude*, and in 1951 there were only two vacant posts to be filled. The normal post-war intake by this method has been about seven every year.

The successful candidate, once appointed, remains on probation for a year before being established. During this time the Prefect or the Minister can ask for his appointment to be cancelled, and then the *jury* in charge of his examination decides whether or not to strike him off. He is not eligible for promotion to Sub Prefect third class until he has at least four years' seniority, unless he has previously been for at least five years an *attaché* of a Prefecture.

The second method of entry is from the ENA. The ENA trains all the future *administrateurs civils*, including those for the foreign service, the *grands corps*, and the Ministries.[1] Competition is extremely keen. There are two kinds of qualification for entry: first, a diploma or degree from a recognized higher educational establishment; second, at least five years' service in a branch of public administration. There are different entrance examinations for these two groups. For the first, emphasis is put upon detailed academic and legal knowledge; for the second, on experience of active administration. Both examinations comprise a written part, followed by interviews with expert committees for discussion, analysis, and exposition of topics placed before the candidate with very little time for preparation.

The successful candidates from both groups join together once they have been accepted into the ENA. As soon as they enter they automatically become *fonctionnaires*, paid by the State and under contract to finish the course and to spend at least ten years in government service.

[1] Details of entry qualifications and particulars of the course are in: *Ecole Nationale d'Administration*. Imprimerie Nationale, Paris, 1950.

They are separated into four main divisions: for General Administration, Foreign Affairs, Finance, and Social Administration. Each division trains for a particular group of Ministries: for example, the General Administration division covers the various branches of the Ministry of the Interior (the *inspection générale*, the *conseils de préfecture*, the *administrateurs civils*, and the Prefectoral Corps), the Ministry of National Defence, the Ministry of National Education, the Secretariat General of the Government, the French Radio Administration and *administrateurs* for Morocco and Tunisia.

The course in the ENA lasts for three years. During the first year the students spend ten months in the provinces, in Germany or in North Africa, serving under a senior administrator such as a Prefect. He trains them in the ways of his own administration and reports on them at the end of the *stage*. Each student must write a short thesis during this period on a subject which attracts his attention, such as the condition of local industries or the possibilities for agricultural development in the Department.

The second year is spent inside the ENA, undergoing intensive instruction in administrative and constitutional law, history, politics, economics, and so on. At the end of the year the students take their final examination. They are graded, and the senior posts open in the various Ministries and *corps* are filled in accordance with the wishes of the students in order of merit. The choice of the students is restricted to those posts for which their division has trained them; if they are in the General Administration division they cannot choose a post in one of the financial or economic Ministries. But students at the head of the list have the option of a post in one of the three highest *corps* of the State: the *Conseil d'Etat*, the *Cour des Comptes*, and the *inspection des finances*. The Ministry of the Interior is therefore rarely the first choice for those who are most successful in the General Administration division[1]. The third year is spent partly *en stage* and partly attending general courses at the school.

[1] In 1954 the Prefectoral Corps became one of those *corps* which the most highly placed students could choose to enter.

Under the existing circumstances the ENA is not producing sufficient graduates suitable for the Prefectoral Corps. At the same time the method of direct entry is not a satisfactory way of filling the gap, because those with the necessary qualifications enter the ENA if they can, and only look upon the examination of the Ministry of the Interior as a second string to their bow.

It is the Government's declared object that the present system should make the *administrateurs civils* the administrative élite of the country, with prospects for rapid promotion. A *chef de cabinet* who is a graduate of the ENA has only to serve for one year in that post before he is eligible for promotion to Sub Prefect third class: the direct entry *chef de cabinet* has to wait at least four years. Similarly, an *administrateur civil* from the ENA can be promoted into the Prefectoral Corps without ever having served as a *chef de cabinet*; he gains administrative experience in Paris, and then when a post becomes vacant he goes out directly as a Sub Prefect.

The present system of recruiting the *chefs de cabinets* has had two important results.

Firstly, the great majority have been recruited by direct entry. Of the twenty-two ENA graduates who went into the Ministry of the Interior between 1947 and 1949, only nine were posted as *chefs de cabinet*, and within two years seven of these were Sub Prefects third class. Secondly, the *chefs de cabinet*, as a body, are being slowly 'proletarianized'. There is an increasing tendency to send the highly qualified and intensely trained ENA graduates out from the Ministry as Sub Prefects rather than to promote the direct entry *chefs de cabinet*. The figures between 1948 and 1952 show that eleven new Sub Prefects third class were appointed; five of them were graduates of the ENA, and the remaining six had never served as *chefs de cabinet* at all, but entered the Corps directly as Sub Prefects from the Ministry of the Interior, from *conseils de préfecture*, or from university teaching. Consequently the length of service for the *chef de cabinet* is gradually extending. Half the present *chefs de cabinet* were recruited before 1948, three quarters of these in 1947. The average age of the *chefs de cabinet* has now risen to over thirty, compared with twenty-six in 1939 and twenty-four in 1925.

This tendency is accentuated by serious overcrowding in the upper grades of the Prefectoral Corps as a consequence of the rapid promotion of the brilliant young men of the Liberation. The chances of promotion for the direct entry *chef de cabinet* are thin, and the general stagnation in the hierarchy of the service means that he does not even gain experience through serving in a variety of Prefectures. Whereas before the War many *chefs de cabinet* held four or five posts before being promoted, the average number now held is two. The direct entrant can probably never hope for more than that he should one day become a Sub Prefect *hors classe*. This damages the spirit of solidarity in the Corps. The only satisfactory solution is to increase the intake of ENA graduates as quickly as possible, and eventually to draw all the *chefs de cabinet* from this source. But this may require some reform of the ENA itself, and it may not be easy for the Ministry of the Interior to obtain this.

2. *The Cabinet*

Before describing the daily work of a *chef de cabinet*, it is necessary first to describe the personal cabinet of the Prefect and its function in the Prefecture.

Every Prefect has his own personal cabinet; but it varies in size and importance according to the importance of the Department. His immediate collaborator is his *chef de cabinet* or his *directeur du cabinet*. Under the supervision of the Prefect's cabinet and of the Secretary General of the Prefecture, the work of the Prefecture is carried out by divisions and bureaux.

In 1942 and in 1946 the *inspection générale de l'administration*, the inspecting staff of the Ministry of the Interior, worked out a standard pattern for the organization inside a Prefecture. This pattern varied with the size and importance of the Department, and enumerated the different categories of affairs to be dealt with by the cabinet, the divisions, and the bureaux of the Prefecture. Individual Prefects have, however, their own conceptions of what is administratively desirable, and there are consequently considerable differences between the practice of Prefectures, even those of the same class.

In the smallest Prefectures the cabinet consists of only two or three typists and secretaries under the supervision of an *attaché* of the Prefecture. In larger Prefectures the staff may number a dozen or so.

In all Prefectures, no matter what their size, the cabinet deals with the Prefect's correspondence, confidential affairs, political questions, and the award of honours and distinctions. In other words it deals with political rather than the purely administrative side of the Prefect's work. Some Prefects have also transferred to their cabinet business normally transacted by the bureaux. In the Prefecture of Ariège (Foix), for instance, elections and the registration of associations are under the cabinet's control; in other third class Prefectures, like the Basses-Alpes and Lot, the Prefect has transferred responsibility for personnel and recruitment from the Secretariat General to the cabinet. In many other Prefectures the cabinet deals with the appointments made by the Prefect to the boards of control of hospitals, *hospices* and welfare centres.

In larger Prefectures more matters tend to be transferred to the cabinet, despite the increased administrative complication. In Allier, Ardèche and Eure-et-Loir some aspects of police administration are dealt with by the cabinet; for instance the control of casinos, lotteries, aliens, the issue of passports and visas, the organization of the fire services, and the inspection of places of entertainment. Other Prefects have deliberately brought under their immediate control matters which they consider require particularly delicate handling. In Indre-et-Loire, for example, industrial disputes and arbitration are dealt with by the cabinet, and in the Sarthe the very difficult problem of executing writs of possession obtained by landlords from the courts. In the Var, the cabinet even deals with prison administration and with requests for conditional releases from jail. It is fairly common in larger Prefectures to transfer to the cabinet powers of control and regulation normally assumed by the division for Police and General Administration.[1] The arrangements often depend on local conditions. Military affairs and civil defence go to the cabinet in Calvados, resignations of local councillors and Mayors in the Manche, public housing projects in the Marne, tourism in the Haut-Rhin. In addition, in many Prefectures of all sizes, the special bureau of National Defence established by a ministerial circular of January 10, 1949, is attached to the cabinet rather than to a division; in some cases it comes directly under the senior *attaché* of the Prefecture in the cabinet, in others it is a part time job for one of the junior officials.

3. *The Rôle of the Chef de Cabinet*

The part played by the *chef de cabinet* in the work of the Prefecture and in the life of the Department depends almost entirely on the individual Prefect. The *chef de cabinet* is never a mere cipher, because he is a member of the Prefectoral Corps, but he may be treated as a collaborator and personal assistant, or he may be used as a mere secretary and deprived of initiative or responsibility. The latter situation is unusual, but it can happen. The Prefect may keep his *chef de cabinet* on the fringe of political and social affairs, or he may immerse him in them.

As a junior member of the Prefectoral Corps the *chef de cabinet* is entitled to free lodging provided by the Department, either an apartment in the Prefecture or a flat in the town. The comfort of its furnishings depends upon the generosity of the *conseil général*. Where, as is the case in many Departments, the Prefecture has been specially built for its purpose he will be accommodated inside the Prefecture. Where, on the other hand, the Prefecture has been, for example, an archbishop's palace, or an old private *hôtel*, the *chef de cabinet* is generally lodged outside. As a general rule, if the Prefecture is not large enough to accommodate the Prefect, the Secretary General and the *chef de cabinet*, it is more often the Secretary General who lives outside. This is because the Prefect often insists that his personal assistant should be always at hand.

[1] See page 126.

Chefs de cabinet seem to prefer outside accommodation; not because they can then escape the Prefect's eye, but because flats appropriated for the *chefs de cabinet* in a Prefecture tend to be those rooms not useful for anything else. These are generally the attics. Even then, they compare favourably with the type of flat that a young official without private means could afford, but they do not stand comparison with the quarters of the Prefect and of the Secretary General.

The *chef de cabinet's* position inside the Prefecture is a curious one. By virtue of his status as the Prefect's personal assistant, he is entrusted with important and confidential knowledge. On the other hand, he is frequently a less able administrator than the *chefs de bureau* and the *chefs de division*, and is certainly less experienced.

The *chef de cabinet* is by custom the man who is always available. In some Prefectures when the day's work is finished the switchboard operator automatically connects the incoming lines to the *chef de cabinet's* private phone. The need for instant action in emergencies has been proved too many times in the past for any sensible Prefect to omit taking precautions. This is very good training for the *chef de cabinet*; it accustoms him to sacrificing his private life to his duties.

The *chef de cabinet* must also play his part in the social and ceremonial functions of the Prefect. Ceremonies to mark the anniversary of Liberation day, Armistice day, the fall of the Bastille, the *fête des mères*, school prize givings, the opening of a new school, technical college or hospital wing; the award of the *médaille de mérite agricole* to a local worthy; the opening session of a local learned society; all require a representative of the State. When the Prefect goes he often takes his *chef de cabinet* with him, partly, if he is new, to see with what aplomb and *savoir-faire* he can conduct himself on public occasions. Sometimes the *chef de cabinet* has to go on his own, when the rest of the prefectoral administration in the Department is attending something else. The *chef de cabinet* is commonly expected to write the Prefect's speeches on these formal occasions, and he must make sure that they are appropriate to the local situation, as in some places local feelings are so intense that an unwitting gaffe can cause a lot of trouble. Social duties vary considerably from Department to Department; they are more onerous, for instance, in the South than in the West. The *chef de cabinet* is seldom expected to entertain visitors at his own expense if they are not his personal friends, but he may have to act as temporary host while the Prefect is away.

As the Prefect's personal assistant the *chef de cabinet* must do anything the Prefect requires of him. His office is always adjacent to the Prefect's and joined to it by private speaker. He often looks after the Prefect's engagement book, keeps the official diary, and makes appointments for those wanting interviews. In most Prefectures the *chef de cabinet* is in charge of the cipher books, and he codes and decodes the confidential reports sent out by his Prefect, and those received from the Ministry or other Prefects.

An administrative task which normally falls to the *chef de cabinet* is the compilation of records and the examination of credentials for anyone in the Department who is recommended (or proposes that he be recommended) for an honour, decoration or award. There are several of these: the *médaille d'honneur départementale et communale*, the *médaille de la reconnaissance française*, and, of course, the *légion d'honneur*. The *chef de cabinet* will, in some cases, have to determine whether the candidate is really eligible, for example, that an applicant for the *médaille d'honneur des sapeurs pompiers* has really been a fireman for the requisite number of years. In the case of honorific titles of some distinction such as the *légion d'honneur*, some tact may be necessary; the timely award of one may pacify a restless politician and be of importance to the Minister, or it may bring the Prefect under fire from rivals. The *chef de cabinet* when compiling the dossier consults whatever official documents are available about the candidate's life and background, and gets in touch with, for example, the Sub Prefect of the *arrondissement* where he lives to obtain any other information he can.

The more strictly 'political' matters which the Prefect must attend to are rarely confided to anyone other than the *chef de cabinet*, for this cuts down the chance of leaks, and restricts the number of people who could use the information for their own ends.

An important part of this work is the preparation of reports for the Prefect. Sometimes they concern detailed information on a general subject which shows signs of becoming important; sometimes they are preliminary drafts and information for a report which the Prefect is making to a Minister. The Prefect may wish to know the incidence of seasonal unemployment in the Department in order to make arrangements for spacing out the public works in the area to the best advantage. The *chef de cabinet* can call upon the expert agencies such as the specialized bureaux in the Prefecture, the Inspectorate of Labour, and he can ask for information from the Sub Prefectures. Or the Prefect may be preparing a periodical report on the state of public opinion in the Department for the Minister of the Interior, or on the popular reactions to a price-cutting programme for the economic Ministries.

Sometimes the Prefect may consider that the situation in a part of his Department is grave enough to require a report from someone more reliable or more politically intelligent than the local *commissaire de police*. During a very acute outbreak of food-poisoning in the town of Pont St. Esprit in the late summer of 1951, as soon as the first reports indicated a number of deaths and a danger of widespread panic, the Prefect of the Gard at Nîmes despatched his *chef de cabinet* to report on the spot the real circumstances of the outbreak, and to reassure the population that those in authority were actively concerned. This went beyond what could be expected from the police, who, with the public health authorities, were primarily concerned with tracing the poison to its source.

There are some political matters of purely private concern or so confidential that the Prefect will keep them entirely in his own hands. There are others which are politically delicate so that the Prefect will keep the strictest possible watch on every step taken on his behalf. There are yet others which apparently present no political dangers, but which experience has shown are likely to lead to difficulties; the *chef de cabinet* will be called in to help in the last two cases. Two instances may help to illustrate these points.

The Minister may instruct the Prefect to take firm action at the first sign of industrial unrest provoked for political motives, in order to prevent political intimidation and to protect the people who wish to work. Obviously the Prefect must find out where to look for potential trouble, the factories and industries most likely to be involved, and the persons most capable of provoking disturbances. He must then formulate counter-measures and lay down a plan of action which can be put into operation smoothly and efficiently when the occasion demands. Both these processes must, by their nature, be conducted in secrecy, the first because of the political troubles which might attend premature publication of the Minister's policy, the second because plans which are known are more dangerous to the formulator than to the opponent. The *chef de cabinet* may be told to analyse past experiences of strikes so as to identify sections of the population which have habitually taken part in disturbances. It is possible that the *renseignements généraux*[1] have already sifted the available material, but it may not be in a form presentable to the Prefect or Minister, or it may lack synthesis, or it may fail to take account of special local factors. A transport strike is normally more important than a hoteliers' strike, but in Vichy the converse is true; the director of the *renseignements généraux* in Moulins may overlook important commercial matters like this.

The second instance illustrates the type of case which is not intrinsically political but which can cause trouble if handled carelessly. On grounds of economy the State Railways may propose to close down some stations in the Department. This might have repercussions on commerce and trade and on public opinion, and the Railways hesitate to act without advice. The Prefect will be asked for his opinion. In itself the closing of a railway station is not a political matter, but local councils in most countries regard

[1] The police intelligence division. See below p. 139.

these measures as an affront, and as a threat to local interests. The Prefect may tell the *chef de cabinet* to collect what evidence is available about alternative road transport, and see whether there are seasonal demands which would justify keeping the station open during part of the year.

Other examples of this kind of quasi-political problem are ministerial questions about the way departmental scholarships are awarded, the profit margins of local agriculturalists, the unemployment which would result from closing down a munitions factory. When these reports need discussion between the Prefect and the heads of the various interested technical services, the *chef de cabinet* may be appointed to act as 'committee secretary'. On the skill of the individual *chef de cabinet* depends how large a part of his time is spent doing these more sophisticated tasks, and how often his work is incorporated into the Prefect's finished report or memorandum.

In sum, a great deal of the work of a *chef de cabinet* depends on two unknowns: the skill and quality of the man, and the attitude and wisdom of particular Prefects. The normal relation seems to be a moderately happy one.

CHAPTER FOUR

The Sub Prefect

THE SUB PREFECTS are the middle cadre of the Prefectoral Corps. They may be appointed as Sub Prefects in charge of *arrondissements*, as Secretaries General of Prefectures, or as *directeurs du cabinet* to very important Prefects. The rules governing recruitment and appointment are the same for all three.

These rules are broadly as follows. Sub Prefects must be at least twenty-five years old, and they are appointed by decree of the President of the Council of Ministers on the advice of the Minister of the Interior. Sub Prefects who have not previously been *chefs de cabinet* or *administrateurs civils* in the Ministry of the Interior must serve a probationary year in office before being confirmed as members of the Prefectoral Corps.

There are four classes of Sub Prefect: in descending order of seniority, *hors classe*, first, second, and third class. Each class is subdivided into echelons for purposes of pay and seniority. In principle a Sub Prefect takes his personal rank from the class of *arrondissement* to which he is appointed; that is, he starts in a third class *arrondissement* as a third class Sub Prefect, and when he is promoted he goes to a second class *arrondissement*, and so on until he is *hors classe*. After that he has to wait, and hope that one day he will become a Prefect third class, but he has no right to expect this.

In special cases a Sub Prefect may obtain personal promotion to a higher class even when he remains in the same *arrondissement*, provided that he has sufficient seniority to justify such promotion. But if he accepts this personal promotion he may be required to move within two years to an *arrondissement* corresponding to his new rank.[1]

The conditions of entry to the various ranks of Sub Prefect are laid down in the Statute of the Prefectoral Corps. But even before the war a decree had formulated in fairly specific terms the conditions of entry to and promotion within their ranks. The new Statute tends to emphasize still more the administrative and bureaucratic nature of the service by restricting direct entry from outside, and defining the necessary qualifications for direct entry almost entirely in terms of service in parallel administrations.

A Sub Prefect third class may be nominated from three types of candidate. First, a *chef de cabinet* can be promoted inside the hierarchy of the Prefectoral Corps, after a year of service if he is a graduate of the ENA, and after four years if he is not.[2] Eight out of ten of all appointments as Sub Prefect must come from the ranks of *chefs de cabinet*.

Second, an *administrateur civil* or *agent supérieur*, or, under special conditions, an *attaché* of a Prefecture, may be appointed Sub Prefect third class without having served as a *chef de cabinet*.

Third, certain other officials within the orbit of the Ministry of the Interior may be posted as Sub Prefects third class. A list of equivalent ranks between these administrations and the Prefectoral Corps has been worked out to standardize such transfers. A *conseiller de préfecture* second class, for instance, can enter as a Sub Prefect third class. Only a quarter of the vacancies which occur can be filled by officials from outside the Corps.

Promotion of Sub Prefects to a higher class is entirely within the discretion of the Minister of the Interior; there are some limits to this freedom, however, for by statute Sub Prefects of the second and third class must serve in that class for three years before promotion, and Sub Prefects first class must serve for at least two years before they are eligible for promotion to Sub

---

[1] This provision is rarely applied.

[2] This four-year period may be reduced if a *chef de cabinet* has had previous experience as an *agent supérieur* in the Ministry of the Interior or as an *attaché* in a Prefecture.

Prefects *hors classe*. Continuous state employment prior to appointment as Sub Prefect for a period between eight and eleven years reduces to eighteen months the seniority required in one class for the second and third class Sub Prefect; it can only be used once.

The most significant feature of the recruitment and appointment of Sub Prefects is its exclusiveness; exclusive not in the social but in the administrative sense. It has always been recognized that the rôle of the Sub Prefects is a great deal less political than that of the Prefects. As will be seen later, the Government still has almost unlimited freedom of choice in appointing Prefects and this freedom may in part counterbalance the very bureaucratic recruitment of Sub Prefects. In the past the Corps has recruited some of its ablest senior Sub Prefects from outside. The strength of the Sub Prefects at the present time may be in some part due to the virility injected by direct entrants at the time of the Liberation. It might have been wise to open rather than restrict entry higher in the scale, in order to emphasize the different character of the Prefectoral Corps compared with other administrations. It has already been remarked by one eminent observer that the Sub Prefects must beware of the growing influence of the *percepteur* and the *inspecteur du Génie rural*: a warning of this nature was hardly necessary twenty years ago.

When the Statute was being discussed several prominent Prefects feared that to codify recruitment closely would diminish the moral authority which an administrator, appointed by the Government, revocable at will, must possess over the career official. This danger is likely to increase as the present generation of in-bred Sub Prefects become Prefects. They will not be able to enjoy both the advantages of a political Corps, and those of an administrative career. Stability is essential in providing the Corps with continuity of purpose and ability, but it is probably a mistake to codify it in legal terms.

1. *Posts and Numbers*

There are nearly 480 Sub Prefects serving in France and her

overseas dependencies. Not all of them are serving in sub prefectoral posts; some have been detached or seconded to other duties in other state administrations; nearly a hundred are either *hors cadres*,[1] *chargés de mission*, or on detached service.[2] There are several who are *en disponibilité*[3]. The great majority of these who are temporarily employed outside the Corps are on detached service; many are serving as *administrateurs civils* inside the Ministry of the Interior, where they are still in fact concerned with departmental and communal affairs, local politics, prefectoral administration, and the police. Other Sub Prefects on detached service have gone to *conseils de préfecture*, or hold special posts in Algeria, the colonies, or the French zone of Germany. Some are Deputies, others are at UNO, and on the staff of other international bodies. Many of these Sub Prefects hope one day to return to prefectoral administration when their present appointment expires.

A Sub Prefect can be called to fill several types of post. In France 216 are Sub Prefects in *arrondissements*, ninety-one are Secretaries General[4] in Prefectures; eight are Secretaries General of Police in the regional capitals in charge of the CATI.[5] There are also certain posts inside large Prefectures which are filled by Sub Prefects. In thirteen Departments the Prefect has an experienced Sub Prefect as *directeur du cabinet*. He has greater autonomy and responsibility than would ever be granted to a *chef de cabinet*.

Then there are the two Paris Prefectures which are so important

---

[1] *Hors cadres* means temporarily employed outside the Ministry of the Interior; he is paid by, and has the right to return to, the Corps, but he has no right to a particular post.

[2] When detached he is paid by the Ministry he is temporarily serving; he has a right to return to the Corps, and a right to be considered for the first available post, but no right to obtain it automatically.

[3] *En disponibilité* means without employment, no salary, no right to a post or to return, but the possibility of so doing.

[4] There are two Secretaries General in the Prefectures of Bas Rhin (Strasburg) and the Alpes Maritimes (Nice); this requires a special decree.

[5] See below p. 138

that the Secretaries General and the *directeurs du cabinet* are themselves Prefects in their own right. They are assisted by several Sub Prefects of some standing.

Finally, nearly forty Sub Prefects serve outside France, either in Algeria or in the Overseas Department of Guiana, Guadeloupe, Réunion, and Martinique. Only one of the Overseas Departments has more than one *arrondissement*, this is Guadeloupe, which has Pointe-à-Pitre and Basse-Terre. Since the Prefect everywhere directly administers the *arrondissement* in which the departmental capital is situated, the remainder simply have a Prefect, a Secretary General and a *directeur du cabinet;* there are no *chefs de cabinet*.

In Algeria, Sub Prefects serve either on the staff of the Governor General as *directeurs* and *chefs de cabinet*, or in one of the three Departments of Algiers, Oran and Constantine. Each of these Prefects has a *directeur du cabinet* and two Secretaries General, one of whom is specially charged with native affairs. These Departments are divided into enormous *arrondissements*, sometimes two or three times the size of a French Department.

The Minister appoints a Sub Prefect overseas only after taking special account of the particular qualities needed in these posts. A military bearing and morale, and an ability to shoulder great personal authority at a relatively early age, are essential. There is the problem of isolation, which is acute in some of the *arrondissements* of Algeria. A Sub Prefect in North Africa has powers of action far exceeding those of his colleague at home. He must have the initiative and character to know when and how to use these powers, for in Algeria there are occasions when it is not possible to lift a telephone to talk to the Prefect. Some members of the Prefectoral Corps specialize in Algerian administration, and many have been recruited on the spot from the ranks of the *administrateurs*, who are the executive authorities in the 'mixed' Communes.

There is no sign yet of a similar branch of the Prefectoral Corps developing for the Overseas Departments. One reason is that there are few posts and little room for promotion; besides, living in the Overseas Departments lacks the physical luxury and rather Byzantine atmosphere of the Sub Prefectures and Prefectures of North Africa. This does not mean that the Overseas Departments are regarded as 'penal' appointments to be used for recalcitrant or unpopular members of the Corps. Those who have gone there have had promising careers up to that date, and when they have returned after three years, their next posts are certainly comparable with those of their contemporaries who had remained in France.[1]

A Sub Prefect in an *arrondissement* and a Secretary General of a Prefecture draw their rank from the area in which they serve. The other posts have no legal class attached to them. The classification of Departments and *arrondissements* is fixed by the decree of October 19, 1946.

Of the ninety-one posts for Secretaries General in France the decree specifies fifty-six which are second or third class, nineteen first class, and sixteen *hors classe*. All the Secretaries General of Police are first or *hors classe*. There are seventy-one third class *arrondissements*, fifty-eight second class, fifty-five first class, and thirty-two *hors classe*.

This is the formal position. In fact the hierarchy of Sub Prefects is very different from this, because many have been personally promoted and are serving in posts below their personal rank.

There are thus 140 *hors classe* Sub Prefects, 125 first class, 140 second class, and seventy-five third class. There is a bulge not a pyramid.[2]

This curious pattern is due in part to the rapid promotion of Sub Prefects who entered the Corps direct at the time of the Liberation, combined with the normal promotion of Sub Prefects who joined before the war and have steadily advanced up the scale. They have reached the top of the Sub Prefects, but the direct entry of young and brilliant Prefects at the time of the Liberation has filled all the posts of third class and second class Prefect to which the senior Sub Prefects could normally aspire.

[1] In 1954 the Prefect of Guadeloupe was recalled to be the *directeur du cabinet* of the new President of the Republic.

[2] The figures change frequently.

This serious situation is likely to last for a long time, unless there is a major political upheaval resulting in a new 'massacre' of the top levels of the Corps. The number of Sub Prefects on detached service is much larger than before the war, since transfer is often the only way in which an ambitious Sub Prefect can continue to rise. The truth is that in the Prefectoral Corps, as in any other crucial political institution, the Minister is mainly concerned with the élite, and a worthy Sub Prefect who feels frustrated is a small price to pay for a brilliant Prefect who knows his job. But it may be that the Corps is slowly reverting to the pre-war pattern, for as veteran Prefects remember promotion was then as difficult to obtain as it is now, and a Sub Prefect seldom became a Prefect before he was forty-five or fifty. The presence of men who benefited by their personal accomplishments and by the strange circumstances of the Liberation has helped to foster an unrealistic conception of the 'normal' prefectoral career.

2. *The Sub Prefect in the Arrondissement*

Three types of appointment open to a Sub Prefect will be dealt with here. First, the Sub Prefect in an *arrondissement*; second, the Secretary General of a Prefecture; lastly, the Secretary General of Police. When a Sub Prefect is a *directeur du cabinet*, he has no statutory duties. He may well be authorized by his Prefect to act independently, and in some cases can be regarded as an assistant Prefect rather than an assistant to the Prefect. He will have far weightier administrative, political and social duties than would ever be granted to a *chef de cabinet*, but the posts are not in their essence very different.

The office of Sub Prefect and his area of administration, the *arrondissement*, have deeper historical roots than have the Prefect or the Department. In 1704 an Edict of Louis XIV conferred on the *sub délégués* powers very similar to those of a present day Sub Prefect; these powers were to be exercised in the *pays*, which by transition through the revolutionary *districts* have affinities with the *arrondissements* of today. The *pays*, furthermore, was in many cases the direct descendant of the *pagi*, the tribal areas of

Gaul and Roman times, and the capitals of *arrondissements* sometimes can be traced back to these origins.[1]

The office of Sub Prefect as instituted by Napoleon had very few specific duties. His presence was justified by the maxim that administration was best conducted on the spot. He was the eyes and ears of the Prefect, and his main activity was to stimulate and guide the work of the communes and Mayors in his area.

During the nineteenth century, his lack of any determinate functions, and his obvious usefulness to the Government as an electoral agent, on several occasions provoked hostile motions in Parliament from members who wished to abolish the office; on the Right for reasons of economy, on the Left from political hostility.[2] In 1876 the Sub Prefectures in the Department of the Seine were abolished, and in 1886 Freycinet's cabinet was overthrown when an opposition motion to strike the salaries of Sub Prefects from the budget of the Ministry of the Interior was carried against the Government. The next cabinet did nothing after proposing to abolish seventy *arrondissements*, but year after year until 1914 motions condemning the Sub Prefects were introduced into Parliament, and in 1903 and 1906 only the opposition of the Senate prevented the Chamber of Deputies from abolishing them.

It was Poincaré, in his drive for administrative reform in 1926, who made the first drastic reduction in their numbers since they had been created. By decree he abolished 106 Sub Prefectures, and amalgamated the remainder into larger units.[3] During the 1930's a mild reaction set in, and with the arrival of Vichy the process of re-establishing Sub Prefectures was greatly speeded up; by 1944 a third of those abolished were restored. No new ones have been added since then.

The point of this brief historical summary is to show that the Sub Prefect is open to attack as superfluous, and he feels that he

[1] A. Grenier: *Les Gaulois*. Paris, 1945. pp. 167–8.

[2] For the details of these proposals, see P. Vacquier: *La suppression des sous-préfets*. Doctoral Thesis; Faculty of Law, Paris. 1922.

[3] L. Trotabas: *La réforme administrative de 1926. Année politique 1927.*

must justify his position. This has been much easier since Poincaré's reforms, which added to his powers and increased his area of administration. In 1946 and again in 1950 he received substantial grants of authority, and to an observer he appears to be an important and integral part of local administration. In a period when powers are deconcentrated from the Ministries to the Prefects, and from the Prefects to the Sub Prefects there should be no serious opposition to his existence; and a growth of social legislation might well make it extremely important.

In fact abolition of the Sub Prefects could now only be seriously considered as part of a major overhaul of the whole French local government system, and such an overhaul is very unlikely while national political life is so firmly based on the Department. It is the more improbable because to have any real chance of success the administrative overhaul would have to be preceded by a social revolution of some magnitude. At the present time only 450 Communes out of 38,000 Communes have over 9,000 inhabitants; 26,000 have under 500 inhabitants, 16,000 under 200 inhabitants. To amalgamate these Communes into units of greater strength would in very many cases run into serious geographical and social difficulties, for the weak Communes have such small populations precisely because they are geographically, socially and economically isolated from one another. Even after the most judicious programme of amalgamation had been carried out, there would still remain many thousands of Communes in need of technical assistance and expert administrative advice. Financial and material assistance can come from the State or the Department. A source of administrative assistance must be nearer home, and this rôle falls squarely on the Sub Prefect, and is his principal *raison d'être*.

The Sub Prefect lives in the Sub Prefecture in the capital of the *arrondissement*. This town may be as important as Toulon or Bayonne, or as unimportant as Castellane or Barcelonnette. The extreme differences between the various units of local government and the wide diversity of culture, occupation and politics makes it difficult to generalize about France. They also contribute to the variety of a Sub Prefect's career. His *arrondissement* may include something between fifty and two hundred Communes with a population ranging between 5,000 and 550,000. The *arrondissement* may be agricultural or industrial, mountainous or flat, civilized or savage, isolated or part of a conurbation. Its main interests may be forestry or wine, coal or tourists, smuggling or aircraft and munitions. Sometimes there is a real conflict between sections of the *arrondissement*, economic conflicts between Communes, personal struggles between their leading politicians. A single Commune may be divided by internecine political or religious conflicts. Some towns in the *arrondissement* may possess great wealth, a flourishing trade, a buoyant budget, many schools, parks and social services. In others the Town Hall and the school may be the same building, and together with the Church constitute the entire communal estate.

The Sub Prefect may be a young man in his late twenties arriving for the first time amongst suspicious and endemically hostile peasants in the Massif Central or the mountains of the Var. Or he may be a wise, sober and mature administrator who has in his time pacified outraged Mayors, stood up to Deputies, tempered the excesses of resistance justice, prevented the bankruptcy of Communes and exposed the shortcomings of local financiers. But when any Sub Prefect arrives for the first time in his new Sub Prefecture, he knows about it only as much as he can learn from reference books. By long-standing custom a new Sub Prefect does not take over from his predecessor in person. The latter should already have left.

In fact the rule makes sense. A prefectoral career is still one in which the highest importance must attach to personal contact and individual judgement; it is up to the Sub Prefect himself to get to know his *arrondissement*, to formulate his opinions about its leading characters, to discover the faces and idiosyncrasies of those he is to administer and advise. This is not to say that the Sub Prefect has no prior knowledge. He may know his predecessor well enough to exchange private letters with him, though the timing of appointments is generally done in a way which leaves no time to engage in anything but the most cursory exchange of letters before catching the train to take up the appointment. But in the weeks after, some contact may be made with the outgoing Sub Prefect; they may meet in Paris, for example, or on a private visit.

Also the Sub Prefect will normally call upon his new Prefect within a day of his arrival; he will learn the Prefect's general policy and the situations in which he is to obtain the Prefect's prior consent to action. The Prefect will also discuss local personalities and political influences in the *arrondissement*, and advise him of particular traps and dangers. The Sub Prefect will try, in the course of the first few months, to visit every Commune and become acquainted with the hundred or so Mayors of the more important Communes. Generally, a Sub Prefect estimates that he needs four to six months before he can begin to claim to be adequately acquainted with his area.

The incoming Sub Prefect is assisted by the permanent staff of the Sub Prefecture, and especially its head, the *secrétaire en chef*. By law every Sub Prefecture must have at least a *secrétaire en chef*, a *rédacteur*, and two *commis*. The largest Sub Prefectures will have a staff of a dozen officials. The *secrétaire en chef* provides continuity through his knowledge of the *arrondissement*. He is paid by the State and belongs to the national cadre of *attachés* of Prefectures, and he is subject to the Prefect. But while working in the Sub Prefecture he is entirely subordinate to the Sub Prefect, and he can obviously be a source of great strength to a new Sub Prefect.

But the Sub Prefect must never forget that he alone is responsible for the work of the staff of the Sub Prefecture. He cannot regard the *secrétaire en chef* in the same way and with the same trust that a Prefect can ragard the Secretary General. Whereas a Secretary General is already a prefectoral administrator of some experience, the *secrétaire en chef* has little acquaintance with the great world of politics. A Sub Prefect who leaves too much to the *secrétaire en chef* will soon lose contact with his *arrondissement*. A situation which a prefectoral instinct would judge to be delicate will not appear so to one who will not be held responsible if administration breaks down. The Sub Prefect must himself decide what he should see, which subjects he should follow personally, and which can be dealt with rapidly and filed away.

A second danger is that he may lose touch with the Mayors. Rural Mayors are not long deceived. If the real authority in a Sub Prefecture is the *secrétaire en chef*, it is to him that they will turn. They may address their formal letters to the Sub Prefect; they will address themselves to the backdoor, and the ear of the *secrétaire en chef*.

The Sub Prefect always begins his residence in an *arrondissement* with some intrinsic prestige which is very useful to him. This prestige derives from his rôle in the Prefectoral Corps with its traditions; it is enhanced by the Sub Prefecture, a building which not only houses the administrative services but is also the residence of the Sub Prefect. It may be a mediaeval *abbaye*, when its sanitary arrangements may be slightly defective, or it may be a worthy specimen of the administrative architecture of the Second Empire or Third Republic, when it will lack charm. But in most *arrondissements* the Sub Prefecture is a building which for a long time has been regarded as a centre of administration. It seldom arouses the sentiment attaching to a *Mairie* or *Hôtel de Ville* which symbolize local pride and individuality. It has neither the distinction nor the potential menace of the Prefecture itself. The Sub Prefecture is withdrawn, it is the post of the permanent observer, the residence of the 'sentinel of the Republic'. It is aloof.

Some have spacious and comfortable apartments where a rich man could entertain lavishly; the standard of its furnishing depends upon the *conseil général*; the standard of entertainment upon the personal fortune of the Sub Prefect. While better able than most French officials of his rank to stand the burden of entertainment, the days are long past when a Sub Prefect could reasonably be expected to take visiting royalty in his stride, as did Haussmann while he was the Sub Prefect at Nérac. The Sub Prefect has few occasions to entertain officially in these days, though this depends to some extent upon the *arrondissement*;

often a Sub Prefect has no social company within call. In places like Bayonne there is always a regular flow of charming company from Biarritz. The Sub Prefect has an expense account which has been standardized, but it frequently happens that there is no company to entertain, or, on the other hand, too many visitors so that the expense account is inadequate.

The Sub Prefect's duties are administrative, political and social. For several years he is required to immerse himself in the life of his *arrondissement*, to get to know its peculiarities, its problems and its personalities. He must interpret its interest to the Prefect, enforce the Prefect's will, and foster the State's interests in his area. On one side he has to be a man of action, capable of administering roads, rural electrification schemes, hospitals, welfare and security. On the other side he must be the detached commentator of the affairs around him. 'L'observateur et l'homme du monde doivent se fondre dans la personne du sous-préfet.'[1]

His life then is a type of committed existence, only part of which is concerned with the formal attributes accorded by law. But it is these statutory powers which are the source of any influence he may be able to exercise unofficially, and they must be shortly described.

The administrative powers of the Sub Prefect contained in various enactments of the nineteenth century, and in the municipal law of April 5, 1884, were few and secondary. He issued game licences and passports, controlled gypsies, vagabonds and the military service lists; he presided of right over certain administrative commissions, such as the *commission sanitaire*, and attended the annual session of the *conseil d'arrondissement*,[2] whose only function was to divide up the *principaux fictifs* between the Communes. The municipal law stated that all decisions of the *conseils municipaux* and all the ordinances of the Mayors had to be forwarded before being put into effect to the Sub Prefecture (or the Prefecture when the Commune is in the *arrondissement* of the

[1] Jouany: op. cit.

[2] These were in effect abolished in 1940.

departmental capital). Some decisions required at this stage the written or tacit approval of an administrative authority. For these the Sub Prefectures merely acted as a postbox and forwarded them to the Prefect. The decisions which did not require further approval were examined by the Sub Prefect to make sure firstly, that they were legal (*intra vires*), and secondly that they had not been discussed or voted upon at a meeting in the presence of a councillor who had an interest in the matter. In either case the Sub Prefect had to inform the Prefect, who alone could annul the decisions on legal grounds. The Sub Prefect was essentially a watch dog rather than a tutelage authority.

By decree, November 5, 1926, Poincaré, as part of his administrative reform, took certain tutelage powers from the Prefect and gave them to the Sub Prefect, to be exercised in his own name. It is from this decree that the Sub Prefect still derives most of his statutory duties.

The Sub Prefect became responsible for examining and approving communal budgets when they did not exceed 10 million francs in each of three successive years, and this put under his control all the small Communes. In addition, he could sanction the dismissal and appointment of *gardes champêtres* and other minor police officials recruited by any Commune, divide the Commune up into electoral wards for voting in communal and departmental elections, and hold enquiries prior to changing the boundaries of local authorities and to setting up a *commission syndicale*.[1]

This extension of authority in 1926 was timely, even though many powers still remained with the Prefect, to whom the Sub Prefect then had to refer. The Sub Prefect is under the immediate authority of the Prefect, and the latter can always issue binding instructions on his subordinate, even in matters which the law expressly gives to the Sub Prefect.

---

[1] When two Communes are amalgamated, one of them sometimes becomes a *section* of a Commune. Should the *section's* interests or entailed resources be threatened by the *conseil municipal*, a *commission syndicale* is formed to protect the *section's* interests and act in its name.

His rôle remained substantially the same between 1926 and the war; there was a slight decline in 1935 when the financial limit to the communal budgets he could approve was lowered to five million francs. But between 1945 and 1950 legislation has appeared to be working towards the position in which he will be the principal tutelage authority for all the Communes in his *arrondissement*. In 1945 and 1946 he was given extended powers of financial tutelage. He could approve larger communal budgets, and in these cases also approve a Commune's application to raise a loan; he could approve the levying of a retail tax on consumption goods in all the Communes. His administrative powers also increased; for instance, he had greater powers to hold enquiries on his own responsibility into matters affecting the internal life of the Communes, and to sanction contracts and approve tenders which Communes had entered into. He was also given authority to accept the proposals put forward by *conseils municipaux* concerning the size and remuneration of communal staffs, as they were required to do by law after 1945.

Two decrees of 1950 and one of 1953 increased his powers still further. He became the financial tutelage authority for all Communes with under 20,000 inhabitants. This was a far more rational criterion than that of the size of communal budgets, which meant that some Communes had different tutelage authorities every few years as their budgets fluctuated. These decrees also raised the figure for communal loans which the Sub Prefect could approve on his own authority.

It has already been said that certain matters which are specified in the municipal law of 1884 and subsequent amending acts are not only liable to examination by the Sub Prefect for illegality, but also require the approval of a tutelage authority before the decision becomes effective. In this case the tutelage authority can reject the *conseil municipal's* decision not only on grounds of illegality but also merely on the grounds that it is inopportune or unreasonable. Where the Sub Prefect has been given tutelage powers over Communes in his own name, he possesses this overriding discretion. He may say, for example, that it is inopportune to dispose of this piece of communal property at a time when land values are rising rapidly; or he may consider that a contract proposed by a Commune is phrased unreasonably. But since the Sub Prefect is an official with limited discretion, any decision he makes can be over-ridden by the Prefect, or in the last resort by the Minister; the Commune can therefore always appeal. Should it consider the Sub Prefect has acted *ultra vires* or broken the law, it can take the matter before the administrative courts for judgement.

A further point is that in the majority of the cases where the Sub Prefect's approval is necessary, he can only accept or reject the proposal; he cannot modify it. He cannot for instance change the proposed rate of interest in a contract, or alter the period of validity of a lease. However, while the law gives him no authority to modify, he is obviously in a strong position to encourage the Commune to adopt his view. If, for example, he unofficially suggests to the Mayor that he cannot accept a lease in its present form, but that he would consider it favourably if the rights of the commune were more explicitly safeguarded by inserting an escape clause, his advice will obviously carry much weight.

Two aspects of the Sub Prefect's tutelage powers require closer analysis. First, the Sub Prefect's tutelage of the budget is different from his other tutelage powers in that he can modify details as well as approve or reject. Second, he can control the floating of loans by Communes; this is obviously important, and it also illustrates very well the type of discreet and unofficial guidance he exercises over communal authorities.

The Sub Prefect is the tutelage authority for the financial operations of the Communes in his *arrondissement* with under 20,000 inhabitants, and of all the hospitals, *hospices*, public assistance boards and welfare centres. He examines their budgets and checks their accounts.

This is especially important in the case of the Communes, and it is worth noting that there are many *arrondissements*, indeed the majority, in which there are no Communes with over 20,000 inhabitants; the Sub Prefect is responsible for every one. He examines the draft budgets after they have been approved by the *conseil municipal*, and he makes such alterations to them as appear to him to be necessary in the interests of the Commune or of the public. He also checks the financial accounts of each Commune at the end of the financial year. He thus exercises both a prior and a post-mortem check upon the life of the Commune. For one has to remember that a local budget is a resumé of the entire administrative life of the Commune.

A communal budget must contain the whole of the financial operations of that Commune. This is the principle of the 'universality' of the budget. Should the Commune have financial interests in, or control over, an outside service which forms an autonomous entity, then a separate budget may be compiled for that service; but it must be annexed to the main communal budget and allowance must be made there for any profit or deficit. Thus, a transport service run by a Commune, or a communal cinema or dispensary, can have its own budget, but that budget must be approved by the *conseil municipal* as part of the whole.

The preparation of the communal budget is the Mayor's legal responsibility. He presents it to the *conseil municipal*, which after discussion and perhaps amendment approves it. The Mayor then sends three copies of the approved budget to the Sub Prefecture, together with the minutes of the session and the record of the votes of the *conseil municipal*.

The budget is then examined in the Sub Prefecture. First, it is checked to see whether it is properly balanced, whether it contains over- or under-estimates for expenditure or revenue. This is done by a comparison with previous years, and by the mental check that comes from dealing with many budgets from the same area for some years.

Next, any new local taxes or other sources of extraordinary revenue must be examined to see whether the *conseil municipal* is legally entitled to levy them, and whether special permission may be needed from the Prefect, the Ministry or the *Conseil d'Etat*. The *conseil municipal* may fall into two errors. Parliament may not have authorized it to levy a particular tax; no *conseil municipal* can impose a tax on drainpipes or new hats. As the list of optional local taxes numbers nearly two hundred, it is not surprising if every year *conseils municipaux* make this kind of mistake.

The other kind of error is often only disclosed after detailed examination of the budget. The proceeds of certain taxes raised for a specific purpose must in fact be used for that purpose. The money raised, for example, by the local tax called the *prestation* must be used entirely on roads, and it cannot be used to repair the *Mairies*, nor to balance the budget in the ordinary way. Similarly, taxes levied for minicipal services, for instance for drains or the collection of refuse, should in principle only be sufficient to cover the actual cost of those services; but some allowance is made to make sure that future outlay can be covered from current rates.

The detailed examination of the budget is done in the first place by the officials of the Sub Prefecture. This work has been greatly expedited in recent years by the standardization of the forms on which the budget is presented, each section following a set pattern, with the items carefully enumerated. Many minor budgets in fact only spend a morning on the Sub Prefect's desk, for there will only be a dozen items on each side, all compulsory charges, the whole amounting to a few hundred pounds. It is very rare for anything strange or debatable to appear in these, as the Communes are stretched to the maximum simply to provide obligatory services.

More important budgets will also be examined first in detail by officials of the Sub Prefecture who mark items that might be debatable. The Sub Prefect will not only consider the items drawn to his attention, but he will also endeavour to assess in his own mind the total effect of a particular budget on the life of the Commune and the *arrondissement*.

The Sub Prefect has discretion to strike out illegal items of expenditure, and also those which seem unnecessary or liable to jeopardize the Commune's financial stability. Sometimes political difficulties in the *conseil municipal* lead to an artificially balanced budget obtained by over-estimating revenue or under-estimating expenditure. The Sub Prefect returns the budget to the Mayor with his alterations within two weeks. The Mayor convenes the *conseil municipal* within ten days to re-discuss it, and the council must come to a new decision within a week. If the alterations are accepted by the *conseil* the budget then becomes operative. If it refuses to accept the changes, or makes new alterations which again unbalance the budget, the Sub Prefect, on receipt, immediately forwards it to the Prefect who has the authority to draft the budget without more ado, using for this purpose the powers of the *conseil municipal*.

The Prefect can strike out any item of optional expenditure, he can increase the income available by eliminating the provision for unforeseen expenditure, and if after that obligatory expenditure is still not covered, he can raise new local taxes.

This type of conflict is not common. In the first place, in many *arrondissements* the Communes are quiet backward places with no wish to meet more than their obligatory charges. A great number of the smallest Communes are quite without the resources to do anything but provide the most elementary municipal services. In the second place, the Communes have a delicate weapon with which to counter an over-zealous tutelage authority. For the law does not authorize the Prefect to allow expenditure on optional items when he intervenes to regulate the budget; he can only compel the Commune to provide those services declared by law to be compulsory. Optional services however include many matters which are of vital importance in larger Communes, such as street lighting; the Prefect has to be careful or he will cut off the mains, which would certainly not be in the interests of good government.

The Sub Prefect plays a passive rôle once the conflict has been elevated to the Prefecture, but he will if possible try to prevent that position being reached. He may discuss a problematic budget with the Prefect before he alters it and returns it to the *conseil municipal* for a second reading. The knowledge that the Prefect has already supported the Sub Prefect in private may persuade the local politicians not to bring about a rupture with the Sub Prefect, since they have no hope that he will be over-ridden.

Other informal approaches depend largely on local circumstances. If the *arrondissement* comprises large numbers of small rural Communes, the Sub Prefect will frequently be consulted by Mayors before the communal budget is prepared. Many rural Mayors have neither the time nor the capacity to understand the complexities of financial law, and it is left to the communal secretary, the *instituteur*, to deal with the occasional pieces of administration which have to be done, for instance, the registration of destitute persons. These small rural budgets are unlikely to cause the Sub Prefect much trouble since he will be able to intervene at an early stage. It is believed that in some parts of the country the majority of communal budgets are virtually prepared in the Sub Prefectures and Prefecture.

Sometimes instead of consulting the Sub Prefect the Mayor turns to other state officials for advice. He may ask the *percepteur*, the local official of the Ministry of Finance, for help in framing the budget; but the Commune has to pay him a fee. He may go to the *inspecteur du Génie rural*, the local officer of the Ministry of Agriculture, for technical assistance. Their advice is generally sensible and realistic, but the result may still be unsatisfactory for the Sub Prefect. Sometimes it is difficult to persuade Mayors that this advice has no moral binding force on the Sub Prefect.

In larger Communes, and even small ones, there may be budgetary difficulties caused by differences between rival factions or political parties. The budget may then be presented unbalanced for want of a clear majority, and there may be little chance of the Sub Prefect's amendments being accepted. The Sub Prefect may try to use his good offices to arrange a private meeting with the leaders of the factions, and to find a satisfactory compromise. But in many cases these conflicts are irreconcilable and very personal, and there is nothing to do but hope that no majority will be found to reject the amendments suggested by the Sub Prefect. Frequently, in these cases, the only solution is to allow the previous year's budget to continue in force, and, if there is complete administrative paralysis, to request the Minister to dissolve the *conseil municipal* and hold new elections.

There is most to be gained from private consultations with the Mayor. Before returning the budget to the *conseil municipal* officially, the Sub Prefect is often advised to discuss with the Mayor the items which seem to be unreasonable; between them they may be able to find a solution which the Mayor is sure will be accepted by the *conseil municipal*. In this way the Sub Prefect can avoid the appearance of conflict between Administration and Commune which can exacerbate councillors and annoy public opinion. In private, the Sub Prefect can also use the wiles of diplomacy. He may suggest that some expenditure is in a category for which a grant from the departmental equalization fund would be appropriate, and promise his good offices to obtain the support of the Prefect. He may be able to hint that an item would raise no objections next year, whereas at the moment financial stringency argues against it. He may delicately remind the Mayor of other projects the Commune has in mind, which will need the Sub Prefect's active benevolence: a bargain may be arranged.

It would however be quite false to suggest that a Sub Prefect's main task is to prevent Communes doing things which they want to do and which are in their own interest. The number of conflicts that arise are small; the average Sub Prefect's conception of his rôle as tutelage authority is that of administrative auditor, careful to reject the impossible, the unreasonable, and the illegal, but equally careful not to intervene without cause. An active and conscientious Mayor can do much as he pleases and can rely on the sympathetic support of the Sub Prefect. This attitude is encouraged by the Prefects who do not welcome difficulties inspired by the officiousness of a Sub Prefect, which will involve the credit of the Administration. Great patience is needed to repair one rash step, as the public quickly loses trust and good will. In many places the Sub Prefect has, by general consent, become a general inspector of administrative services, who quietly ensures efficiency, prevents abuses, and stops other officials from bullying. He is looked to, in times of trouble, to act as a rallying point from which sensible and constructive proposals will come. If the Sub Prefect can sustain this rôle he is well placed to exercise much quiet and discreet influence in the *arrondissement*.

It is part of a Sub Prefect's rôle to stimulate a civic and social conscience amongst the councillors and Mayors in his area; he has no formal powers of coercion to make them good citizens, he can only rely upon his personality and diplomacy. He frequently has no success. If a *conseil municipal* strictly provides its obligatory services, the Sub Prefect cannot make it do more. He may try to influence Mayors when he meets them, or encourage communal officials to put forward constructive schemes. But he has to take care not to embarrass them, as most local councillors strongly resent the Mayor or their officials acting as if they were agents of the Administration, and trying to curry favour with the Prefect.

It is very rarely possible for the Sub Prefect to see that a Commune uses its special resources to the best advantage. Once he has given his formal approval to the disposal of some property, it is very difficult, if not impossible, to make sure that the proceeds are not wasted. For instance, when a Commune out of misplaced local pride decides to build an unnecessary wing to its *Mairie* with the money it receives from selling part of its timber reserves, the Sub Prefect is unable to compel it to build a decent road which would greatly facilitate the development of those reserves. In some places the attitude of local councillors is so hostile to state intervention that they prefer to do without amenities such as piped water, main drainage, or rural electrification rather than accept state assistance. Some *conseils municipaux* are merely anxious to annoy the Government. Others consider that the principal rôle of a *conseil municipal* is to restrict expenditure to an absolute minimum, and refuse to go beyond their bare legal duties. Generations of Sub Prefects can wilt before this sort of morose hostility, and a Sub Prefect can only try to prepare a climate of opinion that may benefit a future successor.

But when he has an active and progressive community in his area he must be able to slip easily into the rôle of business and financial adviser. The Mayor or *conseil municipal* may regard him with suspicion because he is a Sub Prefect, they may view him with distrust because he is a Doctor of Law, they may bear him secret contempt because he comes from Paris, but they will be prepared to use him if they can. He must take advantage of these occasions.

It may be that a Commune proposes to raise a loan in order to develop some ground, or start a new service, or provide new amenities. When the Commune has under 20,000 inhabitants it is the Sub Prefect who approves the loan. But if it is proposed to amortize the loan over a period longer than thirty years the approval of the *Conseil d'Etat* must be obtained. Two further exceptions are, first, that if the money is to be raised through the *fonds forestier national* for forest development, or if the money is to be used for municipal housing projects, the Sub Prefect can nevertheless approve them even if for over thirty years. Second, there has been since the war a maximum size of loans above which central approval must be obtained no matter what the life of the loan.

A Sub Prefect faced with an application for permission to raise a loan will have first to make sure that the proposal makes good legal and administrative sense. He will probably not, for instance, approve a loan in order to build a home for ex-municipal councillors, but would approve the same project designed to house old people or sick children.

He must satisfy himself that the Commune will not prejudice its future financial stability. A loan for too short a time would involve an excessive burden for a few years. A loan for too long a period would mean that the Commune would still be paying for an installation which had ceased to be productive. The proposed loan should properly be for an extraordinary expense that cannot be met from current expenditure by a slight increase in the rates; allowance must be made for any future revenue that will be brought in by the investment which can be used partly to off-set the cost.

The Sub Prefect is most useful when he has a wider knowledge of outside affairs. He should be able to advise on the possibility of obtaining state aid, and how to ask for it. He must be aware of local resources and skills; it is generally unnecessary to bring experts in reinforced concrete from Marseilles to the Haute Alpes in order to build a school playground.

Medium sized Communes with permanent communal officials will normally prepare schemes which make good sense. Detailed supervision is necessary mainly for the small Communes. But even substantial Communes may require the Sub Prefect's assistance when it comes to floating the loan. Raising a public loan on the open market is a very expensive operation, and normally only a very large loan by an important Commune like Nantes justifies the extra charges involved. The local offices of the Ministry of Finance may offer facilities for collecting local subscriptions, and in some areas this is a fruitful source. Then there are special agencies and trusts which specialize in the development of local services; for example, the *caisse de crédit agricole* which is authorized to grant loans for rural development schemes up to a maximum of £15,000. The *caisse des depôts et consignations* and the *crédit foncier de France* are other possible sources. Private banks usually demand too high a premium or too stringent conditions for local authorities to deal with them, but some local banks, insurance companies and solicitors have funds which they are willing to lend at a reasonable charge, and the local savings banks, the *caisses d'épargne*, often invest locally.

A Sub Prefect should have a general knowledge of the business conditions in his area, even if he cannot claim to be a financial expert. It is important that he at least knows how to find out quickly; the experts in the Prefecture, the *trésorier payeur général's* office, the local *percepteur* or a private banker are invaluable sources of information if he knows when to use them.

So far the Sub Prefect has appeared principally as an administrator with a diplomatic bent, but it is essential to recall that he is, by virtue of his position in the Prefectoral Corps, a member of a *corps d'autorité*, with a reserve of personal, compulsive force. As such he demands obedience to the law.

For one thing he ensures the regularity and legality of communal elections. He divides the Commune into electoral wards and fixes the date of by-elections. He is the channel through whom cases of electoral litigation must pass. A complaint that an election was illegal or held under irregular conditions must be deposited with him inside five days of the election day. He transmits it to the *conseil de préfecture* and informs the Prefect. If the complaint alleges mismanagement or illegal practices, the Sub Prefect will himself conduct a rapid administrative enquiry into the circumstances to discover whether criminal proceedings should be begun.

He is bound continually to watch all the actions of communal authorities, and especially of the Mayor, who, says the law, is responsible for the *police municipale*, for administering the Commune, for executing the decisions of the *conseil municipal* and for performing certain administrative duties for the State. The Sub Prefect is principally concerned with three things. First, that the *conseil municipal* does not infringe the law regarding the division of powers in the Commune; the Mayor alone is responsible for exercising municipal police powers, and the *conseil municipal* must not attempt to control his actions in this field or impose its will. Second, that while administering the Commune or executing the decisions of the *conseil municipal*, the Mayor should keep within the law; that he should not victimize personal enemies (by refusing them a licence to trade in the market, for example), that he should not favour communal interests to the detriment of private individuals, that he should not accept bribes from contractors. Third, the Sub Prefect has the right to examine all the police ordinances issued by the Mayor; if any of them appears to him to be against the public interest he can inform the Prefect who is empowered to annul or suspend it. The Sub Prefect can, however, authorize the Mayor to put a police ordinance into immediate effect in case of urgency; otherwise a police ordinance does not become effective until a month from the day it was sent to the Sub Prefecture.

The Prefect is the responsible police authority for the whole Department, and the use and abuse of police powers can raise some awkward political and social problems. It may require the prestige and authority of the Prefect himself to settle them quietly. But Sub Prefects are called upon to act for the Prefect in restoring order and exerting force. A straightforward riot is a matter for the police, and the personal intervention of the Sub Prefect is never required at the time; it may be required afterwards, for instance, if a Deputy has been arrested in the process. But there are situations where there is a potential threat to public order but no actual breach of the peace, and these need a more diplomatic approach than that normally associated with a *commissaire de police* or a sergeant of the *Gendarmerie*. For instance, a Mayor may refuse point blank to hand over the keys of the communal school to an *instituteur* of notorious political opinions opposed to those of the whole Commune; or a Mayor and his *conseil municipal* may strongly resent the cost to the Commune of maintaining the communal school when the church school is already providing elementary education. To send a section of the *Gendarmerie* to extract the key from the Mayor will only end in a scuffle in the main square, and an administrative strike by all the Mayors of neighbouring Communes. In such a case the Sub Prefect may be told by the Prefect to go himself, supported of course at a discreet distance by Gendarmes. It has been found that a Sub Prefect in uniform has a moral effect entirely different from that of a policeman.

But the Prefect remains inescapably responsible for the good order of the entire Department. The Sub Prefect is his subordinate subject to mandatory orders. No Sub Prefect would take upon himself without prior consultation with the Prefect the responsibility for any action which might provoke political or social difficulties, for the Prefect will have to solve them if they come to a head. A very senior Sub Prefect may be given almost *carte blanche* by the Prefect, and then he is free to act on his own initiative, sure that the Prefect will support him. But if the Sub Prefect is young, or if the situation is really troublesome, the Prefect may lay down a detailed line of conduct, leaving the Sub Prefect initiative only to fill in the gaps, or he may even take the matter in hand personally.

The relations between Prefect and Sub Prefect are difficult to assess because they are usually informal. But the Prefect has a formal authority over all the Sub Prefects, which comes not only from his seniority in the Prefectoral Corps, but also because it is his duty to make annual confidential reports on his subordinates to the Minister.

Such reports are, of course, normal in any administration, and their use in France is to some extent codified: for instance, if there is any question of disciplinary action an official has the right to see his *dossier* in order to meet as fully as possible the charges against him.

But the reports of the Prefectoral Corps are different from those of other administrative services. The Ministry of the Interior uses three report forms, one for the Prefectoral Corps, one for administrative class officials, one for executive and clerical staff. The report form for the junior official is a simple document requiring the superior's assessment of a man's work and conduct during the year. He is given a mark out of twenty, based on questions such as 'Is his memory excellent, good, medium, weak?', and 'Is he punctual?' The report only affects an official's career if it is very good indeed, or very bad.

A more complex type of report is required for the administrative class. It contains comments on the official's personal merits and professional qualities, as well as a general assessment.

The report form used in the Prefectoral Corps demands similar judgements. The Prefect has to comment upon the Sub Prefect's personal merits, on his intelligence, his general culture and education, his character, powers of decision, his personal authority and influence over other men, his morality, and the main traits of his personality. In addition to these, the Prefectoral Corps' report takes into account several external factors: his health, his personal bearing, his family connections, his financial situation, any countries where he has interests. The Prefect is also called upon to comment upon the value, influence and rôle of Mme. la Sous Préfète; to consider her ability as the hostess and mistress of the Sub Prefecture. The Prefect is required to give information about the Sub Prefect's political attitude, noting any relevant political history and indicating his present political orientation. These comments are in ordinary times probably a great deal less important than it is the tradition to believe. Finally, the Prefect assesses the professional value of his subordinate, his administrative and legal competence, his dynamism and ability to act, his method of work, and—this could only happen in the Prefectoral Corps—his facility of expression and talent for public speaking.

The fact that annual reports are made in such detail emphasizes the personal dependence of the Sub Prefect on the Prefect. The Sub Prefect is not however entirely at the mercy of his Prefect; a good Sub Prefect who offends a Prefect to the point of open rupture can, if his past record is good, obtain posting to another job and even promotion. The number of Prefects is small, and the tigers and tyrants well known to the Director of Personnel and to the Ministry.

The converse is also true: there are some prefectoral 'teams', which prominent Prefects have collected round them, by selecting the best men they have come across during their service in various Departments. There are Prefectures where the Secretary General, the *directeur du cabinet*, and several of the Sub Prefects have been associated with the Prefect in different capacities for a long time. This is a very harmonious arrangement if it can be worked without favouritism.

In everyday life, close contact is maintained between the Prefect and Sub Prefects. Weekly meetings are held in the Prefecture under the chairmanship of the Prefect at which problems of common interest are discussed; the problem of housing, a future programme of public works, the transfer of building resources from one part of the Department to another. The Minister may have asked the Prefect to consider the best way of encouraging Communes to develop roads useful to farmers. An active Commune in one *arrondissement* may have put forward an improvement scheme which could be of general interest. Or the meeting may discuss a projected *syndicat intercommunal* for distributing electricity.

Many prefectoral meetings also hear progress reports about

work in hand, and periodic surveys are made of the political situation in the Department. The Sub Prefects may bring their own reports which the Prefect will use in drafting his report to the Minister, or they may comment severally upon the way in which different factors affect their own areas. The Prefect may want to know what active strength local unions now possess, or what will happen if the Government cuts down the subsidy to beet growers.

But the political rôle of the Sub Prefect is small compared to that of the Prefect. He has to know what is going on, but he does not often become involved in the same way as does the Prefect. For many Sub Prefects politics means straightening out local squabbles between rival personalities. In parts of Beaujolais, meetings of the *conseil municipal* are like meetings of elders, and the Mayor is more of a patriarch than a politician. On the other hand in parts of the South *conseils municipaux* with a very small population may suddenly decide to give themselves the status of World Citizens, and may encourage their own municipal services to strike against German rearmament. In the industrial north it is quite different, with densely populated *arrondissements*, a sturdy sense of civic pride, and a phlegmatic approach to administration. The variety of political outlook is as varied in France as her natural products. The Sub Prefect relies to some extent on his acumen and intuition in estimating political forces for the Prefect. Local newspapers and propaganda leaflets are useful to follow the drift of public opinion; there are also the speeches and motions of local councils, election returns, applications for permission to hold public demonstrations, petitions from trade associations or labour unions. A Sub Prefect has little difficulty in keeping his finger on the pulse of his *arrondissement*, and many develop unconsciously a subtle awareness of changing temperatures and fluctuating sympathies which will stand them in good stead when they in their turn become Prefects.

But the danger is not that there may be Sub Prefects incapable of performing their varied but essentially minor functions competently, but that their talents, ambitions, and intelligence may become stultified in a system which takes out of their hands problems as soon as they begin to be of crucial importance. This would not be so bad were they sure that every administrative duty which could be transferred to them from the Prefecture had been so devolved. It is vitally necessary to deconcentrate as many duties as possible from the Prefecture to the Sub Prefecture, not merely to increase the standing and administrative powers of the Sub Prefects, but also to protect the Prefectures themselves from the mass of paper which descends upon them from the Ministries, and the pile of applications, requests and forms which mount up from the smallest village.

The Prefect of the Bouches-du-Rhône in a paper to a prefectoral audience stated the need in clear and forthright terms:

'Les interventions des services publics se sont multipliées à tel point que le flot de papiers d'une Préfecture importante peut difficilement être endigué. Comment juger, depuis le chef lieu du département, avec une note humaine, les quelque trente mille dossiers d'assistance publique? Le Sous Préfet et ses collaborateurs les verront avec plus de chance d'éliminer les abus. Les maires leur feront connaître plus facilement au cours d'une conversation, la vraie situation matérielle d'un de leurs administrés qu'ils ne la déclareront par écrit à la Préfecture. Pourquoi constituer des dossiers de construction scolaires, de travaux communaux à la Préfecture, alors que l'avis concordant de tant de services est exigé? Tout ceci se règlerait infiniment mieux sur place, par des réunions en présence du Sous-Préfet, et les contacts directs remplaceraient efficacement les correspondances interminables et stériles. Certes, des observations tenant à l'armature de nos Sous-Préfectures peuvent être faites. Je ne pense pas qu'elles puissent être valablement opposées aux avantages certains de la déconcentration. Le dilemme est évident: ou les Sous-Préfectures continueront à être des boîtes aux lettres et nous mettrons à la longue leur existence en cause, ou nous leur donnons une vie administrative propre, pour le plus grand bien des administrés.'[1]

[1] M. Paira: *Le rôle du Préfet*. Paper read to the Association of the Prefectoral Corps, June 15, 1950.

3. *The Secretary General of the Prefecture*

The Secretary General of the Prefecture is the Prefect's second in command; he has very few statutory powers in his own right, but his place in prefectoral administration is of the greatest importance. Well-qualified persons consider that in the course of an 'ideal' prefectoral career, the young man is most fortunate if his first appointment when he is promoted from *chef de cabinet* is as Secretary General of a Prefecture. This is partly that he should learn at an early stage to handle the details of administrative work which as a *chef de cabinet* he has been able to ignore; partly because if he goes straight to an *arrondissement* as a Sub Prefect he has to learn administration the hard way—by himself with Mayors and politicians breathing down his neck. The post of Secretary General is an important part of the apprenticeship for a post as Prefect.

He is responsible for the work carried on—outside the Prefect's cabinet—in the Prefecture, its Divisions and its Bureaux.[1] The Prefect himself may have many political preoccupations not immediately connected with administration, but the Prefecture as such is the centre of state and departmental administration. It has to initiate, control and co-ordinate the specialist services in the Department which actually plan and execute technical details. It not only performs a great number of routine administrative jobs, such as registering, examining, inspecting and checking the work of Communes and specialized agencies, but it must be able to view broadly the interests of the Department, and to inform the Prefect accurately on any subject he raises. It is for the Secretary General to see that it does so efficiently.

It goes without saying that the Prefect himself normally spends a great part of his time on administration—though rarely on detail—and the Secretary General does not in a formal sense share

---

[1] For a description of the Secretary General's powers see P. Rix: *Le Secrétaire général de préfecture.* Doctoral Thesis, Faculty of Law, Toulouse, 1938. P. Guerrini: *Origines et pouvoirs du Secrétaire général de préfecture.* Doctoral Thesis, Faculty of Law, Lyons, 1938.

the Prefect's responsibility for the Prefecture. He supervises the work of the Divisions and Bureaux of the Prefecture, acting through the *chefs de division* and the *chefs de bureaux*; he controls the officials employed in the Prefecture, the Sub Prefectures, and departmental services, and sees that they do their work properly. His political rôle is limited compared to that of any other member of the Corps. He attends fewer social functions, and he is not so prominent to the public as his colleagues in the *arrondissements*. Bewteen him and the public there always stands the Prefect. He is much more the anonymous official in the British tradition.

His only important formal power is that he automatically replaces the Prefect as head of the Department when the Prefect is absent or sick, even though he may be junior to a Sub Prefect in one of the *arrondissements*; this is subject to a virtually unused provision that the Prefect can if he wishes delegate this duty to someone else. The Secretary General can also sign official documents on behalf of the Prefect, and, if ever the State and the Department go to law against one another, the Secretary General represents the interests of the Department.

To appreciate the rôle of the Secretary General it is necessary to understand the administrative structure of the Prefecture; this depends partly on the scale of administration.

In the year 1950-51, the medium sized Prefecture of Deux Sèvres (Niort) received the following communications:[1]

Ministerial circulars	1,582
Ministerial despatches	1,365
Letters from Deputies, Senators and local councillors	417
Telegrams	635
Deliberations of *conseils municipaux* and Mayoral ordinances	8,252
	12,251

[1] The following figures, as well as those on p. 129 seq., are taken from a study on the cost and commercial efficiency of a Prefecture by R. Bonnaud Delamare, Prefect of the Aisne (Laon).

During the same period the Prefecture despatched on official business:

Letters to Ministries	3,258
Letters to parliamentarians and local councillors	1,303
Telegrams	208
Circulars	227
Prefectoral ordinances	142
Notices to citizens	2,753
Communications to Mayors and *conseils municipaux* concerning their deliberations and ordinances	8,480
	16,371

In addition to these, 33,162 official documents and certificates were issued to the public, and 25,409 warrants for payment were made.

A large part of this work was done by the staff of the Prefecture, in particular by the three *chefs de division* who were each responsible for a major branch of administration. But of the three members of the Prefectoral Corps in the Prefecture, the *chef de cabinet* signed 5,020 documents and letters, the Prefect 11,420, the Secretary General 69,505. There is a striking disparity between the three, even taking into account the occasions on which the Secretary General's signature is a matter of form only; for instance, he would sign an order sent to all Mayors in the Department asking them to compile a census of Algerians in their Communes, though the order would actually be drafted by the Division concerned with Police and General Administration. Almost all the interesting letters to politicians and Ministries will be drafted by the Prefect or the *chef de cabinet* and signed by the Prefect.

The number of visitors received by the members of the staff is also illustrative. During the year, the Prefect saw 714 visitors, the *chef de cabinet* 957, in his capacity as a 'buffer' for the Prefect. The Secretary General in the same time received only 382, and only during February and March did he receive more than one caller a day, though of course he was continuously in contact with the officials of the Prefecture.

He is not, however, entirely anonymous; he attends meetings of the *conseil général* with the Prefect, and during unimportant sessions the Prefect may leave him there alone to deal with minor questions. He also attends many committees and sub-committees connected with the administration of departmental affairs, some of them entirely official committees with representatives of other administrative services, others mixed committees of councillors and officials. The Prefect frequently nominates him as his deputy to attend special *ad hoc* committees of enquiry, or to preside over, for example, the special committee which is called to examine the budget of a Commune whose budgetary deficit over a period of three years has exceeded ten per cent.

Furthermore, since there is no Sub Prefect for the *arrondissement* of which the departmental capital is the centre, the Prefecture has to do for those Communes what the Sub Prefecture has to do elsewhere. The Secretary General may be given certain delegated powers of tutelage over some of these Communes, especially over their budgets. But in most instances the size and experience of the prefectoral staff and particularly of the *chefs de division* is greater than it is in a Sub Prefecture, so that the Secretary General can afford to rely upon them to identify the difficult or contentious problems. The Secretary General may find that the Prefect wants him to deal with the Mayors who come to the Prefecture to discuss matters, but contact with local personalities is the key to the Prefect's personal knowledge and influence, and it is most undesirable to foist the burden on to the Secretary General and distract him from his proper work of supervising the administration of the Prefecture.

The administration of the Prefecture is carried on in Divisions and Bureaux. A standard pattern for all Prefectures, based on size of population, financial returns and so on, was worked out by the Ministry's Inspectorate General in 1946; according to this eleven Prefectures have five Divisions, twenty-five have four, forty-five have three, and eight have two.[1] In practice, there are difficulties

[1] These figures do not include the Prefectures of the Seine and of Police, which have eight Divisions.

in the way of enforcing this pattern. On the one hand, the Minister does not wish to interfere with the Prefect's autonomy inside his own Prefecture; he is responsible for it, and should have the right to modify its structure. On the other hand, the Minister is very conscious of the weight of prefectoral staffs on the Ministry's budget.

Since 1946 there have also been considerable changes in the number and type of functions assigned to the Prefect, and it is these attributes which finally determine what the Prefecture does. Economic powers which were delegated to the Prefect during the war have diminished with the return to a liberal economy; at the same time, the amount of welfare work, the activity of the Communes, and the extent of public works and investment have all increased. Some Divisions have as a result become heavily overburdened in relation to others. Many Prefects have reorganized the internal structure of their Prefecture in order to provide a more balanced division of function between the departments. Of the forty-five Prefectures which are, according to the Inspectorate General's scheme, supposed to have three Divisions, only one, the Prefecture of Aveyron, rigorously follows the division of functions there laid down.

At the same time, there are many instances where the Divisions have been reorganized and extended for almost entirely personal considerations. The Prefectures of Puy de Dôme, Vosges, and Sarthe, all have more Divisions than they should have, because it was personally expedient to promote a worthy official to *chef de division*, and an extra Division was created for him. In one Prefecture an extra Division was created simply in order to avoid an awkward choice between two candidates for promotion to *chef de division*, a senior official with much experience but little administrative talent, a junior one with initiative and greater ability.[1]

Personal complications also arise when the functions of one

[1] These examples are taken from the *Rapport présenté par l'Inspection Générale de l'Administration, 'L'Organisation et les effectifs des Préfectures'*. 1952.

Division decline as compared with the others; the *chef de division* of the contracting Division becomes very disgruntled, and he may be placated by a quite unjustified re-distribution of functions from the other Divisions.

The same personal issues happen in the Bureaux, the sub-sections of the Divisions. In the Prefecture of Mayenne, three Bureaux are concerned with Public Assistance (two normally suffice) in order to keep at his present status a *chef de bureau* whose previous post has become redundant.

It is part of the task of the Secretary General to build the Divisions and Bureaux into as rational and efficient an administrative organization as possible. He will have to gain the Prefect's permission for alterations, and he may be over-ridden, but it is his job to recommend what appears to him best.

The detailed work of the Prefecture has been divided by the Inspectorate General into nine main headings, each of which is subdivided into sections. Each Division is responsible for two or more of the main subjects, and the Bureaux for several related sub-sections.

The nine main headings are, GENERAL ADMINISTRATION, which includes elections, the census, registry of births and deaths, military conscription lists, litigation; POLICE, under which comes the inspection and control of public meetings, gypsies, peddlars, outdoor markets, public entertainments, gambling, car licences, public morality, public order, and public security; CONTROL OF ALIENS, their registration, naturalization and expulsion; the FINANCES of Department and State, and the use of departmental property; COMMUNAL ADMINISTRATION AND EDUCATION, covering questions of tutelage, communal public works, local officials, *syndicats* of Communes, scholarships and school buildings; PUBLIC ASSISTANCE, through the administration of the various types of welfare services, payment of allowances, and care of lunatics; PUBLIC WORKS, which includes hydro-electric schemes, roads, town planning, public housing projects; COMMERCE, INDUSTRY, AND AGRICULTURE, the feeding of the population and the division of scarce raw materials, frauds, lakes and forests, weights and measures, prices and the cost of living index, commercial and industrial associations. Finally, LABOUR, salaries and prices, insurance and mutual societies, unemployment and industrial disputes.

These main categories of affairs are distributed between the Divisions according to the importance of the Department. In over half the Departments there are three Divisions; the first deals with GENERAL ADMINISTRATION, POLICE, THE CONTROL OF ALIENS; the second Division with FINANCE, COMMUNAL ADMINISTRATION, EDUCATION AND PUBLIC ASSISTANCE; the third Division groups PUBLIC WORKS, COMMERCE, INDUSTRY AND AGRICULTURE, LABOUR, and is known as the Division of Social and Economic Affairs. Where there are only two Divisions in a Prefecture, the second Division above is divided between the other two; where there are four Divisions, Public Assistance is dealt with in a special Division; and when there are five Divisions, there is a special Division for Police Affairs.

This is quite a reasonable organization. The Prefectures with four Divisions are in Departments with a high population density and several important towns; social questions are more numerous and more acute. A special Division for Public Assistance makes it possible to deal speedily with applications for relief, and it allows Labour problems to be dealt with expeditiously by a staff free from the details of outdoor and indoor relief. The Prefectures with five Divisions are either in very large or very densely populated areas, with many Communes and several important cities in which the capital of the Department is a provincial capital in its own right. In addition many of these Prefectures are also the headquarters of the IGAME, and the capitals of military regions. There are therefore many other state authorities, security problems, liaison, control of other civil administrative services and a heavy financial burden. At first sight one might suppose that tutelage of the Communes would be more onerous, but the Inspectorate General has found that the cities in these rich Departments already possess highly competent permanent staffs, so that although the volume of municipal activity is very great, its supervision rarely involves more work than that of much smaller Communes.

The Divisions are subdivided into Bureaux. Again, there is a standard plan for each class of Prefecture: in fact there is little uniformity in the number of Bureaux or in the subjects each deals with, and there is often a lack of balance between them. It is for the Secretary General to try to equalize their duties: a difficult task that is in practice confused by the personal wishes of the *chefs de division*, by consideration for the *chefs de bureaux*, and by the habits of the public.

The rhythm of work in a fairly typical second class Prefecture follows a seasonal and a weekly pattern.[1] The Prefecture's relations with the public are of two sorts, personal visits and correspondence. The number of clients who come to this Prefecture to conduct their business in person reaches its highest points in March, at the end of June, and in late October. These points coincide with the awakening of spring and new hope, departure on vacations and the wish to settle affairs, and business worries after returning from holiday. The smallest number of visitors come during the easter and summer holidays, and during the cold spells of the early new year.

Thursday is the high point of the week; the day of the market and the school teachers' holiday. There are always fewer callers on fine days, when the attraction of the cafés and gossip in the squares is greater than the desire to pass the time with old friends in the Bureaux of the Prefecture. As against this, sudden storms and wintry colds are likely to remind people that they have urgent business in the warm offices of the Prefecture.

The habits of the visitors vary with their personal status and the importance they attach to their business. If the Prefecture is fortunate in its usher his presence and unhelpful demeanour may discourage the timid and the casual caller from asking for an audience, or may successfully divert him to a clerk who knows nothing about the matter. All the officials of a Prefecture except the members of the Prefectoral Corps are permanent residents in

[1] R. Bonnaud Delamare: cit.

the Department. Their friends, acquaintances and family connections know that they have a permanent *laissez-passer*, which they may in turn share with their friends, acquaintances and family connections.

There are in every Department a certain number of amateur experts in the management of prefectoral business. Such a person knows his way round the Bureaux, and can with shrewd precision spot the official who will deal with his affair. If his business is simply to obtain a game licence or a driving licence he goes to see the clerk. If he does not feel sure that he understands his own problem very well he sees the *chef de bureau*. When he begins to suspect that his demand has little chance of success he asks for the *chef de division*, or if he feels confidence in his personal weight, for the Secretary General. When there is no further hope he will ask for the Prefect and complain of the indolence of his staff. Thereafter he may turn to his Mayor or elected representative in order to denounce the discrimination against him.[1]

The hardy practitioner of the art develops a skill in the irrelevant and the ambiguous, sometimes to cover his retreat if his real purpose appears even to him to be somewhat presumptuous, sometimes as a method of indirectly enumerating his great personal merits which ought, he feels, to be shortly rewarded by inclusion in the honours list.

The clerks and the *chefs de bureau* in this Prefecture receive well over three quarters of the callers, an illustration of the amount of work which is concerned merely with legalizing documents, issuing permits and licences, and authorizing payments. In a monthly average of 2,815 visitors, 2,317 were dealt with by the Bureaux, an average of 230 callers to each Bureau. The three *chefs de division* received 326 of the remaining callers, and the Prefect, Secretary General and *chef de cabinet* the rest.

Yet visitors are only a small part of the Prefecture's work. Contact with the public is usually through correspondence. Insistence on documentation is not only characteristic of the bureaucratic mind, but also a protective device against exigent and often crafty

[1] Ibid.

visitors. The slow circulation of a dossier round the Bureaux can chill the most ardent spirit, and nullify any indiscretion extorted from an official by a pugnacious or a wheedling caller. Time may solve the problem more definitely than action. Minor officials also find it easier to say 'no' in long hand than in person.

The result of bureaucratic documentation is very clear. It is mutely evident in the number of times the three *chefs de division* signed documents and papers in this Prefecture. In one year the first *chef de division* signed 22,469 documents, letters and authorizations; the second *chef de division* 118,866; and the third 54,825. On an average the first signed seventy-five papers every working day, the second 396, and the third 182.[1] They must therefore rely to a very great extent upon the efficiency and good sense of the *chefs de bureau* and the assistants who prepare matters for their consideration. The only practical solution is to leave routine matters to subordinates to be dealt with by rule of thumb methods, and to attend themselves only to difficult cases, and those involving differences of opinion. They must decide which of these matters they can settle on their own account, and which should be summarized and sent up to the Secretary General for decision. One of the perennial problems in Prefectures is to find an administrative structure which is sufficiently elastic to allow for local variations of custom and psychology, and yet which does not loosen the chain of authority to a dangerous extent. The more affairs can be compartmentalized, the greater the possibility of evolving routine techniques to be applied by junior members of the staff.

Experiments have been made in some places to take account of peculiar local conditions. For instance, in the Department of the Ariège, which borders on Spain and Andorra, and where a large group of Spanish refugees settled after the Civil War, it has been found expedient to create a special Bureau to control aliens. Such a Bureau would hardly be justified in the Creuse. Again, Departments in the West of France are frequently the scene of rather humourless parochial fights over church and state schools.

[1] Ibid.

Several Prefectures in this area therefore have a special Bureau to deal with public education, separating it from communal affairs so that it can be given proper attention.

In the Department of the Drôme, an experiment has been made by centralizing in one Bureau all matters connected with public security. This Bureau is supposed to work out plans for dealing with future emergencies, such as fires, floods, railway accidents, plane crashes, and for sending emergency aid. It is the nucleus of the ARP and civil defence organizations, and prepares schemes for putting the Department on a war footing for rationing, emergency transport, liaison with the military, radio transmitters, and telephone circuits.

The search for the best administrative formula is part of the Secretary General's job. It is for him in collaboration with the *chefs de division* to re-allocate functions between Bureaux, and to appoint the most capable official to a particular task. It is for him to co-ordinate the *chefs de division* and to arbitrate between them in cases of disputed competence.

The burden of routine work on the *chefs de division* is great, and every effort must be made to standardize procedure so that work may safely be delegated to the Bureaux. For this and other reasons personnel matters take up much of the Secretary General's time. An average second class Prefecture with three Divisions such as that at Carcassonne (Aude) has a permanent staff of eighty-four officials, while larger Prefectures like Lyons, Strasburg, and Marseilles have between three and four hundred. A constant flow of regulations regarding appointment, promotion and conditions of service issues from the Ministry. By law each Prefecture has to have an advisory committee for personnel affairs, with representatives of the staff on it; the Prefect frequently presides over it, but the preparation for its meetings and the execution of its decisions rests with the Secretary General.

In most Prefectures the Secretary General has one or two officials (who comprise the Secretariat General) as a personal staff, and this often deals with personnel management. In very large Prefectures it has proved necessary to set up a special

Bureau for personnel; but the Inspectorate General strongly advocates that the Secretary General should personally supervise this Bureau, for it has been found that favouritism may disrupt staff relations if the *chefs de division* are given too great authority over their subordinates.

In all these matters the amount of autonomy given to the Secretary General will depend upon the Prefect. Normally he has considerable freedom of action, but there are some Prefects who consider themselves to be primarily administrators, and they interfere a good deal in details. The others restrict themselves to questions of policy, major changes in the organization of the Prefecture, and serious disciplinary offences.

The Secretary General is given other duties of a more positive kind. In some Prefectures the Secretariat General is responsible for receiving and despatching official correspondence—elsewhere it is the Prefect's cabinet which does this, for the compilation and publication of the official departmental bulletin, and sometimes for control of the Department's printing press. In other Prefectures one of his personal staff acts as librarian, and to this may be added a press and information service. In the Prefecture of the Basses Pyrénées (Pau) the Secretariat General also deals with national lotteries; in Indre-et-Loire with national defence, and in the Drôme the special Bureau of public security comes directly under the Secretary General's control, although it is distinct from his secretariat. In other Prefectures he also deals with staff welfare, the internal services of the Prefecture, supervision of transactions involving state or departmental property, and even, in the Gironde (Bordeaux), with 'departmental affairs' pure and simple.

He will spend much time drafting parts of the Department's budget with the *chefs de division* whose estimates of the needs of their Divisions require discussion, amendment, and co-ordination before the Prefect can begin to prepare the final draft for presentation to the *conseil général*. He may be asked to produce a preliminary report for the Prefect on a subject verging on the political, though this is generally a matter for the *chef de cabinet*;

he may be deputed to arbitrate in a squabble between two minor branches of other administrations, and he may be asked to make suggestions for nominations to posts filled by the Prefect.

In all, the Secretary General has an uninspiring and unexciting task; but without him the Prefect could not hope to be free to deal with those tasks for which he is, or should be, specially fitted. The Secretary General is essentially the man on whom the Prefect unloads the burden of detail. He pays the price for the Prefect's freedom.

4. *The Secretary General of Police*

There are only eight posts of Secretary General of Police.[1] They were not established by statute till 1948, but comparable officials existed during the Vichy and the Liberation periods. The number of these officials and the intrinsic importance of their work would not in themselves justify lengthy description. But they play an important part in the present organization of the French police services, and in the next chapter it will be necessary to assume some knowledge of these services and the Prefect's place in relation to them.

A description of the French police forces is complicated by the French use of the word 'police' to mean not only a body of men, but a power. The Prefect's 'police powers' not only authorize him to direct police forces, but also to make general 'police' ordinances to protect public safety, tranquillity, and order in the Department, and to regulate the public conduct of citizens.

This confusion of terms creates many ambiguities. The terms *police administrative*, *police municipale*, and *police judiciaire* all have two meanings; one the power, the other the forces responsible for applying and enforcing the regulations made under that power.

The French distinguish between police activities which are preventive in nature, and those which are repressive; this is best explained by illustration. Certain police authorities—for example, the Minister, the Prefect, and the Mayor—are required to make

[1] In the Paris region there is no Secretary General of Police.

regulations which will prevent breaches of the peace, dangers to public safety, and attacks on public morality; the Minister for the whole country, the Prefect for the Department, the Mayor for the Commune. Once made these regulations are enforced by certain police forces, most of them uniformed, who direct traffic, prevent riots, or disperse riotous assemblies, inspect premises, and so on. But once the law has been broken, it is for the police to investigate the offence and if possible bring the offender before the courts. This is the repressive police function, and it is performed in close collaboration with the state magistracy. The police officials who perform these duties of investigation are the detectives of the local and national police forces. Some police officials are concerned with both preventive and repressive police; the most notable is the *commissaire* in charge of a police station who controls both the uniformed men attached to that station, and the detective bureau.

Under the Third Republic there were in all four different police forces, three of which were national, and one local.[1] First, all Communes were responsible for maintaining their own communal police forces. In rural areas this amounted to no more than a *garde champêtre*; in large urban centres it would be a sizeable force of uniformed police and detectives. After 1936 a *commissaire de police* was seconded by the Ministry of the Interior to take charge of all police forces in Communes with over 5,000 inhabitants. He was to act under the general authority of the Mayor who was the Commune's formal police authority, but it was believed that he would be less susceptible to local influence than a man recruited and paid locally.

The police forces of the largest Communes in France were gradually brought under the control of the Prefect. Even during the nineteenth century, the cities of Paris and Lyons had a special status, whereby the departmental Prefects assumed within the Commune some of the police powers exercised elsewhere by the Mayor; the police forces were made up of contingents of the State

[1] Chemineau: *Etude de l'organisation administrative de la police en France.* Doctoral Thesis, Faculty of Law, Toulouse, 1944.

Police. Between 1918 and 1939 this system was extended to places like Toulouse, Marseilles, Strasburg and Bordeaux. The Prefects assumed the task of maintaining public order while the Mayor retained the other communal police powers.[1]

The third police formation was that provided by the services of the *Sûreté Nationale*, a department of the Ministry of the Interior; it provided regional brigades of Judicial Police which investigated major crimes and those beyond the scope of local detective bureaux. It also maintained in each Department a section styled the *renseignements généraux*, responsible for police intelligence and political supervision.

Finally, there were the military police forces, composed mainly of ex-regular soldiers who were recruited and paid by the War Ministry; in war time they could be used as a field force and for provost duties. In peace time they were partly training formations, and partly police groups, deployed by the Minister of the Interior to aid the civil police in preventing and detecting crime. The first of these forces was the *Gendarmerie*, which to a great extent assumed responsibility for policing rural districts. The second was the *Garde Mobile*, which was a reserve force called on to act as riot police.

Under Vichy the pre-war system was modified. In the first place, communal police forces were abolished in all Communes with more than 10,000 inhabitants, and were replaced by State Police. The Prefect controlled these forces, and became responsible for the maintenance of order in place of the Mayor.[2]

The second change was the creation of regional police authorities and police forces. The state police forces were regionalized, and their control passed from the Prefect to an Intendant of Police; he in turn was responsible to the Regional Prefect.

[1] A discussion of the division of powers is contained in Englinger: *L'organisation de la police administrative dans les villes à police d'Etat*. Doctoral Thesis, Faculty of Law, Strasburg, 1938.

[2] For the texts of the Vichy reforms, see J. Laferrière: *Le nouveau droit public de la France. Recueil méthodique des textes constitutionnels et administratifs*. Paris, Sirey, 1941.

Third, a new body of quasi-military police was created, the *groupes mobiles de réserve* (GMR) which was to supersede the *Garde Mobile*. The GMR came directly under the Minister of the Interior, and not the War Ministry; the desire of the Minister of the Interior to have his own troops was one of the motives for the reform. The other was that the *Garde Mobile* was rightly suspected of anti-Vichy sentiments. The GMR were stationed in the regional capitals and other important centres.

The Liberation brought no substantial change to this system, but some names were changed.[1] The Regional Prefect was replaced by the *commissaire de la République*, the Intendant of Police by a Secretary General of Police with similar powers. The GMR were dissolved and replaced by *compagnies républicaines de sécurité* (CRS), and some of the personnel were transferred from one to the other. The CRS were, like the GMR, under the control of the Ministry of the Interior, and were used on the instructions of the *commissaires de la République*.

In 1946 when the *commissaires de la République* were abolished, the regional police services were dismantled. The Department again became the area of police administration, and the uniformed branch of the State Police and the offices of the *renseignements généraux* were put under the Prefect's control, although their administration and recruitment went back to the *Sûreté Nationale*; the latter also took over the CRS, the administration of the Judicial Police and the regional supply and communications centres. Only the police record departments were kept (temporarily, it was thought) on a regional basis, under the control of a secretary.

The general strike combined with attacks by armed mobs in November 1947 threatened a complete breakdown in the police services. The Minister of the Interior and the *Sûreté Nationale* were unable to obtain a clear picture of the situation; communications were cut, railway stations, police posts, town halls, post offices were stormed, and the number of radio messages received

[1] P. Doueil: *L'Administration locale à l'épreuve de la guerre*. 1939–49. Paris, 1950. p. 165.

by the Ministry rose from the normal daily average of 700 to well over 2,000. It was impossible in these circumstances to assess the needs of the Departments.

The Prefects were thrown on their own resources. Some jealously guarded the forces they had in their Department, to the detriment of hard-pressed neighbours. Demands to the local army authorities were sometimes duplicated by messages to Corps and Army headquarters. Prefects competed with each other for military assistance, thus forcing the army commander to evaluate the situation on his own authority, which was a dangerous abdication of civil responsibility. The CRS were in theory only to be used on the instructions of the Minister. The results of this chaos was that the Minister had to contemplate withdrawing all his forces in the South to Marseilles and Montpellier until he was strong enough to challenge the strikers.

The crisis was overcome, partly because the strikers themselves lacked agreed political aims. In the ensuing months the Minister made serious efforts to improve the co-ordination and control of the police forces, and in April 1948 there was a return to the concept of a regional police authority. Eight *inspecteurs généraux de l'administration en mission extraordinaire* were appointed with orders to re-form the police services in their regions, assume complete control in times of emergency, and assist the Minister, and the Government in general, by undertaking missions of information and co-ordination in any matter which required general discussion.

The existing regional police records department was expanded to be a *centre administratif interdépartemental de police* (CAIP) under a secretary. The various security forces were reorganized into the same pattern of regions, and their commandants were to reside in the regional capital; a *controleur général* for the *Sûreté Nationale*, the Group Commander of the CRS, the Colonel commandant of the legion of *Gendarmerie*, and the General commandant of the military region. When the IGAME exerted his reserve powers in an emergency all these officials and their formations were required to act on his instructions.

The *centre administratif interdépartemental de police* was abolished in May 1949, and replaced by *centres administratifs et techniques interdépartementaux* (CATI) which were placed under a specially appointed member of the Prefectoral Corps, the Secretary General of Police.[1]

In consequence, the police organization is now as follows. The Director General of the *Sûreté Nationale* is immediately responsible to the Minister for all branches of police work in France.[2] He has under him nine central Directorates and a cabinet. To the cabinet are attached specialized police agencies like the police schools, the criminal record office, the Inspectorate General of Police, and the automobile pool.

The first of the Directorates is that for *règlementation et etrangers*, and this drafts the laws, decrees and circulars to be applied by Prefects and police officials. It has national jurisdiction. Similarly, the Directorates of Administration, Supply and Transport, Aliens and Passports, Civil Defence and Fire services have national jurisdiction without any territorial branches.

Three Directorates have both a central organization and their own regional services and officials: the Directorates of the Judicial Police, the *renseignements généraux*, and the *surveillance du territoire*, the counter-espionage service. The last is organized in six very large regions, not the military ones; each region or sector has several brigades, 'antennae' and 'listening posts', and there is a special mobile antenna. The internal arrangements of the DST are an official secret. Its officers correspond directly with and are responsible to the *Sûreté Nationale*.

The Judicial Police are based on seventeen regions, each brigade covering several Departments. They are responsible for investigating major crimes, and they have special sections to deal with international crime, vice and drugs, subversive conspiracies, frauds and railway robberies. There are roughly fifty officials in

[1] B. Chapman: *A Development in French Regional Administration; Public Administration.* Winter, 1950.

[2] Except for Paris and the Department of the Seine, for which the Prefect of Police is directly responsible to the Minister.

each brigade. Sections of the Judicial Police are stationed in large towns and departmental capitals to aid the local *commissaires*. In the course of their duties they accept orders only from the State Advocate General in their region, and not from the Prefects. Their administration is a matter for their Directorate in Paris.

The *renseignements généraux* have an office with a director in each Department. It is responsible for informing the Prefect, the IGAME, and the *Sûreté Nationale* on matters of public concern which happen in its area. The central Directorate centralizes and analyses the information compiled by the departmental offices, and reports to the Minister and Director General. The officers of the *renseignements généraux* analyse the press and cinema, collect political information, study social and economic questions, supervise the activities of aliens, investigate financial dealings, gambling and casinos, and keep a watch on race tracks. They obtain a great deal of information on political life, trade union affairs, and the private lives of anyone who takes an active part in public life. They are also in charge of the railway police, frontier control, and passport control.

The final Directorate is now properly speaking a Bureau. Until the police reforms of 1948-9, this Directorate was responsible for all the uniformed State Police in the whole country, their administration, discipline and organization. Most of its administrative duties passed to the regional centres of police (the CATI) and its powers to the IGAME; the uniformed police and their officers and the *commissaires* are now under the day to day authority of the Prefect, but administration, records, and serious disciplinary offences are dealt with at regional level. The Directorate became instead the *bureau d'étude de l'emploi de forces de police*, and it works in close touch with the headquarters of the CRS. It is essentially a planning division.

To return now to the Secretary General of Police. In May 1949 the CATI were set up to replace the CAIP whose jurisdiction had proved to be too small. The CATI fused all the administrative, technical and financial police organizations in the region. They have a civilian staff recruited from employees of the Prefecture.

The Secretary General became responsible for the records, pay, and equipment of all uniformed state police in the area, and he was to unify the supply organizations and transport services and plan their rational employment. In the first instance his powers came directly by delegation from the Minister, and they did not impinge in any way on the rights of the Prefects. They retained their existing disciplinary powers, and their right to transfer men from one district in a Department to another. They were expected to keep the Secretary General of Police informed of these movements, and only the IGAME was authorized to move police from one Department to another. The Prefect remained fully responsible for the operations of the police in his Department, and in ordinary times neither the Secretary General nor the IGAME could interfere with his dispositions.

The Prefects were encouraged by ministerial circular to delegate administrative matters concerning the police to the Secretary General, and in particular to refer questions of discipline to him in order that he might draft documents for the Prefect's approval.

The Secretary General of Police works through the CATI; it has a private secretariat and two Divisions. The first Division, for Administration and Finance, has its own secretariat which keeps the files and deals with correspondence and legal affairs. It has two Bureaux, one for administration, the other for finance.

The second Division is for Technical affairs, and it has its own secretariat, as well as Bureaux which run the workshops, storehouses, clothing stores, office equipment, and armament supplies. It is responsible for all the material needs of the uniformed police in the region.

Finally, the regional wireless and communication centres are under the administrative and financial control of the CATI, but they are operationally independent, and responsible for their own research.

A decree of January 26, 1951, helped to fit the Secretary General of Police into the general prefectoral system. The Minister now delegated to the IGAME all his own powers of discipline over the police personnel, and the IGAME was empowered to delegate in his turn to the Secretary General any of his police powers; those he held from the Minister as IGAME, and those which he possessed as departmental Prefect. The Secretary General now drew his powers from his immediate superior, and not by delegation from the centre.

The significance of this reform was that the IGAME could now delegate powers of administration to him as he would to his Secretary General of the Prefecture, and these did not have to be, although they were, only concerned with police affairs. He could delegate some of his police powers, as well as control of police personnel.

To establish his new position firmly, the Secretary General of Police was formally granted the same status and prerogatives as the Secretary General of a Prefecture, with the right to accommodation at the Department's expense, free transport and an expense account. The IGAME were warmly encouraged by ministerial circular to delegate their authority widely, and they soon took advantage of the new arrangements. In the Prefecture of Metz, the capital of the VIth military region, the IGAME placed under the control of the new Secretary General the special Bureau of National Defence, responsible for preparing civil mobilization in case of war, rationing, price control, evacuation, ARP, and liaison with the military. At the same time he transferred the entire Division of Police Affairs in the Prefecture from the jurisdiction of the Secretary General of the Prefecture to the Secretary General of Police. Similar experiments in delegating part of the ordinary work of the Prefecture to the new Secretary General are being tried in the other regional capitals.

In a very short space of time the Secretary General of Police has become an integral part of prefectoral administration. To complete this section three points of potential conflict need to be described, for should they ever become serious, which they are not now, they could lead to hostile attacks on the CATI.

The first are the relations of the CATI with the Prefects of the region. So far no conflict remotely like that which existed between the Intendants of Vichy and the Prefects has arisen.

There is a simple reason for this. The powers of the CATI and the Secretary General have been taken from the centre by a process of deconcentration, and not from the Prefects. The latter remain firmly responsible for their Department and for the full exercise of their police powers; they are under no kind of regional supervision, and they themselves are still directly responsible to the Minister. The Secretary General's powers are simply those of administration, and the IGAME would not tolerate an attempt to expand this office work into the field of police operations, except perhaps in his own Department, if he is himself a Prefect in office.

Second, in theory a conflict of competence could arise between the Secretary General of Police and the *controleur général de police*, the senior police official in the region, for both have some control over police personnel. But it seems to be firmly settled that the CATI have no powers to investigate individual offences by police officers nor to question their efficiency when on duty. For example, a Spanish gentleman absconded from a bank in Bilbao with three million pesetas. He crossed with his loot into France over the Pyrenees, but was arrested near the frontier by a French policeman who relieved him of 150,000 pesetas (five per cent) and then allowed him to return to his own country. The Spanish gentleman was later arrested in Barcelona, and told his story. The Spanish authorities agreed that he and they had cause for complaint and protested to the French government. The investigation of this case was held to be clearly within the competence of the *controleur général*, and not of the CATI.

Finally, difficulties could arise from the special position of the CRS. Their headquarters are in Paris, and the companies, each of about two hundred men, are stationed in the main towns of the region. Unlike the *Garde Mobile*, which are army formations, the CRS are part of the police services under the Ministry of the Interior.[1] The IGAME as the Minister's delegate is responsible for their use and deployment, and only in cases of extreme need

---

[1] When the question of increasing the strength of the CRS is raised in Parliament, the point is always made that an expansion of the *Garde Mobile* would be preferable, since in peace time the latter acts as a holding and

can a Prefect employ them without the IGAME's permission.

The Secretary General of Police may in a few particulars receive some of the IGAME's powers, but no IGAME would delegate to him responsibility for deciding when and how the CRS should be employed. Too many serious issues can arise from using them as police reserves, for they are heavily armed and very unpopular, and they rarely show much consideration for limbs, heads, or property.

The CATI and the Secretary General are periodically attacked in Parliament when the Minister of the Interior's budget comes up for discussion; the attacks are directed against the efficiency of the police as much as against their cost. They appear to an observer to be an economical and sensible administrative device. They have accomplished the necessary task of overhaul and co-ordination to avert the dangers that arose in 1947 and 1948. They have eliminated much waste and inefficiency which used to characterize the police service, and to some extent still does: excessive overtime, duplication of services, lack of discipline and personnel control. At least the CATI is the only body available that can eliminate these abuses.

The CATI and the Secretaries General of Police were recently examined by the Inspectorate General, and their work commended. As a result the Minister has made it known that he would reconsider their position only after recommendations from a body of the highest authority. The only reform probable in the near future is the abolition of one or two services which are from the police point of view technically desirable, but which are administratively and economically unjustified.

training unit, and in time of war is ready for fighting. The CRS on the other hand only trains policemen, and is not a line formation. The Minister of the Interior always resists these arguments because he prefers to have unchallenged jurisdiction over security forces. But para-military forces of this kind are undesirable institutions if there is a reasonable alternative like the *Garde Mobile* available.

CHAPTER FIVE

The Prefect

THE PREFECT HOLDS a unique position in French public life. He is the intermediary between the Government and the population, between the politicians and the electorate. He is the administrator who is part politician, and the politician who is a first class administrator. He is the representative of the State in the Department, and the protector of departmental interests against the Ministries. He makes the Mayors obey the law and he fights other officials in the Department, and sometimes their Ministries as well, on behalf of the Mayors. He is the executive instrument of the Government, and at the same time the initiator of departmental policy. His rôle is partly administration, partly politics, partly social leadership.

These conflicting duties need careful analysis before a complete picture of a contemporary Prefect emerges. This chapter deals in turn with the main subjects which affect his career and influence his work. It considers first the number of Prefects in the Corps and their legal and social status; second, the process of appointment, which raises political questions. The next section deals with the Prefect's powers, and is followed by a discussion of the interests and pressures which influence a Prefect's administration. It concludes with a description of the way a Prefect reconciles his various duties and of the rôle he plays in society.

1. *Numbers and Status*

There are 148 Prefects in the Prefectoral Corps. Of these 106 are on active service in prefectoral appointments, and forty-two are either *hors cadres*, *chargés de mission*, or on detached service in other state posts. The largest group not in prefectoral posts are those on detached service, and their activities vary widely. One is the head of the secret service; others are in national elected assemblies like the National Assembly and the Assembly of the French Union. Several are serving outside France in the Associated States, in Morocco, Laos and Tunisia. Some have been attached to international bodies like the IRO, and others are on diplomatic mission, for example as observer at Wiesbaden and as French Minister to Monaco. Some are in semi-public bodies, such as the Director of the Gas and Electricity Company of Algeria; and another is director of a psychiatric hospital. The remainder are in central Ministries—Foreign Affairs, Reconstruction, Public Works, National Education, National Defence and Ex-Servicemen—where they are serving as Directors. The Secretary General of the Government of Algeria, the Secretary General of the Protectorate of Morocco, and the permanent Secretary General for National Defence, are all Prefects on detached service. The Prefects on detached service, unlike those who are *hors cadres*, have no right to a prefectoral post when they leave their present appointment.

Ninety-eight of the 106 Prefects on active service are in charge of Departments: ninety-one of them in France, three in the Algerian Departments and four in the Overseas Departments. The remainder are serving in exceptionally important posts under a more senior Prefect; three on the staff of the Prefect of the Seine, who has two Prefects as his Secretaries General and one as his *directeur du cabinet*, two with the Prefect of Police—the Secretary General to the Prefecture and the *directeur du cabinet*—and three on the staff of the Governor General of Algeria, two as Secretaries General and the other as *directeur du cabinet civil*.

Like the Sub Prefect, a Prefect draws his personal rank from the Department in which he is serving.[1] The two highest posts a

---

[1] Prefects who are *hors cadres* or on detached service can be promoted within the Prefectoral Corps even though at the moment they are not performing prefectoral duties. Furthermore, if a Prefect has been in one Department long enough to qualify for promotion the Minister can promote him without

Prefect can hold are those of Prefect of the Seine and Prefect of Police. Next there come fourteen *hors classe* Departments in metropolitan France; in eight of these the Prefect is also the IGAME of the Region. There are nineteen first class Departments, twenty-two second class, and thirty-four third class. The Overseas Departments are not classified.

But as with the Sub Prefects, the hierarchy of Prefects is much more confused than this pyramid suggests. Many Prefects have benefited from personal advancement while holding the same post. Thus, fourteen Prefects who are serving in third class Departments are second class in rank; four of those in second class Departments are first class Prefects; and there are two *hors classe* Prefects in first class Prefectures. To add to the confusion, there is one first class Prefect in an *hors classe* Prefecture and another in a third class Prefecture. On active service there are actually twenty-five third class, thirty-four second class, thirty first class, fifteen *hors classe* and the two Paris Prefects.

These figures are not merely numerical exercises for they reveal two important points. The first is that the prospects of promotion are becoming increasingly bad. Not only is the pyramid of promotion out of shape, but the age span of the various grades no longer makes sense. The average age of the second class Prefects is lower than that of the third class Prefects.

Before the War it was usual for a Prefect third class to be appointed between the ages of forty-five and fifty; thereafter, he would serve in that grade for five years before promotion, with service in two or more other Prefectures. Now the average age of the *hors classe* Prefects is fifty-four, of the first class Prefects forty-eight, of the second class forty-six, and of the third class Prefects, among whom are a substantial number of those promoted from the career Sub Prefects at the end of the War, forty-eight; two years more than the class above them.

This is a disquieting position for many Prefects, and, of course, for all Sub Prefects. The average age of all the Prefects in the

transferring him to another Department. But not more than a quarter of one class of Prefect can have this personal promotion at one time.

Corps now is lower than the normal age of entry as Prefect under the Third Republic. It will take nearly twenty years before the brilliant prefectoral appointments of the Liberation have worked themselves out. By that time the age of the Sub Prefects to be promoted will be very high compared to the past. The Government may, of course, decide to introduce new blood in preference to promoting men with too long a history in subordinate posts, or there may be some startling promotions among the new Sub Prefects from the ENA who have raced up the ladder while serving inside the Ministry of the Interior as *administrateurs civils*.

The second point behind the figures is of wider importance. Is the present system of territorial appointment, whereby a Prefect must move if he wishes to obtain promotion, the best formula? This controversy has gone on ever since the Prefectoral Corps offered a career. Napoleon's Prefects were appointed on a purely personal basis and there was no formal hierarchy of classes. Thereafter at various times either the Prefect drew his rank, as now, from the class of the Department in which he was serving, or he had a purely personal rank which had nothing to do with the Department he happened to be serving in at a particular time.

An eminent author[1] has recently seriously criticized the present arrangement. He maintains that the classification of Departments is out of all touch with reality. The Vendée is a third class Department with 394,000 inhabitants, Yonne a second class Department with 266,000 inhabitants. The Côtes-du-Nord with 527,000 inhabitants is second class, Eure is first class with 316,000.[2] Admittedly there are sometimes strategic or other reasons for giving a small Department a high class. But in many cases the main reason for anomalies in the classification of Departments was only the laudable desire to ensure promotion for Prefects. In others it was to satisfy the demands of local politicians.

The result of the territorial system is that an ambitious Prefect

[1] D. Jouany: *L'Administration telle qu'elle est. Revue Administrative.* March, 1951—January, 1952.

[2] It might be argued that only in an otherwise rational system of classification would these exceptions be noticeable.

must always be on the move. This means not only that he will sometimes go from a socially and economically more important Department to a less important one when he gets promotion; it also means that he is unable to undertake those schemes of long term development and planning in a Department for which he is specially suited. In a world where other administrations are by no means content to accept without question the Prefect's supremacy in the Department, it is only if he can become firmly attached to a particular post, understand the profounder currents of local life, and act as a point of stability as well as of leadership, that he will be able to pursue a steady and purposeful policy.

Serving Prefects sometimes object to remaining too long in one place; they hold, sometimes with apparent justification, that a Prefect who remains too long exhausts his credit. There comes a time when he can no longer exert moral pressure, and reliance solely upon legal powers is the first step towards impotence. It may be difficult for him to remain impartial. The Ministry and the politicians sometimes believe that he has become too deeply absorbed in defending local interests against the Ministries, or that a desire for stability means that he has found a sinecure.

On the other hand there are many precedents for Prefects remaining for very long periods in one post without obvious disadvantages. The greatest Prefect of Police, Lépine, served in this most difficult of all posts with only one minor interruption (when for two years he was Governor General of Algeria) for twenty years, from 1893 to 1913. He served under twenty-three different Ministries. Many others in the nineteenth century and a few under the Third Republic served in one post with distinction for up to twenty years in conditions that were not obviously easier than those of today.

M. Jouany's proposal to amalgamate into one class all the third and second class Prefectures seems eminently sensible, for it would cut down unnecessary movement. But in any event one result of the present overcrowding in the Corps may be to encourage, if not to force, the Ministry to accept as normal a much longer period in one place.

The Prefects are among the best paid state officials. Their salaries range from 1,388,000 francs (roughly £1,388) for a third class Prefect, to 1,900,000 francs for the Prefects of the Seine and of the Police. In addition, they receive free furnished lodging in luxurious quarters reserved for them in the Prefectures. They draw an expense allowance which varies with the class of the Department, but which seems reasonable. If they are married they benefit from various children and marriage allowances. The Department in which they reside provides them with a car and chauffeur and pays its running costs. They can travel first class on all State railways. If they are more than 600 kilometres from Paris they are permitted to fly on business, but they must themselves pay the difference between the cost of air passage and first class rail fare.

They have other prerogatives. Like Deputies, Senators and Ministers, they are entitled to wear on their cars a tricolor identification 'target'. They are allowed to enter the private rooms of the National Assembly and the Council of the Republic without formal permission. They have a special uniform which must be worn on official occasions, and they take precedence over other officials and are entitled to military honours. If they are accused of a criminal offence while in office they are tried before the regional *cour d'appel* and not by the local courts.

The Prefect of the Pyrénées Orientales (Perpignan) exercises the prerogatives and duties of the old Counts of Foix in the Republic of Andorra, which were vested in the Crown of France in the first instance, and later in the President of the Republic. His co-sovereign is the Bishop of Urgel in Spain. The Prefect controls the public services set up there by France, such as education, posts and telegraphs.

The Prefects of Paris—the Prefect of the Seine, and the Prefect of Police—have very special powers and duties. The Prefect of the Seine, who is normally regarded as the most eminent official in the Corps, is not only a departmental Prefect, he also assumes the powers and jurisdiction of mayor of the city of Paris. The Prefect of Police has a unique rôle in that he controls all the police forces throughout the Department of the Seine, and exercises many of the ordinary communal and departmental police powers both in the Department and in the city of Paris.[1]

The Prefects are marked off from any other type of official. They pay for this special status by the fact that more is expected from them than from any other official. They must be politically loyal to the Government of the day, whereas other officials are free not to be provided their work does not suffer. The Prefects are appointed by a decree of the President of the Republic and can be dismissed without cause or explanation; other officials are protected except in cases of grave misconduct. Both Prefects and their wives are forbidden to take up any paid job in their Departments, and a Prefect may hold no other office of profit under the State. He is ineligible to stand as a municipal or departmental councillor in his area, or as a Deputy or Senator anywhere. He is forbidden to belong to the central organization of a political party or take part in local political activities. He may not attend any public or private rally of a party political character. The Prefect is forbidden to receive deputations from demonstrators when they are drawn up outside the Prefecture[2]. He is required to reside in his Department, and must obtain approval before leaving it, even if only to call on the Minister. Prefects' actions are subject to the Minister, who can suspend or annul any of their measures or decisions. They have no right to their post, and, for a long time, this principle was carried to the extreme of not requiring them to contribute to their pension; but this favour has now disappeared.

Prefects can be dismissed without compensation; they can be retired; they can be put *en disponibilité*, which means that through an error of taste or an error of psychology they no longer have the full confidence of the Minister: they do not then receive any

---

[1] I have dealt with the work of these two Prefects in some detail elsewhere: 'The Government of Paris', in *Great Cities of the World*. Ed. Robson, London, 1954; and 'The Prefect of Police' in the *American Journal of Criminal Science*, December, 1953.

[2] Regulation of February 23, 1950.

salary,[1] but contributions towards their pension continue. They can also be put *hors cadres*, which means that they receive their salary, up to a maximum of five years, and that they have the right to return to the Corps.

As in Napoleon's day, the Prefects remain one of the most favoured bodies of the French Administration, but they pay for it by the strain under which they live.

2. *Appointment*

The Prefect's importance is such that no Government has ever been prepared seriously to restrict its liberty of choice in appointing him.[2] In broad terms any man who is qualified to be a *fonctionnaire* of any sort can be a Prefect. These elementary qualifications amount to little more than being a French citizen, in possession of civil and political rights, and free from infectious disease. An applicant for the police force must not have been to prison for more than a fortnight; this is quite immaterial in a Prefect.

There are however minor restrictions on the Government's liberty of choice, and these are set out in the Statute. They concern the promotion of Sub Prefects to Prefects, and the transference of officials of the Ministry of the Interior to the Prefectoral Corps. Only *hors classe* and first class Sub Prefects can be promoted Prefect, and in the latter case only if they have at least four years seniority in that rank. An assistant-director or sub-director in the Ministry ranks as a Prefect third class, a director with less than three years seniority as Prefect second class, a director with between three and five years seniority as Prefect first class, and a director-general or a director with more than five years seniority as Prefect *hors classe*. Assistant- and sub-directors must serve at least a year as a Prefect before they can be promoted to the second class; but thereafter their service in the Ministry counts towards their seniority in the Prefectoral Corps.

[1] Sometimes as a favour they are put on half pay, but this can only continue for a year.

[2] In December, 1934, a decree arranged eligible Sub Prefects in a *liste d'aptitude*; it was abolished within nine months.

Promotion within the ranks of the Prefects has also been formalized by the Statute, for Prefects of the second and third class can be promoted only after three years service in that rank, while a first class Prefect needs two years seniority before promotion to Prefect *hors classe*.

It will be seen that the limitations upon the Government's freedom of choice are concerned only with those already in the Corps or the Ministry of the Interior. It is a formal framework designed to prevent the spectacular and unjustified promotions which were at one time fairly common. The Government's freedom of choice in appointing men from outside the career is virtually unlimited. An industrialist, a jurist, a professor, an army officer, a trade union official can enter directly at any stage in the hierarchy. If a first class Prefecture becomes vacant, the Government may consider the second class Prefects and the directors in the Ministry; it may consider transferring a first class Prefect to the post. But it may decide to ignore them all and appoint someone from outside the service.

There is no restriction whatever upon the Government's right to dismiss, transfer or suspend a Prefect without cause or explanation. The protection that other state officials have against unjustified dismissal is not applicable to the Prefectoral Corps.

A great deal has been said about the 'politics' which attend the appointment and choice of a Prefect, and this point needs discussion. There is a good deal of exaggeration about the amount of political favour customary in appointments as about so much else connected with the Corps. It is true to say that, in 'normal' times, that is between changes of régime or real changes of political direction, the Corps is, and has been now for many years, very much a career, in which men rise from *chef de cabinet* at the bottom to Prefect of the Seine at the top. The best way to become a Prefect is to be a really good Sub Prefect. All the Prefects now in office who entered the Corps before the war began either as *chefs de cabinet* or as junior Sub Prefects. There were, of course, Prefects in the 1930's appointed from outside the Corps, several on political grounds, but those that have lasted the course came from inside. In normal times it is also customary to find as Prefects a few administrators from other branches of the state service, for example, *maîtres des requêtes*, who add a leaven to the career officials.

In exceptional times, and when there is a real change in political direction, political appointments are the general rule, though even then many will be appointed from inside the service if they show that their sympathies lie with the régime. Vichy packed the Corps with men who supported its philosophy and politics. Some genuinely considered that they were serving their country, others served their ambition. The loyalty of some Sub Prefects was bought by a promotion.

The Liberation followed the same pattern. All Prefects in office at the time of the Normandy landing were automatically suspended; they were replaced by Prefects nominated by the Provisional Government and agreed to by the internal Resistance. Many had had no previous association either with the Prefectoral Corps or the Administration. All the Resistance Prefects were appointed provisionally, and later the most successful were integrated into the Corps and the remainder were dismissed.

During the immediate post-war period several of the Prefects of the Third Republic returned to office, when they returned from captivity or when their war records had been cleared; some of them had successfully performed the formidable and exhilarating task of serving the Resistance under the noses of the Germans, the Militia, and the police intelligence groups.

Since 1947 the career element has once again tended to rise, and new Prefects are most frequently promoted from the Sub Prefects or sub-directors of the Ministry; several of these were, in their turn, liberation entries at a junior level.

The present composition is this. About half the Prefects in the Corps joined before the war, the great majority as *chefs de cabinet*. A few of these entered directly as Sub Prefects after having previously been on the personal staff of a Minister, though not always of a Minister of the Interior. Many of those who entered as *chefs de cabinet* had already had some experience, since the average

age of entry was twenty-seven; some had been teachers, others *rédacteurs* in Prefectures, and others *rédacteurs* in the Ministry of the Interior or occasionally in other Ministries. The majority who entered before the war came with some experience of administration.

Very few of the present Prefects entered during the war, about one in ten. The reason is clear. If they entered between 1940 and 1944 as *chefs de cabinet* or Sub Prefects, they did not have the seniority when the Liberation came to be acceptable at once as Prefects. Those who had political energies which they used as Sub Prefects under Vichy were *ipso facto* ineligible, and they were sometimes fortunate to be left alone as Sub Prefects. The few Vichy entrants who are now Prefects either benefited by being dismissed by Vichy for activities hostile to the Government, or took part in activities which brought them to the favourable notice of resistance leaders. Almost all were previously either officials in a Ministry or *rédacteurs* of Prefectures. This group also contributes to the 'administrative' background to the Corps.

About two-fifths of the present Prefects entered at the Liberation, some of them as Sub Prefects, but the majority directly as Prefects. Only a minority of this group of Prefects had had previous experience in comparable forms of administration before they joined the Corps; those that had, came from Ministries, Prefectures, Algerian and Moroccan governments, or the *conseils de préfecture*. The remainder (that is, between a quarter and a third of the whole body of Prefects) came from outside posts and from the liberal professions: several men of law, several professors, an actuary, a banker, a police official, a naval construction engineer, an aeronautical engineer, an army officer. Two of them began as *commissaires de la République*. Others began as Prefects. Others did not go directly to a prefectoral post, but rose quickly after a short spell on the staff of a *commissaire de la République*; some entered first the private cabinet of a liberation Minister, others first went to responsible posts in the *Sûreté Nationale*. They were then posted out as Prefects after making their mark at the centre; their colleagues who entered at the same time and are still Prefects were the cream of the 'parachuted' resistance Prefects.

The balance between the career Prefects with long administrative experience and the direct entry Prefects from other walks of life is well exemplified in the fifteen *hors classe* Prefects. One-third joined at the Liberation, two-thirds were members of the Prefectoral Corps before the war, some of them already Prefects, some still Sub Prefects: those who were Prefects left the Corps during Vichy, a few to take up non-political posts such as director of a hospital, a few to escape from the country to De Gaulle.

At the very top of the career there is a striking comparison between the Prefect of the Seine and the Prefect of Police. The present Prefect of the Seine entered the Prefectoral Corps after the 1914-18 war in which he received the highest decorations and permanent disability. He joined as a *chef de cabinet*, and gradually worked through various posts as Sub Prefect and Secretary General until in 1934 he was appointed Prefect third class at the age of forty-three. By 1939 he had become Prefect second class, but in September 1940 was suspended by the Vichy government for his attachment to the republican form of government. During the war he was a regional director of the Ministry of Health, and in August 1944 re-joined the Corps on being appointed by the Provisional Government as Prefect of the Seine-Inférieure. Within four months he had been transferred in haste to take up the post of *commissaire de la République* at Marseilles, where conditions had deteriorated badly. In 1946 when the *commissaires* were abolished he went as Prefect of the Alpes Maritimes (Nice), a post of great difficulty, since it combines with social duties the strategic importance of a crucial frontier and the difficulties of dealing with a volatile and mixed community. He was appointed Prefect of the Seine in 1950.

His colleague in Paris, the Prefect of Police, had a very different career. He began by taking a diploma in forestry, and before the war was an inspector of Posts and Telegraphs, at one time in charge of a technical research division. He was a militant trade unionist of some notoriety. As a result of his resistance activities, he was appointed Prefect of the Basses-Pyrénées (Pau), his place of origin, in 1944 at the age of forty-seven, and two years later, since he had shown many qualities, he went as Prefect at Toulouse. At the time of the grave scandals which affected the Food Ministry under M. Gouin as Minister in 1947, a strong figure was needed to take administrative charge; this was his next post. When the situation in Marseilles again became serious after the strikes of 1947, and the police force there was partly demoralized in face of a very active Communist Party, he was sent to take charge, and successfully and ruthlessly brought order; he acquired a reputation as a stern disciplinarian and took an active part in social and intellectual activities. For a time he acted as IGAME to the region, then in 1951 he was appointed Prefect of Police when his predecessor was posted to Algeria as Governor General.

These short biographies show two different types of career, and the same pattern can be found at all levels. The amalgam of administrative experience with experience of other kinds is essential to the Corps. A purely administrative Corps would lose its special status and conform to the stereotyped pattern of a civil service career. A purely direct entry Corps would probably offer a temptation which the politicians could not resist, and it might not provide that sense of continuity and stability which is the mark of administration by permanent officials.

One point is worth notice. The Prefects who enter from other walks of life are in virtually all cases of the type and calibre of an intellectual élite. The Corps can and does attract men of the highest standing and intelligence. It is well to remember this when ungracious remarks are made about the Corps. On the other hand few Prefects enter the Corps directly from other branches of the Administration without some training either as Sub Prefects or inside the Ministry of the Interior. It is not a post that can be held down by any high administrator; he requires a particular flair and understanding which rarely comes to those whose contact with the public has been limited to interdepartmental committees and the study of files. If statistics show anything in this case, it is that it is safer to appoint a man of law, a professor, or an engineer as a Prefect than it is to transfer an *inspecteur des finances*, or a director of the Ministry of Economic Affairs.

The events of 1940 and 1944 confirm, if that was necessary, that the Prefect's place in the administration of the country is of such importance that a real change in political direction must be accompanied by a profound modification in the composition of the Corps. This, to the French, appears reasonable. The selfless administrator without clear or profound convictions is of little use either to a Government or to a society when called upon to deal with matters as fundamental as the control of education, police, and industrial conflict.

But now a further question is raised: how far do political considerations affect the appointment of Prefects during periods when the country is enjoying political stability, when changes in the Ministry are changes in political nuance and not political direction?

A salient point is that even in ordinary times a good deal more than seniority is involved in the promotion of a Prefect. During the first half of the Third Republic appointments were sometimes blatantly made on the ground of membership of a political party. Today this is rare, because too many qualities are required from a Prefect for enrolment in a party to be a qualification in itself. If a man possesses these qualities, membership of a party may or may not be an additional assistance to him in his career. Generally speaking, to be known as an outspoken advocate of one party is a handicap; discreet sympathy with one or other of the centre parties can be helpful. This is not high minded caution, fearful of sullying administration with politics. It is a very practical calculation. A Prefect who is known to be the protégé of a party or prominent politician as often brings discredit to his patron and to the Government as influence. If, as Prefect, he takes steps to benefit his Department, the good he does will have the aura of political machination, and will be derided as demagogy and partisanship. When he is forced to take an unpopular line public hostility will reach the patron as well as the Prefect. A once prominent Deputy bewailed that his political decline dated from the appointment of his protégé as Prefect of his

Department.[1] Blatant political patronage is dangerous: for the Government because its servant's loyalty is divided; for the Deputy, who stands to gain as much unpopularity as influence; for the Prefect, whose position hangs on that of his Deputy.

It would be unrealistic to suppose that there are no mediocrities among the career Prefects nor political adventurers among those appointed from outside the service. There are weak Prefects who fear to take decisions lest they make a political mistake, and there are bombastic Prefects whose main activity is personal advancement. Such persons are inevitable in any body of officials, but the demands made upon the capacities of a modern Prefect uncover his weaknesses more ruthlessly and speedily than in any other *corps* or administrative service. If the Minister knowingly keeps such people in office it is with the knowledge that one day he may be held accountable for their failings. He may gain some immediate political advantage, but the risk is considerable.

There is a further check on partisanship. By convention no Prefect is appointed by the Government if any member of the cabinet firmly opposes the nomination, and since virtually all French governments are coalitions this veto presents an automatic counter to gross favouritism. It might be expected that Cabinets would in consequence agree to divide up the Prefectures between the parties, each in effect naming its own nominee. In practice, this is next to impossible. The problem of assigning Prefectures between political parties would arouse so many political passions and personal rivalries that the trouble would be out of all proportion to the tenuous advantages. Cabinets are too short lived for such arrangements to have lasting effect; if it was decided to let parties allocate the Prefectures as they fell vacant, many years would elapse before the pattern was complete. The only alternative would be to massacre the existing Corps, and this would so far endanger the stability of the country, and so arouse public opinion, that no party or group of parties would consent to it.

[1] Mentioned by G. Poulat, a former Prefect, in *Tribune Libre*, Bulletin of Prefectoral Corps, April, 1951.

In addition to the unanimity rule in the Cabinet, it is also customary for the Minister of the Interior to consult prominent party leaders, particularly when the post to be filled is one of the highest in the Corps, or when it involves the politician's own Department. This is normal courtesy, and it will be extended to members of parties not at the moment in the Government. If the Prefecture of Hérault fell vacant, a Minister of the Interior would make known to M. Moch the man he had in mind as the next Prefect, or even (on some occasions) ask him for suggestions. The same would be true for nominations to the Rhône, when the advice of M. Herriot would undoubtedly be taken. In other words prominent party leaders may on some occasions have the option of putting forward the name of the man they would personally consider most satisfactory for the post, in others the right of veto over some names on the list of candidates. It naturally depends to some extent upon the character of the Minister of the Interior at the time how far he will go in order to be conciliatory, and how far he will ignore objections. But there is little credit to be obtained by appointing a notorious free-thinker to M. Schumann's Department.

Prefectoral appointments are political in that they involve choice between men of intelligence and ambition, who are to exercise powers of control and initiative in matters important to politicians. The outlook and capacities of these men are known, and are taken into account when one man has to be preferred to another for a particular post. Members of the Prefectoral Corps have often served in a Minister's cabinet during their career. Others acquire a political label from the way they handle matters in their Departments. Unless a Minister remains in office for a long time he can hardly become personally acquainted with all the Prefects, and he naturally seeks the impressions of his colleagues in Parliament who have an opportunity to judge as a result of daily contact with the Prefect in local administration. It is obvious that these impressions are sometimes biased more by the way the parliamentarian considers the Prefect treats him than by an objective evaluation of his strength of character or administrative worth. Against this, however, the Minister also has the personnel division of the Ministry to advise him; the Director of Personnel, who is frequently a member of the Prefectoral Corps of some standing, is in a position to balance the parliamentarians' assessments by indicating the non-political merits of the man. It is difficult to obtain accurate information on the way that prefectoral movements are drawn up; it is probably fairly near the truth to say that the script presented to the Minister for consideration is the joint work of the Director of Personnel and the *directeur du cabinet* of the Minister. If this is so, it symbolizes the balance between politics and administration to be found in prefectoral appointments.

For the most important posts of all the Minister will have political consultations with his colleagues, party leaders, and perhaps the President of the National Assembly and the President of the Republic. These posts are those of the IGAME and the Prefectures of the Police and Seine. It is not certain who takes the intitiative of putting forward the names of candidates, it may be the Ministry, the Minister, or anyone with a good idea. For the highest posts there may only be two or three serious candidates all of whom are *hors classe* Prefects, and the final choice may depend on the political nuance of the Minister of the Interior himself, a socialist Minister leaning slightly towards a Prefect known to have socialist sympathies, a zeal for reform and welfare schemes, a radical Minister tending towards the Prefect of substantial administrative worth, capable of strong action in an emergency. Both Socialist and Radical Ministers are likely to count membership of a Masonic Lodge as an additional qualification in a Prefect. Many members of the Corps are freemasons, and it is a traditional aid to a man's career to join a lodge at an early stage. Freemasonry in France has long been recognized as a political force, and some prefectoral careers and appointments are only explicable with it in mind. Its influence extends into much of the political world and the other *grands corps*, but it has been particularly noticeable in the Ministry of the Interior from the days of the Church and State struggles when the Prefectoral

Corps was the spearhead of the drive against the congregations. Control of the Ministry of the Interior by a convinced anti-clerical has long been regarded by vociferous elements of the public as the guarantee of the lay State, and before the war the Radicals had a virtual monopoly of the Ministry. Between 1944 and 1949 the Socialists assumed control, and now the trend is for the Radicals to become entrenched there again. There is an additional political reason for this. The influence of the Interior is so great on the internal affairs of the country that in any coalition of parties the one nearest the centre of the political spectrum is the least likely to abuse the post. As a result the Prefects themselves take the moderate complexion of their political masters, and the possibility of a Prefect in high office holding extreme views or marked prejudices is as improbable as an extreme Minister of the Interior in a normal French cabinet.

But the term 'political considerations' applied to prefectoral appointments extends beyond the simple enumeration of political affiliation. Because of the Prefect's influence on local affairs the Minister must consider other aspects of his character and person. A politically difficult Department like the Var requires a Prefect of strong character, acute political sense, and an unhesitating, brusque manner. Other Departments would feel insulted at the idea of a 'vulgar man' as Prefect, one with radical leanings and a contempt for social niceties. Prefects appointed to Nancy, Tours, Angers or Bordeaux should be distinguished gentlemen, at least in manner, capable of being accepted by the local aristocracy and bourgeoisie. A Prefect must have the entrée to the important centres of local influence in order to carry out his duties; the qualifications vary. The personal character of a Prefect has a political value. If the Prefectures of the Nord (Lille) and Gironde (Bordeaux) fall vacant simultaneously the same man may not be a serious candidate for both. On the other hand, there are several Prefects who would be fully equipped both intellectually and socially for both types of Department.

Finally, one comes to the extent to which Prefects themselves enter the arena in search of appointments and develop their careers by their personal efforts and contacts. Many of them have the capacity and ambition to use the politicians' weapons on their own behalf.

Some Prefects are content, at least during the early stages of their career, to wait their turn without calling attention to themselves. They believe that the febrile activity of the careerist tells against a man with the Minister, and they are often right. These wait in their Departments, entertain wisely when they can, and learn of their promotion or movements from the press.

The second type of Prefect combines caution with action. He chooses a particular Department in the grade immediately above his own, and then firmly and persistently assures all his callers and those he meets on his trips to the Ministry that he wishes to be considered only for that post. He does not chase after the first post vacant but seeks to create a climate of opinion at the Ministry that he is the natural successor to his chosen Department. He may already be assured of the sympathy of the most prominent politician who represents that Department, or he may seek it. This approach needs tact and patience, but seems to be fairly successful.

The last type of Prefect boldly tackles the problem of promotion in a political way. When it becomes known that the Ministry is preparing a prefectoral movement, he takes every possible occasion to go to Paris on business. He sees the Director of Personnel and the *directeur du cabinet*, he contacts his political friends, he calls into play what influence he has. He watches with vigilant hatred his colleagues who come to Paris on the same errand, and tries to discover their manoeuvres and to oppose them. He risks more than his cautious colleagues, for a rebuff makes a noise, but he stands the chance of more rapid promotion, or alternatively of the pleasanter posts. It may be found that the overcrowding in the Corps, the stabilization demanded by some experts, and the formal provisions of the Statute will lead to this approach eventually becoming less effective.

The ideal for a Prefect is to be admired as a personality by the Minister, to be known to his colleagues as an administrator of high quality, to have the favour of several parliamentarians of different parties, yet be tied to no one party or personality, and to be equable in temperament. It is also desirable if possible to serve in Paris for some time, or in a Department within easy striking distance, so that he becomes known. For a serving Prefect a period in the Ministry demands sacrifices, since he loses some of the perquisites such as free lodging to which he is entitled in a Prefecture. The more fortunate Prefects are able even while serving in the provinces to maintain an apartment in Paris to act as a pied-à-terre, but this is possible only if they have private means or benefit from the rent acts, which give security of tenure at very low rents.

It will be seen that many considerations affect these appointments. They are not the blatant political jobs they once were (some still believe them to be so today), nor are they official appointments of the ordinary type for which seniority as much as personality is the key to advancement. The rules are more subtle and variable and are perhaps more like those applicable to service in the Diplomatic Corps than to any other branch of the Administration.

3. *The Prefect's Powers*[1]

The Prefect's powers have been the result of a long and steady growth. Until 1850 his duties and authority were couched in very general terms. This helped to establish his absolute supremacy over all other officials, for none knew the real extent of his powers, and he assumed that authority which seemed necessary to himself and desirable to the Government. But after 1851 his powers were gradually codified by successive laws placing upon him some new burden of administration or giving him some explicit right of inspection and supervision. The result, once the Third Republic was established, was to weaken his authority in some directions,

[1] The remainder of this Chapter is concerned only with Prefects in continental France. Those in Algeria and the Overseas Departments have different powers and a much more direct political influence. They should properly be studied in a 'colonial' context.

for it could be plausibly argued that he had no powers outside those granted him expressly by law. While the Prefects were under a political cloud, in the first comparatively stable decades of the Third Republic, their authority diminished. It revived with the war of 1914 and the fresh internal weaknesses which became evident between the wars, and today few laws connected with the internal administration of the country do not foresee prefectoral intervention at some stage, whether they cover national elections, compulsory purchase, welfare services or town and country planning. By now the total enumerated powers amount to over 5,000. In 1861 it was 177.

It is impossible to list them here, and they cover such a variety of duties that it is difficult to synthesize them into a coherent pattern. The Prefect's constitutional position is simply stated in Article 88 of the Constitution of 1946. 'The co-ordination of the activities of state officials, the representation of national interests, and the administrative supervision of local authorities are secured, within the Department, by the delegates of the Government appointed in the Council of Ministers.' Article 1 of the Statute of the Prefectoral Corps states that the Prefects are the delegates of the Government, and it goes on to repeat this section of the Constitution almost word for word.

The Prefect then has constitutional authority in the Department, but the phrases in the Constitution are too general to explain the extent of his powers. Sometimes he acts as the general representative of the State, exercising what almost amounts to a prerogative power. Sometimes he acts under specific statutory authority; sometimes his powers are delegated to him by a Minister. Sometimes he acts as the general administrator of the Department, sometimes as chief executive of the Department, sometimes as *tuteur* of the Communes, sometimes as chief of police.

The Prefect's personal accountability is twofold. In the first place he is accountable to the Government. He, more than any other official, is held politically responsible for his acts. The Government does not have to find any pretext for removing him from office. Whenever an individual Minister delegates powers to a Prefect these powers are exercised under the control of that Minister, who can annul the Prefect's decision, alter it, or substitute a new one in its place.

In the second place the Prefect is responsible to the courts. If he commits a civil or criminal offence he will be judged by a civil or criminal court. His official decisions, his ordinances, and his refusals to exercise his powers can all be challenged before the administrative courts; his decision can be annulled for illegality, or damages may be awarded to the plaintiff. Such damages are awarded against the State if the Prefect was acting in his capacity as a state official, or against the Department if he was acting as chief departmental executive. Damages will be awarded against the Prefect personally if he is guilty of a *faute personnelle*.[1]

The Prefect is not politically responsible to any local elected body, although he is legally bound to put into effect the lawful decisions of the *conseil général*: if he fails to do so the *conseil* can either appeal to the Minister to order the Prefect to do his duty, or take the case to the administrative courts on the grounds of *excès de pouvoir*.

The following analysis deals (a) with the Prefect's position as general administrator in the Department and, (b) with his position as chief departmental executive. Something must be said (c) of the wide range of personal powers which he exercises in his own right, and to give this section some form it will be subdivided into the Prefect's police powers, his judicial powers, those which come to him as *tuteur* of the Communes, and others which can best be described as his social powers. These distinctions are uncomfortably artificial, as any classification must be, but at least they have some degree of clarity.

(a) *General Administrator*

It is from his constitutional position as the sole legal repre-

---

[1] I have attempted to state the elementary principles of French administrative law in: *Introduction to French Local Government*, London, 1953. Chapter 5.

sentative of the State in the Department that the Prefect obtains his legal supremacy over all other officials. This supremacy was not explicitly assigned to the Prefects when the Corps was founded, but since 1850 the phrase that 'the Prefect is the only representative of the State (or of the Head of the State) in the Department' has been included in several laws.

In 1939 the Prefect's supremacy was practically unchallenged, but during and after the war Ministries managed partially to free their local officials from the Prefect's control. Sometimes this was done at the instigation of the Ministers themselves, many of whom had long resented the Minister of the Interior's supremacy in local affairs.[1] Frequently it was because central officials incited their departmental colleagues to evade the Prefect and to correspond directly with the Minister, and sent instructions directly to them without notifying the Prefecture. Some Ministries provided their officials with funds outside the Prefect's control, and one or two local officials, such as the *inspecteur d'académie*, received a direct delegation of authority from the Ministry in place of the Prefect. For instance the nomination of *instituteurs* to their posts was given to the *recteur d'académie* in place of the Prefect: a highly desirable reform.

Some trespass on the Prefect's powers was inevitable. The Prefects of the war years were too preoccupied with the major problems of security, air raids, refugees, housing and rationing to be able to check these practices. The war also greatly increased the complexity of administration by specialists and the intricacies of regulation, control and inspection. Many Prefects had no time to follow this tendency, and just before and after 1944 many Prefects were not of the calibre to understand either the technicalities or the encroachment on their powers.

The most important result was the marked centralization of affairs concerned with the activities of technical officials, for their Ministries frequently left them powerless while local business was transacted without local knowledge in the offices in Paris. In addition services multiplied and there was a wasteful duplication

[1] Doueil: op. cit. pp. 288–291.

of effort without any arbiter at the departmental level. Some Ministries pursued policies in conflict with those of others. Some expanded their local staffs without sense or logic; they would appoint two different officials to perform different aspects of the same task, yet would give neither of them official seniority over the other,[1] and in some cases appointed them to different towns in the same Department. The tendency to regionalize services raised further problems, for each Ministry fixed its own region. Some Ministries regarded the regional official as an inspector of departmental services, others made him both a regional inspector and a departmental official, others regarded him as the direct administrator of the whole region. Ministries either corresponded directly with the regional official, or with the departmental official, or with both, or with both and the Prefect, or with both and the Prefect of the Department and the regional Prefect. They tacitly refused to acknowledge the members of the Prefectoral Corps as the legal authority in the area, and yet gave no legal autonomy to their own official. This did not lead to good administration.

In 1949 the Minister of the Interior began to re-establish the Prefect as unchallenged authority in the Department. He was helped in this by the reiterated demands of the associations of Mayors, of *conseils généraux*, and of local authorities, to return to the traditional and understandable system of government with its single tutelage. The Minister of the Interior took the initiative by returning to the Prefect several powers of decision assumed by the Ministry during and after the War, and he consistently pressed for further large measures of deconcentration of authority to the Prefect by other Ministries. The discipline of administration grew tighter, as was bound to happen as wartime practices were eliminated. But Ministries retained powers of decision which before the War were held by the Prefect, and their technical officials in the Department were no longer in practice subject to

[1] The Ministry of Agriculture once went so far as to say that leadership of its services in the Department belonged to the one (of two) who was the most zealous.

the Prefect in all matters, since they frequently had instructions to act only with the agreement of their own Ministry. There was diffusion of responsibility, unjustifiable delay through continual reference to Paris, and neither Ministries nor their local officials possessed the local knowledge of the Prefect, nor were they under the same daily pressure to arrive at a prompt decision. The Prefect, unlike some other officials, knows to his cost that the best possible decision today is better than a perfect one in a fortnight's time.

The major obstacle to this deconcentration was undoubtedly the officials in the Ministries. Some of them feared loss of personal power, others, more penetrating, feared that the Prefect's intervention in technical affairs would introduce political considerations. A critic held that this desire to free technical affairs from political considerations frequently meant only a desire to disregard local conditions, and created in France a 'régime of circulars', where local affairs were dealt with as if every part of France were at least a thousand miles from Paris: directives poured forth from the Ministries to their bewildered local representatives so that individual projects were swamped in abstractions.[1] The whole strength of French local government has been that the Prefect is a point of centralization qualified and willing to translate into action general principles of policy.

In order to remedy this situation the Government decided in 1953 to enunciate clearly and emphatically the old principles of administration. A set of decrees was passed on September 26, 1953, to clear up many of the worst abuses of local administration.

In the introduction to these decrees the Government roundly declared that the Prefect was the sole legal representative of the central authority in the Department and the personal delegate of *all* the Ministers. The heads of the external services of the Ministries in the Department were reminded that they were under the Prefect's authority in all matters of general administration. Although they preserved their initiative and responsibility in the exercise of their technical functions, and although they were em-

[1] D. Jouany: op. cit.

powered to draw from public funds in the ordinary course of those functions, the Prefect alone was to control the funds allowed by the State to the Department for optional expenditure, for grants in aid, and for subventions.

The Ministers were called upon to transfer to the Prefects all the powers they had previously delegated to their own local officials; in exceptional cases they could continue to grant powers to the latter, but this delegation was to be expressly renewed before January 1954, and thereafter new delegations of powers should always be to the Prefects.

The Prefect's position was considerably reinforced by these decrees. Not only was he confirmed as the lawful superior of all other state officials in the Department with the right to make annual reports on their conduct to their Ministers, he was also placed in a strong position *vis-à-vis* the central administrations of the Ministries. A new provision in these decrees laid down that whenever a Prefect's decision was subject to ratification by a Minister, the Prefect's decision became automatically effective if, within two months, the central administration had not commented on it. The delays of Paris had for too long been a bad joke.

These Decree Laws decisively confirmed the Prefects' position as general administrator. In addition the Prefect is the official source of information concerning the Department, and all other officials are required by law to give him the information and assistance he requires. Decisions even on technical matters should be communicated to him: in most cases detailed technical information is sent directly from the technical service to its own Ministry with a copy to the Prefecture. Most Prefects only compile reports themselves when these are needed for the preparation of general policy. For instance, if the Government wishes to analyse the internal economic situation, or forecast the probable results of floating a national loan, it is the Prefect who drafts the report, using the information supplied to him by the technical experts.

There is a complicated relationship between the Prefect's administrative staff in the Prefecture, and the offices of the Ministries in the Department, and it is necessary to examine the other state administrations in the Department to get a clear picture of the Prefect's position. He works through these offices as well as through the Prefecture, and the heads of these services are his technical advisers on financial, agricultural, industrial, labour, health and welfare matters.

The internal organization of the Prefecture was described in the previous chapter. Each Division deals with a broad category of affairs for which the Prefect is responsible—finance, public assistance, agriculture and industry, and so on. The Bureaux deal with specific aspects of the administration for operating these services.

The technical side of these services is performed by the offices in the Department of the responsible Ministries. Thus the Ministry of Agriculture has seven technical branches in the Department, each with its expert head: they are the *directeur départemental des services agricoles*, the *ingénieur du génie rural*, the *conservateur* (or *inspecteur*) *des eaux et forêts*, the *directeur départemental des services vétérinaires*, the *contrôleur de la protection des végétaux*, the *contrôleur des lois sociales en agriculture*, and the *inspecteur départemental de la répression de fraudes*. There are at least thirty other ministerial technical services working in each Department on various aspects of production, transport, highways, education, finance, taxation and social welfare,[1] and these do not include services run by the Ministry of the Interior such as the police, nor the Judiciary and the judicial police, customs, nor services organized directly by the Department such as fire brigades.

In 1917 there were seventeen different areas of regional administration; one expert has estimated that there are now forty-nine. They are completely unstandardized, ranging in number from five *circonscriptions de haras* and six for the DST, to seventy-five regions for the *génie rural*; the Ministry of Agriculture alone administers through 10 different sets of regional areas.[2] Complete confusion is avoided only because the Department is always used

[1] See Appendix A.
[2] See Appendix B.

as a further area of administration. Inevitably, departmental officials are torn between the Prefect, their regional officer, and their Ministry in Paris. Even when the law is obeyed and these officials act under the general control of the Prefect, his authority is diminished.

This tendency has gone much too far for the Minister of the Interior to obtain a complete return to the 1939 position; indeed, it is by no means certain that that would be desirable. Many technical services in the modern world can only be organized efficiently on a broader basis than the Department. But undoubtedly a tidier system would increase efficiency. Three matters require particular attention.

In the first place there are technical services in the Department which duplicate each other's work. For instance, the Ministry of Public Health's two officials, the *directeur départemental de la santé* and the *directeur départemental de la population* both administer the laws relating to public health and social hygiene: and in addition the bureaux of the Prefecture are charged with supervising and applying these laws. Two out of these three organizations would appear to be superfluous.

In the second place, since 1939 many of the newly created departmental offices have been authorized to use funds allotted to them by the Ministry without the countersignature of the Prefect. Before 1939 only special administrations had this right, among them the Post Office and the *trésorier payeur général*. The Ministries may be right to lessen the old subordination to the Prefect, but the traditional reasons for his supremacy—unity of direction, proper control of public funds, and economy—are still valid.

In the third place—and this is the most serious point—the bureaux of the Prefecture and the offices of the technical services both do roughly the same administrative work. This duplication has nothing to commend it, and every person or body who has studied the question recommends change. How this is to be secured is a subject of much debate.

One school of thought, whose most authoritative exponents

have been the *comité centrale d'enquête sur le coût et le rendement des services publics* and M. Le Gorgeu,[1] see the solution in making each technical service responsible for its own administrative work; the corresponding bureaux in the Prefecture would then be abolished. This may look as if it were based on a bias against the Prefect; but these critics go on to say that the Prefect's personal position in the Department should be strengthened. Ministers should delegate to him personally all powers devolved to a departmental level, all the funds used by these services, except those used for modernization and re-equipment, should be under his control, and he should have the right to suspend on his own authority any official serving in the Department guilty of misconduct. He should arbitrate between different services with power to decide conflicts.

The result of these reforms would be to make the Prefect into a sort of administrative commander-in-chief, surrounded by a small and brilliant general staff; he would have no body of troops under his immediate command.

The opposing view is taken by administrative bodies like the *inspection générale de l'administration* and the *commissions départementales d'économies*. They reject the general staff picture of the Prefect and his immediate collaborators, since they believe that administration is itself a specialized task which technical officials are not competent to do properly: 'l'administration régente les hommes, tandis que les services techniques régissent les choses'.[2] It is the task of administration to orient, utilize, control and co-ordinate the technical services. Reports of *inspecteurs* of the central Administration show that many technical heads do not in fact do their proper job; they are forced to devote much time to administrative chores, for which they are neither properly equipped nor personally qualified, to the detriment of their proper functions.

These critics say that without his own officers and methods of inspection the Prefect would be completely in the hands of the

[1] *Revue Administrative*, July, 1948.

[2] *Rapport de l'inspection générale de l'administration*, cit.

technical heads from whom he would obtain information only on sufferance. His control of activities in the Department would be illusory, and local authorities and politicians, becoming accustomed to treating with the technical heads, would soon ensnare these different administrations. At the moment they have to concentrate on the Prefect, who at least knows what is going on, and normally has the insight and experience to cope with the politicians on their own ground.

This school of thought proposes to return as far as possible to the traditional conception of the Prefecture as the '*maison centrale d'administration générale*'. The office of the Prefecture would deal with the administrative work of the technical services. The technical heads would be freed to do their expert job without other preoccupations. The Prefect would have the means to co-ordinate and direct.

There are many weighty theoretical and practical arguments on both sides, but their analysis would be out of place in this study. It is at least clear that both camps are agreed that a further extension of the Prefect's powers is desirable. The question posed in the controversy is a practical one, whether or not the Prefect can properly perform his duties without having an administrative staff of his own; but there are larger issues behind this. The vitality of French local government is largely due to the prefectoral system. The personalization of executive responsibility in the Prefect, the crystallization of local political activity round the Prefect and the Mayors, and the balance of forces between administrators and politicians at a local level, are the backbone of French local government. But very few modern administrators and Ministries have any regard for local government. They look upon pressure groups, local interests, minor obstinacies, and parish pump politics as a source of vexation and a bar to efficiency. They are probably right, but these are perhaps not the only criteria. However badly economic and industrial efficiency are needed in many parts of France, they do not automatically bring any increase in civic responsibility or political maturity; these may be equally desirable in the modern world.

(b) *Executive of the Department*

The Constitution of 1946 says that the executive head of the Department is the chairman of the *conseil général*: not the Prefect. In practice the Prefect is still the Department's executive. The relevant article of the Constitution is apparently quite explicit: 'les collectivités territoriales s'administrent librement par des conseils élus au suffrage universel. L'exécution des décisions est assurée par leur maire ou leur président' (Art. 87). However, since it was impossible to work out the new division of powers in the Constitution itself, a further article (Art. 89) postponed the details to be dealt with in a later law. Meanwhile, as a temporary arrangement, the existing laws were maintained, with the proviso that when the Prefect acted as departmental executive his actions were subject to the 'permanent supervision' of the chairman of the *conseil général* (Art. 105).

No permanent law has yet been passed. The Departments are therefore administered under the provisional arrangements sketched in Article 105; and will presumably continue to be so.

The reasons for this failure to implement the Constitution are not hard to find. Several projects have at various times been presented to Parliament for consideration, but they have all been either withdrawn or buried.[1] Ministers of the Interior during the first legislature were extremely reluctant to take steps deliberately designed to loosen control on the country; the critical post-war years were not the best time for such experiments. Under the reform the Prefect would remain state representative and *tuteur* of the Communes, but would lose part of his job. The possible loss has been exaggerated, for it has been reliably estimated that the work done in the Prefecture which concerns only the Department occupies two Bureaux out of a total of nine in a medium-sized Prefecture. This may, however, understate the administrative effects of change; there would be real inconvenience from the loss of contact between one part of the administration and the

[1] For the various proposals, see J. Gandouin: *La Constitution et la réforme de l'organisation départementale et communale*. Doctoral Thesis, Faculty of Law, Paris, 1950.

other. The Prefect would find himself forced into the position of watchdog over the *conseil général's* decisions; and if this were all he did in the affairs of the Department, he would soon become either immensely unpopular or useless. He would also lose that close supervision of work in the Prefecture which provides him with his information and enables him to control and co-ordinate.

There is clearly a good case for the old system on administrative grounds, but it has in fact been maintained largely for political reasons. There was the danger that such a reform would transform some Departments like the Haute Vienne (Limoges) into red 'fiefs'. This caused the centre parties to hesitate. Then the politicians and the chairmen of the *conseils généraux* themselves began to have second thoughts. Several chairmen were loath to undertake the job. For some it was because they would be unable to continue as chairmen, since if they accepted these new duties, their own livelihood would suffer. Clearly, a reform would inevitably lead to a demand for the chairman to remain in office for a minimum of three years, and perhaps even six, in order that the continuity of administration might not suffer. The alternative would be to adopt the English model, which gives more real power to permanent officials than to the chairman or Mayor; but in this case why change the Prefect, who was better fitted for the task than any of his subordinates?

Some chairmen feared that such an increase in authority would render them personally responsible before the public; they would be compelled sometimes to take unpopular decisions and their political position with the electorate would be endangered.

These political preoccupations were echoed by the politicians in Paris. If the chairman were an active politician his increased stature in the Department would constitute a dangerous threat to his colleagues. If he were not already a Deputy or Senator, it would justify his casting covetous eyes on their seats in Parliament. If he were, his status would overtop his colleagues in Parliament.

Neither the politicians, the chairmen, nor the Government want the reform but none considers it tactful to say so in public. There is every reason to believe that Article 87 will remain a dead letter, and that the provisional status will be permanent.

For a long time the major problem about these provisional arrangements was to interpret in practical terms what the Constitution meant when it said that the Prefect, when acting as departmental executive, did so under the 'permanent supervision' of the chairman of the *conseil général*. This phrase could mean many things, and in particular it might mean that the chairman should act as permanent supervisor, always looking over the Prefect's shoulder, demanding justifications, insisting upon compromises.

The French tradition of unity of direction and responsibility was opposed to this conception, which in some cases would have paralysed administration. The ministerial circular of November 22, 1946, was issued to clarify the situation. The fields of administration in which the chairman had any rights at all were 'the preparation of the departmental budget, the execution of the decisions of the *conseil général* and the *commission départementale*, the appointment of officials paid from the Department's funds, litigation involving the Department, the passing of contracts, and the administration of the Department's estate.' These duties were performed by the Prefect in his capacity as departmental executive, and they alone were subject to the chairman's supervision. But even 'in these matters, the application of the transitional régime (Article 105) must not be permitted to slow down departmental administration. . . . It is not under any circumstances to take the paralysing form of requiring prior agreement between Prefect and chairman of the *conseil général* on every matter that comes up for decision. It is rather to be an agreement of principle on the lines of general policy to be followed in defence of the Department's interests.'[1]

This circular concluded with the banal reminder that the chairman should be informed of all that goes on, and should be consulted before decisions on particularly important matters. Anyway, ended the circular, this is what Prefects do already.

Since 1946, as the prospect of new legislation has faded, the

[1] Quoted in R. Bonnaud Delamare: *Loi du 10 août 1871*. Niort, 1950. p. 5.

Prefect has regained the moral initiative which in the first years passed to the chairman. Observers estimate that the relations between Prefect and chairman, and methods of departmental administration, are virtually the same as they were before the war. The relations between the Prefect and the elected authorities in the Department will be dealt with later in this chapter, since they are a very important factor in the life of the Prefect. It is desirable first to consider shortly the extent and variety of the Prefect's powers. This is inevitably a brief account, but will indicate their extent and importance.

(c) *Personal Powers*

A cursory glance at the *Recueil des Actes Administratifs* of any Department shows the range of the Prefect's influence. Prefectoral ordinances restrict the use of public hoardings, authorize communal budgets, control the elections of agricultural social security organizations, create joint boards, fix the wheat content of bread, repress 'debauch and prostitution', regulate the pasteurization of milk, nominate minor officials to local offices and doctors to hospital boards, organize anti-mosquito campaigns, accept town and country planning schemes, lay down the conditions of employment for forestry workers. Circulars to Mayors reminding them of future administrative requirements, suggestions to improve communal services, advice on points of general interest raised by local authorities, are the daily reminder to the public and the officials of the Prefect's influence.

The Prefect's powers will be dealt with here under four heads: (i) his police powers, (ii) his powers concerning the administration of justice, (iii) his tutelage powers, and (iv) his 'social' powers.

(i) Police powers are dealt with first because the maintenance of law and order is the primary responsibility of the State, and therefore of the Prefect. He exercises in the Department what the French call the *police générale*.[1] This means that he has to ensure

[1] The other persons who are responsible for the *police générale* are the President of the Council of Ministers, the Ministers, *commissaires de police*, and

the internal and external security of the State by guarding against plots, outrages, espionage, and seditious meetings, and by supervising aliens, the press, public meetings, private associations, and so on. He is required to see that all laws and ordinances are obeyed and in particular those concerning public health, public order, public security, and public morality. This covers for instance measures to prevent the occurrence or spread of epidemics, the use or continued existence of unsafe property, the inspection of dangerous and harmful trades, the maintenance of public order, the control of lunatics, and the safety of theatres.

This formidable list gives the Prefect a general reserve warrant entitling him to act, in an emergency, without other consideration than for the general welfare and safety. The list involves two distinct things: the organization and control of forces of men who are responsible for ensuring that no one breaks the law; and the use of a legal power by which the Prefect is authorized to make regulations and ordinances designed to limit the chance that there may be a breach of the peace, or a danger to public morals, or public health. Consequently the Prefect can be regarded from one point of view as chief of the police forces in the Department: from the other, as an authority empowered to issue binding regulations and ordinances.

The Prefect's rôle as chief of police has been mentioned in the section on the Secretary General of Police. The Secretary General and the CATI, his organization, are concerned with the administration of police personnel, technical affairs, and finance. Inside the Department the Prefect has wide authority over police activities: he can transfer units and men from one station to another, he has extensive disciplinary powers, some of which he can delegate to the Secretary General of Police. He has in the Department a senior *commissaire de police* who is responsible for technical matters like patrol areas and the investigation of crimes. But if the Prefect fears an outbreak of violence in a particular area, he can instruct his police commander to concentrate forces

Mayors; the last two do so under the jurisdiction of the Prefect, and the Prefect does so under the jurisdiction of the Minister of the Interior.

there. For example, when a part of Vaucluse (Avignon) was terrorized by a series of murders committed by lunatics allowed out on parole in plain clothes by a progressive asylum, the Prefect, disturbed by the danger to the public peace, at once reinforced foot and highway patrols in the area. He also ordered the asylum's authorities to be a little less progressive.

He also has under his authority the director of *renseignements généraux*. From the information compiled by this department, the Prefect is able to understand not only the surface movements of opinions and tactics, but also the causes and the inspirers. In most Prefectures, the director of *renseignements généraux* issues a daily confidential report, a copy of which goes to the Prefect, a copy to the *Sûreté Nationale*, and (in some regions at least) a copy to the IGAME.

Sometimes the close relationship between the Prefect and the police forces results in rather tenebrous activities designed to protect the police from public opinion when they have been guilty of abusing their powers. There have been one or two recent cases in which the police have ill-treated and extorted confessions from suspected persons. In one case seven years elapsed before the policemen concerned were called to court to answer the charge, and some responsible jurists alleged collusion between the police, the Prefecture of Bordeaux, and certain elements of the judiciary itself to prevent the case ever coming before the courts at all.

The Prefect also has general authority over the activities of the companies of *Gendarmerie*. The CRS are in a slightly different situation, since, except in case of immediate peril, the Prefect can only employ these forces with the permission of the IGAME. It is for the Prefect to request their assistance, and, once the IGAME has authorized reinforcements or agreed to the use of these forces, to be responsible for their deployment.

Finally, the Prefect is empowered to call upon the Army for assistance, should the maintenance of public order be beyond the capacity of the police, the *Gendarmerie* and the CRS. The Army must never intervene in civil affairs on its own authority, and the requisition for armed force must be accompanied by a written warrant signed by the Prefect stating the place, the reason and the duration of the requisition.

The Prefect loses his powers as chief of the police forces in two special cases. First, if the IGAME is forced by the widespread nature of serious disturbances to use his Letter of Service, which delegates to him personally the powers of the President of the Council, the Minister of the Interior and the Minister of Defence; this Letter confers on him absolute powers of direction over all civil and military authorities in the region.

The second case occurs if the Government declares a state of siege, the effect of which is to transfer all civil powers to the military authorities. This is martial law, and the Prefect then exercises only those powers not exercised by the military: their extent is for the military commander to decide.

The police and military forces available to a Prefect depend upon the strategic position of his Department, and upon the size and importance of the towns inside it. In a town of 15,000 inhabitants, the contingent of State Police has a *commissaire* in command, two detective sergeants, and fifteen patrolmen. These may be supplemented by communal policemen recruited by the Commune. An important city with over 100,000 inhabitants is normally divided into four quartiers: there is a *commissaire central* in charge, and each quartier is controlled by a *commissaire*: there are 200 patrolmen, and a detective bureau under a *commissaire* with fifty detective sergeants. In Marseilles, with a population of 636,000, there is a *commissaire central*, twenty-six *commissaires*, some 420 detective sergeants, and 2,370 uniformed patrolmen. Paris (for a population of about four million) has a total force of nearly 20,000 men operating under the control of the Prefect of Police.

In addition to the police, the Prefect of an average Department with some strategic significance such as the Haut Rhin (Colmar), has within call a company of the CRS, and a company of *Gendarmerie* divided into sections, one for each *arrondissement*, and a sub-section for each canton: a section of the *Garde Mobile*, a regiment of artillery and a battalion of infantry. The number of troops available will, of course, increase if the Department includes a Parachute School or some other major military establishment.

We come now to the other side of the Prefect's police powers: his position as a regulation-making authority.

It will be remembered that many matters included under the *police générale* are not primarily the concern of the Minister of the Interior, at least not until they threaten a breakdown in public order. The Ministry of Public Health is the proper authority for regulating public health, the Ministry of Agriculture for regulating the affairs of agriculture, the Ministry of Industry and Commerce for industrial safety, and so on. But the general responsibility for public health, industrial safety, and agriculture rests with the Prefect: he is said, for instance, to be responsible for the *police industrielle*. This means that ministerial officials work under his supervision, and it is the Prefect and not these officials who make ordinances in these matters.

The following are some of the detailed powers conferred on the Prefect in these various fields.[1] From the Minister of Agriculture he draws powers to ensure the protection of game, plant life and nests, and the destruction of vermin and pests; he pays rewards from a fund provided by the Ministry. He supervises the inspection of food and the repression of agricultural and viticultural frauds; he is responsible for the veterinary services. He declares the hunting season open and closed, and enforces laws for the protection of wild life. He is responsible for the security of forests and the control of forest fires. This can be very important in areas like the Landes, which had a major disaster from forest fires in 1949.

From the Ministry of Public Works the Prefect receives authority to control rivers, lakes and canals, whether open to navigation or not. In Departments on the coast he has to organize sea defences and protective works in ports. The Ministry of Public Works is also responsible for highways, railways, telegraphic and telephonic lines of communication, and the Prefect supervises all

[1] R. Bonnaud Delamare: *Attributions juridiques* etc., cit.

these. He can insist on security devices, and impose safety regulations on passenger and goods transport services. He is responsible for the security of the highway, and he can suspend driving licences of drivers arrested by the police for dangerous driving, pending the decision of the courts. He is also responsible for the security of the air, and he registers and regulates the use of private aerodromes and the holding of local air pageants and circuses.

The Prefect has a variety of special duties devolved by the Ministry of Industry and Commerce. He supervises the operations of Stock Exchanges and money and produce markets, the conduct of auction rooms and second-hand dealers. He controls the inspection of weights and measures.

From the Ministry of Education he receives authority to regulate the display of outdoor advertising, with authority to ban hoardings on highways, and to remove objectionable items.

He is responsible on behalf of the Ministry of Labour and the Ministry of Public Health for many matters connected with public and social welfare. He has to ensure the proper observance of the law in all matters pertaining to industrial law—conditions of work, safety regulations, working hours, minimum wages, holidays, the employment of women and children. He can, for example, arrange a roster of the times that bakers or chemists shall remain open in a particular district.

He supervises in the Department the regulations affecting public health—sanitation, the public analyst, protection against disease, the registration and prophylactic treatment of infectious disease, and the prevention of epidemics. He also supervises the qualifications of members of the medical profession, and ensures that no unqualified or debarred doctor, chemist or osteopath practises.

Finally on behalf of the Minister of the Interior, the Prefect controls and organizes the fire services and civil defence services in the Departments, he registers the keepers of carrier pigeons, issues gun licences, and authorizes public officials, when necessary, to break into private dwellings.

It may be useful here to give an instance of the way in which the Prefect exercises his regulating powers. There is no set form which ordinances must take, but they must be written, signed and dated, and must state their object clearly. A trivial instance is perhaps more striking than a complicated, legally impressive document.

The Prefect is responsible for protecting public morality. The Prefect of the Bas Rhin (Strasburg) in pursuance of this duty issued the following ordinance, dated March 18, 1950.

'The Prefect of the Bas Rhin... Having taken into account the law concerning judicial organization ... and the law relating to the family and the French birthrate, and the instructions of M. le Ministre de l'Intérieur, and in view of the moral danger to which young persons especially are exposed by the exhibition on the public highway of certain illustrated publications devoted to crime and prostitution, and of journals of a licentious character:

Orders that:

Art.1. The exhibition of the following publications in windows, shop doorways, kiosks and shops in such a way as to be visible from the public highway or in public places is forbidden:—

TAM-TAM

MUSIC-HALL FOLLIES

Art. 2. The Secretary General of the Prefecture, the Sub Prefects, the *commissaire central de police* of Strasburg, the Squadron Commander, officer-in-command, the Company of Gendarmerie in the Bas Rhin, the Mayors, and all other Agents of Public Authority, are charged, each in so far as he is concerned, with the execution of the present ordinance, which shall be inserted in the Bulletin of Departmental and Communal Information, and in the *Recueil des Actes Administratifs*.'

(ii) The Prefect has a number of duties relating to the administration of justice, and some of these are important. It is his duty to publish the laws, and to keep a record of them. He has some minor powers such as determining the sums due to *greffiers* of courts, and the legalization of documents. He supervises the administration of prisons, with the right of inspection and the duty to investigate complaints.

In some matters the Prefect can on his own authority initiate legal proceedings on behalf of the State without waiting for the intervention of the State Advocate's department. He can refer highway offences to the civil courts, and can refer such administrative offences as suspected *détournement de pouvoir* and *excès de pouvoir* directly to the *Conseil d'Etat*.

He has the right to intervene in matters affecting the jurisdiction of the civil and criminal courts; should he believe that a civil court is attempting to judge a case which is properly within the jurisdiction of the administrative courts, he can force the civil court to suspend consideration of the case until the supreme civil and administrative tribunal has determined to which court jurisdiction belongs.

In his capacity as sole legal representative of the State in the Department, the Prefect is responsible for all litigation in the State's name. This is no empty formula, when one considers that the Minister of the Interior had to call his Prefects' attention to complaints of his ministerial colleagues in the Circular of March 2, 1951. He had to remind them that they were supposed to obtain from the technical Ministry concerned the best possible case before undertaking an action. Several Ministries had protested that they had often known nothing about litigation until after a judgement had been given, and they believed that had they known in advance they could have done much better. The Minister instructed Prefects to obey the rule of prior consultation and to make use of the legal and technical experts of the Ministries.

It seems likely that in the complexity of modern administration it would be better if each Ministry were responsible for its own litigation. It would damage the theory, for the Prefect could no longer properly be regarded as the sole legal representative of the State in the Department, and it might harm the practical unity of direction; the solution might be to compel the Prefect by statute to consult the Ministry concerned.

We come now to the formidable authority conferred on the Prefect by the famous Article 10 of the *Code d'Instruction Crimi-*

nelle. The article was repealed in 1933 because of the abuse of power that it seemed to sanction, but it was re-established in 1935 with some modifications[1]. It allows the Prefect to act without any formal warrant should he suspect a person, or persons, or an institution, of acts prejudicial to the internal or external security of the State. He is then, on his own authority, empowered to search suspected premises, to seize documents, and to arrest individuals without warrant, without necessarily informing any other administrative or legal authority: even the State Advocate may be unaware of his action.

The threat to individual liberties appeared to be so great that the exercise of these powers is now subject to certain precautions. The Prefect cannot use these special powers merely because he has grounds for suspecting illegal activities: they must really involve, or appear to involve, the internal or external security of the State. Furthermore, there should be some reason why absolute speed and secrecy were necessary. In time of war and international tension the Prefects' acts would be less restricted than in peacetime. Otherwise the State Advocate or the Military Prosecutor should be called upon to deal with the case in the ordinary way. Finally, the Prefect must inform the State Advocate of the measures he has taken within twenty-four hours, at the same time forwarding the evidence he has seized. The police officials who acted on the Prefect's orders are also held personally responsible for informing the State Advocate's department without delay.

These powers are not conferred on the Prefect on the assumption that they will never be used. Obviously they were used, and widely used, during the War and the Liberation. But they are also a reserve power that can be used in peacetime. For example,

---

[1] The Prefect's powers under the old system are dealt with in J. Marizis: *Les pouvoirs judiciaires des préfets et l'Article 10 du Code d'Instruction Criminelle*. Doctoral Thesis, Faculty of Law, Paris, 1913–14. The new system is dealt with in P. Lantecaze: *Les pouvoirs du police judiciaire des préfets. Article 10 du Code d'Instruction Criminelle*. Doctoral Thesis, Faculty of Law, Bordeaux, 1938.

in 1950 the French Communist Party was conducting a very strong and sometimes violent campaign against the Atlantic Treaty and the organization of the West. In Marseilles and Toulon the agitation reached a point where war material was being thrown into the sea by rioters, and attempts were constantly made to block trains, hinder transport and cause breakdowns in public services. The IGAME of the Marseilles region instructed the Prefects in the name of the Minister to take all lawful measures against the wrecking propensities of the CGT. The Prefects were to use their powers under Article 10 to prevent the spread of tendentious newspaper reports and incitement to violence; they were reminded that they could seize leaflets, confiscate newspapers, and arrest their authors.

There is another side to the Prefect's relations with the judicial authorities. He is the executive authority in the Department, and many legal judgements cannot be executed without his support. Marshal Lyautey once said, 'quand un règlement vous empêche de bien faire, ne l'appliquez pas'. The Prefect assumes, on occasions, even greater discretion, even to the extent of ignoring the binding force of a legal judgement.

A striking illustration was given by the present Prefect of the Seine, with reference to complaints that had been levelled against his administration by the judicial authorities while he was serving as Prefect of the Alpes Maritimes (Nice). He had, it appears, refused to allow the police forces to execute eviction orders served on tenants at the instance of the landlords. M. Haag said at the time: 'Some latent conflicts exist between the judicial authorities of the Alpes Maritimes and the prefectoral authorities, as a result of the non-execution of certain judgements of the courts. The judiciary appear to believe that the situation is simpler than it really is; they apply the law when strict interpretation requires them to do so. But this leads to judgements which may be perfect in law but which are very far from what we consider to be equitable. And when these judgements concern people with large families, ex-servicemen, ex-prisoners, deportees, the aged and sick, we are inevitably obliged to consider the consequences of such decisions upon public order. Not only because we fear a riotous demonstration in the district around the homes of the people who are expelled, but also, and principally, because we consider the decisions gravely unjust to a class of citizens who have deserved well of the country.

'It is then that the Prefect intervenes, not so much in order to obstruct the execution of a legal judgement, as to impose a standstill until a solution can be found; either by making an order to requisition the property concerned, or, if we can—and we are frequently successful—by coming to a friendly agreement with the proprietor so as to avoid the people being thrown out into the street.'[1] This is a bold affirmation of the right of the Prefect to regard himself as the custodian of the public interest, and it was made by a Prefect of long experience and high esteem. In the interests of public order, which is interpreted in the widest sense, is included the well-being of the inhabitants. It should not, of course, be forgotten that the Prefect's decision is always subject

[1] Speech by M. Haag to a session of the Assembly of the Prefectoral Corps: June 15, 1950, reported in the *Bulletin du Corps Préfectoral*, No. 9. 1950.

Prefects remained for a long time torn between their duty to execute legal judgements and their concern for public welfare. They came to adopt increasingly M. Haag's estimate of where their duty lay in face of the National Assembly's abdication of responsibility in this domain. In January 1954, under pressure from his political friends, M. Martinaud-Déplat, Minister of the Interior, issued an instruction to the Prefects pointing out that the *Conseil d'Etat* was taking a serious view of the unenforced warrants, and granting damages to the landlords against the State. He himself considered their non-execution was 'an attempt on the authority of the State', and he instructed them to enforce within a period of three months every expulsion order granted by a civil court; they remained free to appreciate local circumstances, and to choose the right moment to send the police along with the bailiff, but they must enforce the orders within the three months. Since the instruction was dated January 14, 1954, at the beginning of an extremely cold spell, the ethical and political sense of the Minister compared very unfavourably with that of his Prefects. It may be noted in passing that when the issue had arisen in the summer of 1951, M. Baylot, Prefect of Police, had been forced to give instructions to the police to execute the writs at first light, as only in this way could they avoid a *fracas*. See oral answer by the Prefect of Police to the *conseil municipal* of Paris, June 28, 1951.

to attack in the *Conseil d'Etat*, but that court might well find that when faced with the conflicting duties of enforcing law and maintaining order, the Prefect's first duty was to maintain order. In this instance the thinly disguised threat to use his powers of requisition, and the delays that would arise from an appeal to the administrative courts, were obviously likely to influence landlords.

(iii) The Prefect is the *tuteur* of the Communes in the Department; this means that some of the actions of the Mayor and some of the decisions of the *conseil municipal* are subject either to his veto or to his positive approval.

The Mayor has three functions: he is the agent of the State in the Commune, he is responsible for the *police municipale*, and he is the Commune's executive responsible for putting into effect the elected assembly's decisions and for organizing the Commune's administration. When the Mayor acts in either of his first two capacities, as agent of the State or police authority in the Commune, he is subject to the control of the Prefect; as executive of the Commune he is subject only to his *conseil municipal*, but this body is itself partly under the tutelage of the Prefect.

As agent of the State the Mayor has to perform certain administrative functions in the Commune on behalf of the State: for example, to compile conscription lists, register births, marriages and deaths, and collect statistical material needed by the central authorities. His exercise of these powers is subject to the regulation and control of the Prefect, who can, for instance, insist that he makes the returns by a specified date, or that he uses particular forms for presenting his information.

The Mayor is also charged, under the supervision of the Prefect and Sub Prefect, with the *police municipale* and the *police rurale*, and for executing orders by a superior authority relating to them. He is responsible for publishing and enforcing laws and ordinances affecting public safety and for performing any special functions assigned to him by law. He is empowered to make local ordinances which will amplify or give effect to general laws and ordinances in such a way as to fit local circumstances. Before they are valid these ordinances must be forwarded to the Sub Prefect or Prefect who can annul them or suspend their execution.

The *police municipale* concerns safety and free passage on the highway, the prevention of riots and public disorder, the security of the public, the decent burial of the dead and the decorum of cemeteries, the inspection of food, the destruction of mad and vicious animals, the apprehension of lunatics, and the prevention of and precautions against public calamities and natural disasters.

In all these matters the Mayor is entitled to make ordinances valid throughout the Commune. They can either be general or individual: they can require all pedestrians to cross the road by special crossings, or they can order a landlord to repair his property if it is a danger to public health or security. Sometimes the Mayor's police powers will amplify ordinances made by the Prefect for the whole Department: for example, the Prefect may order that all sewage must be treated before being deposited in a river, and the Mayor may add the more detailed prescription that all the inhabitants of the Commune are to use the communal refuse collection service. If the Prefect has not made any ordinance on a particular subject, the Mayor is entitled to make his own; if, however, the Prefect later issues a general departmental ordinance this supersedes all existing mayoral ordinances. If the prefectoral and the mayoral ordinances should conflict, it is then usual to regard as valid the stricter of the two ordinances.

In two other cases the Prefect can replace the Mayor in making ordinances for the Commune. He can do so if public order is threatened in two or more adjacent Communes; he can then assume both the Mayors' control of communal police forces, and their powers of regulation. He can also do so if the Mayor refuses or neglects to do his duty; the Prefect or Sub Prefect must first draw the Mayor's attention in writing to the matter requiring attention, and only if the Mayor makes no effort to remedy his shortcomings can the Prefect substitute his authority for the Mayor's.

In Communes of over 10,000 inhabitants where the communal police force of *gardes champêtres* and *agents* is replaced by a State

Police contingent under the orders of the Prefect, the Prefect is responsible for maintaining public order, and the Mayor for public security and public health. The State Police must obey the Mayor's instructions whenever he is dealing with any matter within his competence; he can, for instance, put an extra patrol on the market, or close down an establishment which is a danger to the safety of the inhabitants.

Finally, the Prefect has the right to suspend the Mayor for a month if he is guilty of actions harmful to the good order of the Commune or the efficient working of communal administration. The Minister of the Interior can dismiss a Mayor, but this is done only for very serious offences.

The Prefect's powers over the *conseil municipal* and over the Mayor when acting as communal executive, are restricted to seeing that they obey the law, and to approving or rejecting their decisions on matters specified by law.

It will be remembered that in the absence of a Sub Prefect in the *arrondissement* of the departmental capital, the Prefect is the only tutelage authority for all the Communes in that area, and that the Sub Prefect has no powers over any Commune with more than 20,000 inhabitants. In both these cases the Prefect's tutelage is exactly the same as that described under the chapter on the Sub Prefects.

In addition, however, the Prefect can settle matters of great importance which are outside the scope of a Sub Prefect. These involve the positive use of legal authority: for instance, the Sub Prefect can alter details in a communal budget, but if the *conseil municipal* is obstinately determined to throw on the Administration the burden of writing the budget entirely on its own authority, the new budget can be issued only by the Prefect, and never by the Sub Prefect. Similarly, the Sub Prefect may point out that a decision of a *conseil municipal* is *ultra vires*, but only the Prefect can legally annul that decision, and only he can annul a Mayor's police ordinance.

The Prefect also has a variety of tutelage powers on specific matters. He can approve or reject the creation of joint boards, although he must first obtain the *conseil général's* opinion. He can challenge on his own authority the validity of local elections. His authorization is needed before a Commune can write off bad debts. He must sanction a new scale of charges for municipal funeral undertakings, and for any changes in the local tax on food. His approval is necessary for many appointments in communal administration.

He arbitrates between communal and Administrative authorities. If the Mayor and the Departmental Controller of Indirect Taxation fail to agree on the *principal fictif* of the Commune, the Prefect decides. If two or more Communes together run an intercommunal school and disagree about the share of the cost, the Prefect decides.

Like the Sub Prefect, the Prefect mainly looks for illegal proposals, and for attempts to spend money outside a council's lawful field of action: for example, payments to party funds; to official or unofficial bodies with ends considered desirable by the council but not sanctioned by law, like the Propagation of the Faith; or excessive expenditure on a totally unwarranted optional service, like putting stained glass windows in the Town Hall of a Commune which has not yet got drains, a water supply, made up roads, or a decent schoolroom. But he has no legal powers to compel Communes to put their resources to the best use, or to follow an enlightened social policy.

(iv) The Prefect's influence in the field of social policy can however be exercised by a judicious use of miscellaneous powers, which may loosely be called social powers. The majority of these powers were originally designed for control and not for construction, but it is not an abuse of these powers that they should now be used to initiate and encourage. The difficulty is that a substantial part of the population, though still probably a political minority, regards social welfare as something to fight for, and considers that the policy of *laissez-faire*, for which the Prefect's powers were framed, is completely outmoded. The Prefect may personally consider an increase in social welfare desirable and may resent the economic backwardness of French industry caused by selfish sectional interests. But it is Parliament's responsibility to give a clear lead in this field, which it has seldom done. The Prefect, however, apart from his own desires and aims, may have good reason to interfere in the social policy of the Department, for a consistent and aggressive demand for social advance by the most active part of the population threatens social order, and he must intervene to maintain public security and tranquillity.

In some cases the Prefect has an opportunity to intervene directly by virtue of an official position. He is by right president of many departmental commissions, the *commission départementale des opérations immobilières*, for example, with jurisdiction over the acquisition of property by local authorities, leases, and compulsory purchases. He also presides over the *conseil départemental de l'enseignement primaire*, which has powers over the number and siting of communal schools, over syllabuses, and over the discipline and recruitment of teachers. He has many powers over such matters as expropriation, public assistance, and town and country planning.

The Prefect's influence is gradually being increased in that Ministers devolve to him control of funds to be used for local development. The Minister of Education has put under his control a fund to be used for school repairs and modernization, with which to aid local authorities, and this will add weight to his encouragements. The Minister of the Interior has authorized Prefects to draw up schemes to be partly financed by State funds. He has granted them global credits allowing them to make grants of up to 15 million francs a year on any project in the Department. The Ministry intends to raise this figure to 50 million francs as quickly as possible.

But this financial assistance is too small to provide for all needs, and some local authorities tend to relax their own efforts and wait for the State to pay for everything. In others the mere possibility of State intervention raises the strongest reactions amongst local councillors, who foresee no good from anything in which the State has a hand, and prefer, by custom, to stay as they are, and by principle to avoid all contact with the State, especially a control which might threaten their independence.

In the field of social welfare, the Prefect is the tutelage authority for hospitals, *hospices*, workhouses, asylums, orphanages and welfare centres. In many cases he nominates representatives to serve on the governing boards of these institutions, and he may be able to influence administration through them. He acts as the legal representative and guardian of wards of the Department, and he protects the interests of children and war victims in need of care and protection. Social campaigns against venereal disease, tuberculosis, and cancer are organized under his direction.

In the industrial field he has the right to inspect and supervise (but not direct) the distribution of electricity, reconstruction, war damage repairs, piped water supplies and public housing programmes. He can compel unwilling landowners to join organizations for work in the public interest; for example land drainage and river defence schemes. He can also forbid development schemes which endanger the public interest; for example proposals to convert historic houses into cinemas, or to destroy a famous park in order to build a dirt-track.

He intervenes to maintain industrial peace in the Department: this responsibility comes to him because it is his duty both to enforce public order, and to ensure observance of the law in the industrial field, the *police industrielle*. His relations with the representatives of capital and labour are of the highest importance, for in a critical situation he must arbitrate between them. He is not now the official arbitrator. Until 1946 the Prefect could intervene as soon as an industrial dispute arose, but this rôle is now played by the Inspector of Labour in the Department, and in law the Prefect only intervenes when a dispute threatens public order, and it becomes necessary to close a factory or disperse an aggressive picket line. Informally, however, the Prefect uses his credit and authority as far as possible to arrive at a prompt and equitable solution to a dispute. The manager of a factory in an eastern department was instructed by the general manager in

Paris to dismiss twenty-one workers. The local union immediately called a strike which went on for several days. The Inspector of Labour was unable to get both sides round a table and feared that the conflict would spread; the manager of the factory feared an outbreak of violence and a complete stop to production; the union anxiously watched its funds run down, and feared the factory might be permanently closed. The Prefect learnt through his sources of information that the unions' maximum concession would be the dismissal of the nine men most recently taken on. On the Prefect's word the local manager obtained permission from Paris to accept this compromise. The Prefect is most influential when there is fear in the air.

He is entitled by law to some acquaintance with the internal affairs of capital and labour organizations; elections within Trade Unions, and elections of employees to the boards of social security organizations are subject to his supervision, and he has the legal right to enter meetings of the Chamber of Commerce. It is one of the Prefect's most important informal duties to strike up and maintain contacts with leaders of both sides; many industrial disputes have been happily resolved through the Prefect's 'comprehension, his knowledge of economic and social life, his art of negotiation, his faculty for convincing, his clarity and his impartiality'.[1] This can only be done through countless informal private meetings and unofficial contacts. It would be too much to hope that all Prefects have sufficient credit with both sides of industry to be successful, or that all Prefects use their social capital to the full. But the desire to do so is widely diffused, and their social influence in many parts of the country goes some way towards making up for the ineffectiveness of the national politicians, and the inertia of many local authorities. It is perhaps in this field that the Prefects' future is to be found.

4. *The Prefect's Government*

This cursory glimpse at the Prefect's legal powers has indicated the wide fields in which he has the right to intervene. In

[1] Jouany: op. cit.

dealing with administrative authorities he has the right to inspect and direct, in dealing with elected authorities his influence is essentially political—encouragement, initiative, stimulation. This is the key to understanding of the Prefect's rôle.

When M. Queuille was Minister of the Interior he described the Prefect's place in modern government in these broad terms:

'The Prefect, as representative of all the Ministers, is not bound by any bureaucratic rules; it is more important that he should understand the general problems facing the country than the detailed rules which govern the administration of the services put under his control.

'Representative of the Government, it is for the Prefect to animate all those who help it with that "virtus" which Montesquieu considered to be the basic principle of democratic régimes. Should that "virtus" weaken, democracy can be swept away by demagogy.

'It is for the Prefect to explain within the Departments and the Communes, where reside the deep roots of the country, the guiding principles of government action. It is he who must apply the laws, and adapt a general measure to the individual susceptibilities of the population he administers; and he must never forget that in a democracy it is above all else the spontaneous support of the citizen which guarantees respect for the law.

'To govern, to administer, is essentially to seek out the points of contact between men, to bridge their points of disagreement: it is a permanent effort to discover the unity of the Nation beneath the different tendencies which divide public opinion.'[1]

The question is how does the Prefect really live. One ex-Prefect has described a day in the life of a Prefect in the following way: 'One passes from the relative value of different methods of construction to the wheat content of bread, from the rates of local taxes to the co-ordination of transport, from the mating season of bulls to contracts for fire engines, scales of family allowances and identity cards for deportees to the college of

[1] Speech of M. Queuille: June 15, 1950, commemorating the 150th anniversary of the Prefectoral Corps.

domestic science; from tourism, hotel equipment and highway police to the price of a sirloin of mutton, from hydroelectric barrages and from abattoirs to lockouts and religious processions; from the security of cinemas to campaigns against mildew to clandestine organizations and to military affairs; from lunatic asylums to plots against the State.'[1] This account may be a little highly coloured, but it contains a strong element of truth, and it brings to life the abstract lists of powers compiled by administrative lawyers. M. Queuille places the Prefect in a position of considerable political authority, but he does not ask how the Prefect can deal with the politicians on their own ground, without either dominating or being dominated by them. This point is discussed in the remainder of this chapter.

The idea of politics involves two different approaches: in one sense it is the elaboration of policy, in the other it is the actuation of policy. In the first it is the determination of ends, and the general principles upon which conduct of a given category of affairs is to be guided. In the second case it involves finding means to bring these intentions to life.

To do either of these things in a democratic system involves an understanding of the political forces at work in society; these must be understood not only in the abstract sense of social or historical trends, but also in the practical sense of pressure groups, individual interests, personal jealousies, economic resources, financial possibilities, and so on. In France this understanding is complicated by several fundamental divisions of opinion which are not susceptible to placid negotiation round a table.

The French Left has never really accepted the fact that to act a State requires a good deal of compulsive authority. It demands that the State should act, and that it should intervene positively in social and economic life, sometimes in a drastic way, to redress the balance of social life. But it reacts strongly if a Government, even one of strong republican sympathies, attempts to acquire those powers which would make effective government possible.

[1] V. Ventour: *Petite contribution à la philosophie d'une carrière. Revue Administrative.* September, 1951.

They believe that any strong Executive will turn against themselves.

The Right on the other hand has failed to recognize that the elementary condition of social peace is to remove the basic causes of social unrest. Traditionally individualist, they strongly oppose compromise with social 'forces', especially when directly associated with a class whose demands are collectivist. The Right regards the power and organization of this new political collectivity as a menace not only to economic and social privilege, but also to the innate character of the 'real' France, the France of the provinces, of the countryside, and frequently of the Church. It is hostile to interference with the individual in social, economic and political fields, although it sometimes accepts the need for authoritarianism in religious and moral matters. The Right sees the Left as a mass of incomplete individuals, who reject the validity of individualism because of personal incompetence, but who nevertheless constitute a threat to the peace of right-minded citizens. The State should intervene, if necessary by undisguised force, to prevent the mass from overturning the 'real' France. For the Right, the Executive should act as the gendarme, and nothing more.

The Left rejects the intervention of the State without which none of its programme can be fulfilled; the Right accepts the intervention of the State, but in none of those fields in which it could be useful. This dilemma of power in French life lies at the root of many of her political difficulties. By the same token it is the ever-present background to the work and rôle of the Prefect. He works in the knowledge that there is no agreed standard of administrative control or of administrative initiative, and that whatever he does with his power is likely to be wrong for one or other group; sometimes for both.

The Prefect, both in the part he plays in the formulation of policy, and in the part he plays in actuating policy, is bound by the conflicting political forces. This is equally true whether he acts himself or has to procure the action of others. To take a simple instance: if he refuses to allow a cycle race over the

Department's roads after 10 a.m. because of the traffic jams they invariably cause, he will be vehemently attacked by the local newspapers and cycle clubs that organized it, the cycle manufacturers, the advertisers who have put up the prizes, and the shopkeepers and Communes who expected to make money from the crowds. Even a simple matter of highway control may involve interests of considerable financial and political influence.

(a) *The Government*

The first and most important influence upon the Prefect is obviously the Government, and this must be understood to mean both the Cabinet as a whole and the Minister of the Interior in particular. The influences at play inside the Government at the time of the Prefect's appointment have already been described.

The Government can always insist upon a Prefect strictly following a specified policy. It can tell him that under no circumstances is he to approve any more applications for permission to raise loans. He then has no choice. He is also expected to conform to a general line of policy, even though the initiative remains with him. If the Minister tells him to help the formation of centre party coalitions he must exercise all his abilities to calm local feuds, placate personal rivalries, and arrange common meetings. In a recent case a Prefect in a Department of the West arranged by judicious conversations to heal a breach between Independents and MRP which had previously resulted in giving the RPF a clear majority in elections. As a result of the Prefect's activities the RPF were put in a minority. This is very different from giving a Prefect precise instructions. The outcome in most cases does not depend upon him, or upon the Minister's will; he cannot be ordered to patch up a centre party coalition, he can only be ordered to use his good offices to make alliance possible, if the politicians can find a common basis of accord. The Minister must rely on his Prefect's ability and loyalty.

As public representative of the Government the Prefect must bear the brunt of maintaining the Government's authority in the Department. He may have to act as scapegoat. A Prefect who one day left his Prefecture for a day's shooting in the hills returned at night to find it in the hands of strikers. It was pure chance, but the authority of the State and the prestige of the Government required that he should be removed. When Carnot, the President of the Republic, was assassinated at Lyons in 1894, the Prefect of the Rhône was on the following day promoted in the *légion d'honneur* for his behaviour during the incident. The unfortunate Prefect of the Hérault, however, was dismissed on the spot when investigation showed that the assassin, Caserio, had entered France irregularly through the port of Sète, which was in his Department.

Sometimes a Prefect is dismissed for a fault which would normally have no serious consequences but which is the prelude to a difficult situation. The Prefect of Corsica, Allain, was dismissed in 1919 because the police failed to prevent the escape of the Greek Ministers interned on the island. On other occasions the Prefect is sacrificed to international politics. The Prefect of Seine-et-Oise, Chaleil, was dismissed when a hostile crowd hissed the German plenipotentiaries to the Peace Conference of Versailles in 1919. On several other occasions the head of an innocent Prefect pays the price for an international incident or government ineptitude.

There is no way in which a Prefect can 'deal' with the Government, except by being a good Prefect, avoiding bad luck, and remaining loyal to the Government's policy in all its aspects, the part which is implied as well as the part which is written down. He is expected to inform the Government as accurately and objectively as possible of the situation in his Department, and to keep it in order. When the Government has no policy he must substitute his own. If the general paralysis of political institutions renders impossible a clear and general solution of a problem, he has to build up in his Department by gradual process an alternative policy, as far as possible in accordance with what the Government's line would be if it had power to act. He must, for instance, make up for the bankruptcy of Parliament in face of the immense problem of housing, by encouraging local authorities wherever he can to undertake schemes within their own resources, even though these may only result in one or two cottages in the depths of the country. He must fight weary legal battles to try and find space for building against associations of landowners and property owners who on principle begin legal action whenever the State uses its powers of compulsory purchase.

One must not of course overestimate the complete subordination of the Prefects to the Minister. Governments have a habit of changing quickly, and although some Ministers of the Interior develop an expertise in the affairs of the Ministry during successive governments, the effect must not be exaggerated. The Prefects are strengthened by the instability of Ministries, and also by the threat of serious political and social disturbances. The Deputies' freedom to be irresponsible is often due to the Prefects' efficiency. The latter have certainly had more to do with maintaining internal stability and with promoting internal welfare than have many of the national representatives.

(b) *The Politicians*

Very closely related to the Prefect's position *vis-à-vis* the Government is the influence of parliamentarians, and to some extent of local politicians. The essential factor in the relations between Prefect and politicians is that the Minister obtains much of his information about a Prefect through the local Deputies and Senators. The holders of important posts, such as the Prefects of Police, and of the Seine, the IGAME and those Prefects sufficiently close to Paris to attend at the Ministry regularly, will probably be known to him. But about half the Prefects will be names and faces, whose capacity and personality he will have had no opportunity to judge for himself. He will hesitate to rely upon the views of the Director of Personnel who has a heavy administrative job, has not much chance to travel around, and is himself a member of the Corps.

It is the politicians who have to live with the Prefect, and it is they who may know him from three sides. Many of them are municipal councillors, who see his handling of local affairs from the roots; many of them serve on the *conseil général*, where they come into close personal contact both in the council chamber and in the corridors; and third, they view him with the eyes of a member of a political party with a special outlook, its own clientèle, and its vested interest. They not only see the Prefect as an administrator but as a local political force. He is an important, though exaggerated, element in their livelihood, which is punctuated at nearly annual intervals with new elections. And success in politics in France depends to a large extent upon having a firmly established local base, with a hard core of political friends and supporters. It often means taking an active part in local politics both at the communal and the departmental levels. Yet municipal elections are one year, departmental elections another, national elections another. The politician is therefore continually up for re-election in one political arena or another, and the results of a council election often have considerable, though not decisive, effects upon a Member of Parliament's national position.

He is then by force of circumstances keenly interested in everything the Prefect does which may affect the electorate. The exercise of administrative powers by the Prefect is not disguised by the anonymity of the bureaucrat. The politicians know what is going on.

They also have their political 'friends': the Mayors of important towns, the influential leaders of local pressure groups, the leaders of the unions and of the business associations which help to finance elections. These friends are the '*grands électeurs*', whose intervention can swing blocks of votes. The politician is interested in their fate: if a favourite project is discarded, if they appear to the public to lose their influence, their decline may carry the politician with them. If they become seriously annoyed at the politician's alleged shortcomings, his seat may be in jeopardy at the next election.

Politicians also have their own close supporters who rely upon their protection: they form a very useful hard core for the politician. It is alleged that the *Sûreté Nationale*, worried at the lack of policemen in a very large city in the South, discovered that a substantial group were employed exclusively in the police band, without any other kind of duty. When the Prefect and the *Sûreté Nationale* tried to remedy the situation, they were met by outraged remonstrances from certain Deputies, whose voters and agents these men were.

If the politician is a member of a party in the governing coalition, and supports the Government, he weakens his own political position by partaking of the unpopularity which is the eventual lot of every Government in France. He will expect the Prefect to help him to offset this unpopularity by granting certain favours within his power.

An additional difficulty lies in the fact that under the present system of proportional representation with the Department as the constituency, there may be Deputies of several parties. Very rarely is the Prefect subject to pressure only in one direction. But he *can*, of course, be faced with unanimity; for example, in some Departments much valuable land has been requisitioned for building NATO aerodromes, but it seems to require a lengthy and weary process before actual construction begins and before any payment is made to the expropriated farmers. On such occasions the Prefect will be faced with a united front of Deputies from Communists to Moderates, each no doubt inspired by his own preoccupations and clientèle, but the whole constituting a formidable pressure group. However, the few issues which could force Deputies to act together are usually of such a magnitude that they are entirely out of the Prefect's hands, and he can, rather smugly, refer them to the Minister.

There are Prefects who boldly affirm that Deputies give no trouble provided they know that the Prefect is not afraid of them, and there are less assured ones who consider that Deputies give no bother provided the Prefect handles them carefully. The more senior a Prefect is, the more forcefully he can express his mind and opinion to a Deputy. There is common agreement that Members of Parliament have no longer the influence, nor the presumption, that they had in the past.

There is moreover a compensating factor resulting from the present system of proportional representation. A number of Deputies and Senators of different parties tend to neutralize each other's direct influence. It is difficult for them to expect the Prefect to do things which only favour themselves.

Further there are several ways in which a Prefect can oblige the parliamentarian. He appoints many minor officials in the Department, men like *cantonniers* and *facteurs*, and it is an easy method of pleasing to consult the politicians first, and often to be guided by them. The granting of some types of trading licences, for example the sale of alcohol, can also be granted after prior consultation. A politician may be able to persuade the Prefect to include in the draft departmental budget some grant or subvention to a project in which he is particularly interested: it stands much more chance of being accepted than if it is proposed during debate, with all the other parties and persons holding the floor.

All applications or proposals for the award of decorations must go through the hands of the Prefect, who compiles the report which the Minister considers. The favour of a complimentary report is sometimes sufficient to provide the Prefect with an ally, though he is normally rather small fry.

The Prefect is also very useful in expediting business: minor branches of the French administration are as lethargic as their opposite numbers in other countries, and the word of the Prefect can bring the application for relief, or the request for a building licence out from its resting place. Successful intervention by a politician at the Prefecture will enhance his prestige, and is a legitimate occupation for a public figure.

The Deputy may want the Prefect's assistance in larger matters, a loan from the Government for a local authority, plans for land reclamation. These matters can be expedited by the Prefect while they remain in the Prefecture, and their future fate may depend partly upon the report he forwards to the Ministry. If they are blocked there the Prefect may be able to expedite affairs in Paris too.

His influence in Paris is rather curiously parallel to that of a parliamentarian. There is fairly common agreement that Ministries, and not only the Ministry of the Interior, are not displeased when a Prefect calls upon them, and if there is a matter which requires more expeditious treatment than it is receiving, and must be extracted from the clutches of a Bureau, the Prefect and the senior ministerial heads can understand each other, and arrive at a prompt solution and a ready answer. But should a Deputy or Senator intervene in the Administration, a wall of glass sometimes descends: not because the officials do not fear the politician, nor because they are unaware of his influence, but because they fear even more being trapped in the web of political intrigue. The proper place for a Deputy to intervene is with the Minister's cabinet. There he may be able to get the same speedy decision as the Prefect does by dealing with the officials. The dossier can be extracted at the demand of the *directeur du cabinet* as quickly as at the wish of the official directors. But a politician has only a certain amount of credit he can count upon with his political colleagues; daily interventions to extract minor matters of no real importance end with his waiting in the anteroom of the Ministry longer than is polite.

There are also occasions when less honest favours are granted to Deputies and Senators. For example, a Prefect may deliberately omit to enforce a local ordinance forbidding the use of loudspeakers in public on the occasion of an eve of poll speech; this obviously gives the candidate an unfair advantage over his opponents.

The extent to which a Prefect is liable to political pressure depends a great deal upon where his Department is, upon local attitudes to politics, and, in part, upon the Minister's attitude. There was a time when a great part of the political pressure brought to bear on the Prefect was coldly and deliberately aimed at rigging elections.[1] In 1922 the Prefect of the Aisne (Laon) was dismissed by a Minister for incompetence merely in order to make a place for a protégé who was a Sub Prefect and who could

[1] This is still true in Algeria and in the Overseas Departments.

be expected to favour the local politicians by using his powers for electoral purposes. But even in those days this caused considerable disturbance in the Chamber of Deputies and the protégé was ejected at the next change of Government.

Nowadays the Prefects 'calculate rather than orientate' electoral results. But it must be remembered that Prefects are in a highly strategic position at election times. They, more than anyone else, are likely to be aware of the programmes, platforms, and secret intentions of the various candidates. Odd conversations with political leaders, hints from labour and business leaders, information from Sub Prefects and the *directeur des renseignements généraux* provide them with a picture of the electoral battlefield and campaign which is often very accurate. The Prefect may know the 'red herring' which is calculated by some party tactician to stampede the electorate at the eleventh hour; his general knowledge of his Department's psychology suggests which issue is most likely to attract public attention.

His advice then is of very real value to the rival candidates. It can be very helpful to know in advance that your opponent intends to concentrate all his guns on the cost of living, or on the European Army, or on the air force authorities' reckless requisitioning of agricultural land, or on the illicit *amours* of your party agent. You can nullify a hostile whispering campaign by spreading it first yourself and applying it to your opponent. If you know that at the last moment an irresponsible opponent intends to reprint in poster form a speech of admiration for Hitler you made in 1933, you have the time to find a speech in which he paid a passing compliment to Stalin in 1934. A politician's platform must be a judicious mixture of national and local issues, and the Prefect's advice about the most telling combination can be invaluable for success. The Prefect may reserve his best advice for one of the candidates, and merely pass a pleasant half-hour's fencing with the others. How far a Prefect may discreetly mislead an unfavoured guest is a matter on which there is little reliable evidence. Certainly several joint party lists have been arranged through the Prefect's ability to distinguish the issues which least divide these parties, and his forecast that if they do not all hang together they will hang separately.

But no evidence has been produced for a long time to show that the Prefects encourage or threaten electors to vote in one way. They may indicate in private discussions their, or the Government's, preference, but nobody has produced evidence that even this allegation is based on fact, and in many parts of France it is highly probable that such intervention would provoke the electorate to vote the other way. This would certainly be true in the south, for it is usual there to see political significance in every act of authority. It is significant if a Prefect attends one inaugural ceremony rather than another; it is significant if the Secretary General appears at a reception in a canton rather than the Prefect himself; the nomination of a doctor to a hospital board is seen as a repayment for secret services rendered; the distribution of grants by the Department is an illustration of the way the *conseillers généraux* have bought the Prefect, or vice versa.

In the north and east administration is assumed, in default of positive contrary evidence, to be objective. A political decision is recognized as such; but local opinion does not go out of its way to gild every action with an unexpressed design. Departments vary in this respect, and one of a Prefect's first task is to learn local psychology.

Not many Deputies or Senators or Prefects would find anything seriously wrong with this description of themselves by a serving Prefect: their relations 'ont parfois l'allure du vaudeville et parfois l'allure du roman de cape et d'épée, mais, quant à l'essentiel, il (est) fort décent et fort sérieux sans excessive galanterie ni noirs dessins.'[1]

(c) *The Administration*

The great majority of heads of technical services dislike being entangled with political matters. They fear that they will be

[1] E. Pisani: *La fonction préfectorale*, in *Encyclopédie permanente de l'administration française*.

hauled before the public if they 'arrange' anything for a politician; they fear that subterranean pressure will handicap their careers if they refuse to accede to his demands. Probably neither is true, but the political danger modifies the technical service heads' conception of administrative autonomy. They are prepared to act autonomously provided they are not likely to be held publicly responsible. This is a depressing phenomenon not unusual among officials in most countries. In France it enhances the status of the Prefects, who are generally willing and competent to deal with political questions and bear the burden of public responsibility.

The Prefect must maintain his personal superiority over other administrators in the Department by being a first class administrator in his own right. The Prefect who trusts innocently in the good sense of his subordinates may one day lose his post for a mistake on their part.

These administrative duties are the lot of the highly placed administrator. The Prefect must, however, make sure they never get out of proportion; they may take much time, but they are only subsidiary tasks. They help him to retain supervision over the technical services since his Bureaux can often provide them with assistance and information and with the administrative resources they do not possess. Technical services are apt to heed their Ministries too much, and the Ministries on their side are apt to lay down detailed rules which may be theoretically desirable but which, by their nature, ignore local conditions. Some heads of services know this quite well, and are aware that their own schemes may be faulty, even from the technical point of view, through lack of detailed local knowledge. The Prefect now influences the officials of other Ministries less because of his legal supremacy than by virtue of his greater knowledge, special abilities, and qualities which the technical heads recognize as lacking in themselves and in their organizations.

No comment on the Prefect's relations with other Administrations would be complete without mentioning his relations with the Army and with the Catholic hierarchy. By the nature of things the observer is unable to know what takes place at meetings between Army commander and Prefect, or between Bishop and Prefect. Their public comments about each other appear sometimes to be barbed, and not unmalicious. Their public salutations are marked more by politeness than warmth. Their joint appearances in public show a certain joylessness in each other's company. What happens in their private relations is known only to those who have had experience of one of the careers. A serving Prefect, commenting on prefectoral relations with the Bishop, speaks of, 'le mystère d'une double confession où nul ne sait lequel des deux donnera l'absolution.' He adds that, as regards the Prefect and the soldiers, their encounters are 'tout semblable à un poème héroi-comique chanté sur un rythme martial; il aurait eu pour refrain ce "cedant arma togae" auquel le Préfet est tellement attaché'.[1] Only the parties concerned will know how much mockery to discount.

(d) *The Local Authorities*

The local authorities are another and confusing source of political pressure upon the Prefect. The term 'local authority' includes not only the three or four hundred *conseils municipaux* and Mayors in the Department, but also the *conseil général* and the *commission départementale*. First, then, the local authorities of the Communes.

It is difficult to picture the precise situation which any one Prefect will have to face. There may be national politicians among the Mayors of Communes or members of *conseils municipaux* who will try to use their national position to increase their status in the local assembly. Sometimes the Mayor of a Commune is amenable, but his *conseil municipal* is aggressive and awkward. Arrangements with the Mayor may then be overturned by the local assembly, when everything appeared settled; this is especially likely to happen on financial questions.

There are extreme differences between the size and importance of Communes within the Department. There are several third

---
[1] E. Pisani: cit.

class Departments which contain only two Communes with a population of over 10,000; the rest are scattered rural villages. Other Departments have a large number of strongly established Communes with a long tradition of municipal government, divided from each other by local feuds and political interests. The task of the Prefect of the Nord (Lille), a densely populated area with many large Communes of this sort, is perhaps an extreme example. Some Departments are split between two major centres of activity, each attracting the economic and social life of the Department, and each hostile to the influence of the other; for example, the rivalry in the Basses Pyrénées between Pau and Bayonne; this rivalry is exacerbated by the simple fact that the Prefecture can only be in one of them, in this case Pau.

Other Communes may be in conflict because of competing economic interests; for instance the ports of Calais and Boulogne in the Pas de Calais (Arras). In tourist centres rivalry of this kind is often worse because the Communes are smaller and the competition more personal. Attempts to modernize or develop one of these centres will be regarded as a direct challenge to the others, to be fought by political and financial means. Some towns may be so important to a Department that their decline threatens a wide hinterland, yet it may not be very obvious to the rest of the Department that its immediate interests are connected with those of the major centre. The tug-of-war in the *conseil général* then becomes acute, and the Prefect must assume part of the responsibility for explaining simple economics to indignant personages who feel they are being exploited on behalf of the 'big town'. The decline of the port of Bordeaux is a very serious matter, yet a great part of the hinterland is wine growing country, and with the decline of the overseas markets, the wine growers appear to have no immediate interest in expanding the port again by the development of oil refineries and of easier means of access. Yet if Bordeaux really declined the prosperity of a very wide area would suffer: this is elementary, but someone has to say it sufficiently frequently to make an impression.

The amalgamation of neighbouring Communes is also a delicate task, which is inevitably a source of trouble for the Prefect. In the ordinary way, modifications in communal boundaries and the absorption of one Commune by another is done by decree of the *Conseil d'Etat* on the proposition of the Minister of the Interior. This method will always be successful in the end if the case is a good one, but it is a lengthy business, and is likely to arouse much local bitterness. Administrators are reluctant to initiate it; yet it can sometimes be highly desirable to strengthen one Commune by adding another. In the east of France, there is a long drawn out story of the decline of Mulhouse *vis-à-vis* its Swiss neighbour, Basel, which is partly due to the existence of the small Commune of St Louis which runs between Mulhouse and the frontier. To strengthen Mulhouse, which would benefit the inhabitants of Mulhouse, St Louis, the Department and the State, would involve its amalgamation with St Louis. If the Prefect can obtain the consent of the two *conseil municipaux*, and a favourable motion in the *conseil général* he can amalgamate two Communes on his own authority, provided they belong to the same canton. This is much more expeditious, does not leave the bad feeling, and can be worked out by local men rather than lawyers in Paris. But it demands from the Prefect a most persuasive tongue, a clear and well thought out programme lasting for some time, and an ability to sense when to be outspoken, and when, for a time, apparently to abandon the whole scheme.

Nor must one forget the awkward little squabbles which blow up inside small Communes, squabbles which are insignificant in themselves but can cause trouble for the Prefect, because they involve issues or institutions of more than purely local importance. When a Communist Mayor in a small village in Burgundy learnt of Stalin's death, he draped the Commune's tricolor with black mourning and flew it from the *Mairie*. When no one was looking the priest took it down and replaced the flag by a broom, and decorated it with an umbrella frame. The Mayor indignantly held a protest meeting and marched a squad of party stalwarts round the church. He also, as a responsible civil authority, informed the Magistracy, and served a writ on the priest alleging 'profanation sacrilège' of the national flag. The priest claimed on his own behalf that several men in the Commune had died in Indo-China as a result of Stalin's policies. This type of squabble can sometimes arouse the fervour of both sides to the point where public order is threatened and the Prefect, or the Sub Prefect on his orders, has to intervene. It can be worked up by the local Communist press into a general anti-State campaign, or worse, the Bishop might intervene; if he decides to cover the priest with his authority he will try to do so through the Prefect; if he admits that the priest is wrong, he may try to placate the communal authorities through the good offices of the Prefect.

Some of these local incidents require quick thinking. The Mayor of Tarbes, who was elected to office in 1953, was a Communist. On the occasion of VE day festivities, he departed from the customary sonorous platitudes, and regaled his audience—which included on the platform with him the Prefect of the Hautes Pyrénées and the colonel commandant of the regiment scheduled to march past—with the current party line on international affairs. To remain on the platform in uniform under such circumstances would be personally embarrassing and a delight to ill-disposed persons in the crowd; it might also be regarded by the politically uneducated as an official blessing upon the views expressed by the Mayor. The Prefect had to decide rapidly to withdraw his recognition from the proceedings, to march the other State representatives off the platform, and to arrange for the regiment to march back to barracks by a route different from that planned for the official march past.

A sense of humour is sometimes equally essential. In Ajaccio (Corsica) one municipal election resulted in a curious, if not unique, majority coalition between Radicals, Communists, and Independent Bonapartists, to elect a Dissident Bonapartist, M. Maglioli, as Mayor.

The outgoing Mayor, M. Serafini, a member of the RPF who had orthodox Bonapartist support, decided to resign with fourteen colleagues in order to force new elections, and thus remain in office in the meantime. Their resignations were never apparently received at the Prefecture. In order to prevent the remaining sixteen, now a majority, from meeting to elect M. Maglioli as Mayor, the outgoing Mayor, M. Serafini, took the precaution of surrounding the Town Hall with police. Unable to reach the council chamber, the new majority adjourned to a room in the vicinity of the Town Hall and there elected their Dissident Bonapartist Mayor. They drafted the results of the election and their deliberations on municipal notepaper taken from the Town Hall.

M. Serafini, now in Paris, promptly declared that he alone was legally competent to convoke a meeting of the council, that no council meeting outside the Town Hall could be regarded as valid, and that the notepaper from the Town Hall had been stolen. He threatened to start legal proceedings against everyone involved. With two soi-disant Mayors, Bonapartists, Dissident Bonapartists, and Independent Bonapartists divided against each other, and half the council threatened with legal actions, the Prefect had to intervene to prevent the breakdown of municipal administration in the capital of Corsica; and his own Prefecture was involved because of the curious story of the missing resignations.

The influence of an important Commune in departmental affairs is not much less, as far as the Prefect is concerned, than that of the *conseil général*. But the latter acts as spokesman of the Department's interests, and is therefore a political force which can never be ignored. Some of its members will be associated with Communes, others may be national politicians, a few may be both. It is in the sessions of the *conseil général* that the Prefect's public reputation is made, and it is there that he comes into direct contact with the political elements of the Department—Deputies, Senators, some Mayors. It is also there that he meets representatives of the countryside.

A *conseil général* is elected by cantons, and the geographical distribution of these electoral areas is heavily weighted in favour of rural districts: only in large cities like Montpellier is one Commune divided into more than one canton; otherwise an urban Commune is part of a canton including the surrounding

Communes, and so loses its chance of separate representation on the departmental council. This makes little allowance for the representation of urban interests, which are often, in France as elsewhere, opposed to agricultural interests.

In an average Department about a quarter of all the departmental councillors are employed in agriculture, either as landowners, farmers or in rural industries: another quarter are professional men such as doctors, veterinary surgeons and solicitors who are effectively spokesmen of the rural areas in which they work—they may have homes in the cantonal capital but are compelled by their profession to travel around and become known. A third quarter are officials of one kind or another, many of them retired, and they too are in fact frequently representatives of the rural areas in which they live. Only the last quarter, the businessmen, architects, shopkeepers and journalists, really represent urban interests.

The Prefect may be faced with a *conseil général* composed of rather slow and unintelligent rustics who can be touched more often by interest than by reason. He may have an assembly in which one or two politicians of national importance are busy forwarding their own projects. Some assemblies include a mixture of the two.

This distribution of interest groups naturally affects the Prefect; it affects him in the same way as the national life of the country is affected by a distribution of power which favours the economically static parts of the country to the detriment of the economically dynamic areas. It complicates the Prefect's task of administering the Department, and it handicaps him in taking steps to overcome conflicts.

As departmental executive the Prefect puts into effect all the decisions of the *conseil général*, he appoints officials paid by the Department, he represents the Department in legal affairs[1], he authorizes expenditure from departmental funds, he advertises

[1] Except when the State and the Department are involved in litigation: then the Prefect represents the State and the Secretary General the Department.

tenders for departmental contracts and signs them on its behalf, and he directs all the administrative, technical and welfare services organized by the Department. He has the right of entry to all sessions of the *conseil général*, and the assembly is not entitled to take up a matter for discussion unless it is accompanied by the Prefect's report. No committee appointed by the *conseil général* can be ordered by the parent body to assume the responsibility for preparing an original report in place of or parallel to that made by the Prefect; no official can report directly to the *conseil général* without the Prefect's approval, even when the matter is entirely of departmental concern. The *conseil général* can, however, set up its own committee to study and report on a particular matter once the Prefect has already done so.

The Prefect has to be careful in his relations with his *conseil général* not only out of the respect properly accorded an elected assembly, but also because of the legal powers of the *conseil général*. A hostile *conseil général* can play havoc with the Prefect's draft budget and hamper constructive action. In recent years a Minister was forced to replace a Prefect whose *conseil général* showed their hostility by refusing to meet while the Prefect was present.

The *conseil général's* powers of decision include the acquisition, exchange, lease or sale of departmental property, the use to which it is put, the departmental budget, the classification and construction of departmental highways, the supervision of intercommunal roads, of public works financed by the Department, concessions for using or organizing services of departmental interest, legal representation and litigation involving the Department, the organization of all welfare services set up by the Department, and arbitration between Communes when they disagree among themselves. The *conseil général* has a general warrant to deal with any matter of departmental concern brought to its attention by the Prefect or the *commission départementale*. It is also empowered to go directly to the Minister if it wishes, and can pass motions on matters of general economic interest.

These very large formal powers are to some extent offset by

financial considerations and by statutory duties. The *conseil général* must allow in the departmental budget sufficient funds to meet the cost of maintaining certain buildings used by the State—the Prefecture and Sub Prefectures, barracks for the Gendarmerie[1], the civil tribunals and *cours d'assises*, and the teachers' training college; they also have to finance part of the educational service, and a large part of the health, welfare and highway services. Some wealthy Departments can cope with these duties without too great strain, but for many the cost of highways and assistance services together account for more than two thirds of the total departmental budget; after the other compulsory charges have been met, there is very little left for optional and constructive expenditure.

The departmental budget requires the approval of the Minister and his permission has to be obtained for raising most loans. The Prefect has no tutelage powers over the *conseil général* as he has over the Communes; but if he considers a decision *ultra vires* he can refuse to act upon it until the *Conseil d'Etat* gives its judgement.

Only on rare occasions is the Prefect called upon to exercise legal supervision over the council's actions. The most frequent abuse, not always deliberate, is for the assembly to attempt to discuss matters outside its competence; for example, votes of censure on the Government, the Prefect's use of his police powers, and general political questions. If the council refuses to accept the Prefect's contention that the matter raised in discussion is outside its authority, the Prefect and his subordinates leave, thereby automatically suspending the validity of the session.

The meetings of the *conseil général* are relatively short; the first in April and May lasts a fortnight, and the second lasts a

---

[1] The Department can now transfer these buildings to the State which assumes all responsibility for them. In practice several barracks so transferred were allowed by the State to fall into such decay that on humanitarian grounds the *conseil général* has felt it necessary to undertake improvements even though it is no longer responsible. This was the case in the Department of the Lozère: see report of the IGA, Vol. I, 1950. p. 27.

month between August and October. But the *conseil général* can hold extraordinary meetings at any time if it is convoked by decree, or at the Prefect's request or on the demand of two thirds of the *conseil général* or at the request of the *commission départementale*. The result is that some *conseils généraux* extend their sessions, and especially the autumn session when the budget is passed, for an inordinate length of time, sometimes until the end of the year. This may not be due to malicious tactics or filibustering, but to an inefficient chairman or a loquacious or irrepressible assembly. On such occasions the burden on the Prefect is heavy. For months on end he has to attend the council to deal with unforeseen circumstances and to reassure the *conseil* of its prestige. The session lasts generally from 2.30 until 7.00 in the evening; the Prefect has to perform his other duties early in the morning or late at night. He has continually to be alert and to give the appearance of omniscience in answering or parrying the questions and speeches which are to be expected from a self-assertive assembly. Many of these questions are irrelevant and many are in fact illegal since they relate to matters outside the assembly's competence. It is not uncommon for a Prefect to find himself forced to answer the irrelevant questions because he has already had to refuse to answer so many illegal ones. If he insists on remaining within the strict letter of the law he is likely to arouse opposition in the assembly for imputed lack of respect.

The *commission départementale* is a body in intimate contact with the Prefect. It is elected annually by the *conseil général* from among its own number, and can have delegated to it powers of decision on matters within the *conseil's* competence. It must by statute meet once a month and it can meet more frequently if it wishes. Each month it checks the Prefect's accounts relating to departmental affairs. He must also present it with the draft budget ten days before the budgetary session of the *conseil général* begins and it can present its own report after the budget speech made by the Prefect.

The *commission départementale* is a tidy body from the Prefect's point of view. By law it can include no member of Parliament, nor the Mayor of the departmental capital, normally the most influential political figures in the Department. When the Prefect differs from the *commission*, he can suspend all action until the *conseil général* has had the opportunity to decide. This may not be for several months, unless the Prefect or the *commission* convoke it especially. The *conseil général* can then if it wishes dissolve the *commission* and appoint a new body.

Nevertheless, despite its potentially subordinate position, it performs a very useful task, and its relations with the Prefect are normally most satisfactory, for the *commission* knows better than the *conseil général* the difficulties of detailed administration. The *commission* is a valuable sounding board for foretelling the probable attitude of the full assembly, especially in financial matters. Of the notable influences in the departmental assembly, the chairman of the *commission départementale* ranks next to the chairman of the *conseil général*, and, not far behind, comes the *rapporteur* of the departmental budget.

(e) *Local Interests*

'Local interests' is a phrase used to cover a wide variety of institutions; some are organized on a permanent basis, some coalesce only when occasion demands it, some are merely attitudes and sentiments widely held. All these can have a considerable effect on a Prefect's life and policy.

In many Departments the strongest organized interest is the agricultural interest: Parliament itself knows the blackmailing propensities of some sections of this group—the cider growers, the beet growers, the small distillers. The activities of farmers' associations are of great importance to Prefects all over the country. For many years, for example, each summer has brought scarcely veiled threats to withhold agricultural supplies from the towns unless the farmers obtain more satisfactory prices; the Prefect fixes the local price for many food products. In 1951, for instance, the area farmers' association in the Rhône (Lyons) demanded an increased price for their milk in the normal way; when the Prefect offered them an award which they considered inadequate, the association called upon its members to stop supplying the city of Lyons. It was only when the Prefect, exasperated, issued warrants for the arrest of the President and Secretary General of the association on charges of criminal conspiracy, and successfully opposed their applications for bail when they were committed for trial, that the association discovered that it might after all be able to meet the city's needs without going bankrupt. In this instance the Prefect had several particularly strong cards in his hand. He was himself a man of the highest authority and prestige in government quarters, he had the support of a city whose Mayor was President of the National Assembly, and the demographic as well as the political balance of power in the Department was heavily weighted on the side of the urban area.

In several Departments there is only one main agricultural interest: the Hérault (Montpellier) for example, produces a large proportion of the *vin ordinaire* for the whole of France, and therefore has a formidable viticultural pressure group which neither Deputies, Senators or Prefects can ignore. The effective pressure which a particular group can bring to bear on a particular Prefect will depend upon its relative position in departmental life. For example, the viticultural interest in the Basses Alpes is nothing like so strong as that of the Gironde. The beet-growers' associations in Departments like the Marne have every chance of effective pressure, whereas in the Hautes-Pyrénées they have none.

These interests do not of course limit themselves to correspondence with the Prefect; departmental councillors, and even some members of Parliament, may have their campaigns financed by them. There is a solid rural vote for most *conseils généraux*, and the tactics adopted by agricultural interests follow a fairly uniform pattern throughout the country. They object to all proposals which involve the compulsory purchase of land, except in urban areas; they tend to object to any large expenditure of public funds on work which benefits the towns in the Department, except work connected with marketing, storage, and transport. Their representatives on the *conseil général* generally press for a budget balanced at the lowest level, and, if there is a surplus, they ask for expenditure on anti-mildew campaigns rather than anti-tuberculosis campaigns, on the construction of silos rather than main drainage, on the construction of local roads with an agricultural purpose, rather than an extension to the teachers' training college.

They react strongly to any threat of alteration in the grants, allowances, subsidies they have obtained from the State or Department. When the Government proposed to restrict the right of fruit-growers freely to distil part of their own produce and to levy a tax on alcohol so produced, the Prefect of the Haute Saône was faced with this statement in the *conseil général*: 'La défense de leurs libertés (of the bouilleurs de cru) est entièrement distincte de la question de l'alcoolisme, fléau contre lequel il importe de lutter.' The *conseil* thereupon invited all the members of Parliament representing the Department 'à agir d'urgence pour obtenir le retrait ou le rejet des dispositions particulièrement injustes et contraires aux libertés traditionelles des producteurs de fruit.' A Prefect with an eye to the future and a taste for logic is often unhappy in provincial France.

Some Departments have special local interests. A Department like the Lozère has substantial forestry interests, and a proposal to close down a branch railway on grounds of general economy is regarded as a serious personal attack since it would involve transferring awkward loads of felled trees to long distance road transport. Several uneconomic lines which no longer accept passenger traffic are kept open for this purpose. The Prefect is expected to plead the case before the Government and the SNCF, and he will be thought inefficient if he does not succeed.

Occasionally such local interests have a positive programme which they press. For example, they may wish to devote whatever sums the Department can afford to the construction of new weighbridges to facilitate the checking of loads.

Besides rural interests there are the economic interests of urban workers. The trade unions in particular constitute a permanent pressure group. Sometimes the various unions can work in harmony, especially on major issues of social policy; for example, their representatives are naturally anxious to expand housing programmes, welfare services, trade schools, and so on. Sometimes however their interests conflict. If unions representing municipal transport workers demand higher wages, they are likely to run up against those representing industries whose members have to travel long distances to work. Christian Democrat, Socialist and Communist trade unions may also speak with different voices. If the Prefect is called upon to intervene he will be subject to pressure from many sides.

Sometimes representatives of labour and employers agree to press for the extension of certain services by the Department or by the State. In the past coal miners' and coal owners' organizations have formed a temporary common front to lower the cost of coal transport and delivery.

Other urban interests are the shopkeepers and traders, and the Chambers of Commerce. Their strength obviously depends upon the size and importance of the industrial and commercial activities in the Department. In many Departments such as the Creuse (Guéret), the commercial as well as the urban interest is numerically very small; no more than two or three towns. In the affairs of other Departments trade plays a vital part. For instance, the transport, cold storage and entrepôt functions of Limoges make its trading associations very powerful; and since the continued prosperity of much of the surrounding agriculture depends upon the good offices of commerce—the beef of the Haute Vienne supplies Paris—the agricultural interests tend to follow the traders' lead, or at least not to oppose them.

Another urban, or mainly urban, interest is the hotel trade which is linked in many Departments with the tourist trade. On many issues hoteliers are likely to side with the traders in opposition to agricultural and perhaps industrial interests. They have an interest in improving communications, in providing modern amenities in towns and in developing certain areas and Communes, all of which from the agriculturalists' point of view are of very little use. To create new ski centres or summer resorts often demands expenditure on roads and electrical installations to open up areas which are of no interest to wine growers or fruit producers. It sometimes leads to real conflict when, for instance, the development of a Commune well situated from the tourist point of view means interference with forestry or pastures. Then an alliance may be struck up between that Commune and commercial interests in the big town of the district, to combat neighbouring Communes and the other big towns in the Department who fear competition.

Economic interests give place in some Departments to less specific but equally pressing difficulties arising from history, geography or social problems. The latent nationalisms of the Alsatian, the Basque and Breton can often be ignored as political factors until an incident occurs.

The trial in 1952 arising from the massacre and burning of the entire village of Oradour by a company of an SS battalion, aroused such a political outcry in Alsace that Parliament itself had to intervene. The SS company included several young Alsatians who had been conscripted by the Germans and were present during the massacre; they were put on trial at the same time as the Germans. The Prefects of the Bas Rhin (Strasburg) and the Haut Rhin (Colmar) were faced with large scale nationalist Alsatian protests. The fact that these protests remained peaceful to the end was almost certainly due to the speed with which the National Assembly amended the law, so as to prevent the Alsatians being tried in the same dock as the Germans. When this failed to appease Alsatian opinion, they passed another amendment to provide that, for the Alsatians, simply to have belonged to the SS did not constitute presumptive evidence of guilt, as it did for the Germans. The whole trial was a thoroughly unsatisfactory piece of business from which no one emerged with any credit, least of all the French Government and Parliament. Such faults of timing, justice and common sense are a burden that Prefects have to accept philosophically; there appears to be little doubt that in this case both Prefects in the Alsace

Departments had accurately informed the Government of the state of public opinion some time before the trial was arranged. The Prefect of the Haute Vienne (Limoges), where Oradour is situated, was faced in his turn with widespread protest meetings when the Alsatians were amnestied, for it was regarded as an insult to the memory of the massacred; the new Commune returned to the Prefecture the cross of the *légion d'honneur* which De Gaulle's government had awarded it *in memoriam* in 1945.

Incidents involving Basque institutions or religious leaders can also arouse strong local passion. The kidnapping of two Jewish children by their legal guardian, who had them baptized in the Catholic faith and opposed their return to relations and the Jewish faith, involved the connivance of members of the Catholic hierarchy. The children were smuggled to Spain with the active support of Basque priests. When these priests were arrested the Prefect of the Basses-Pyrénées (Pau) received protests and demonstrations both from Basque nationalists and from indignant Catholics. As in Alsace, once local nationalism has been seriously aroused the central Government usually has to intervene to pacify it. In the meantime, while the Government considers, the Prefect has to ride out the storm.

In some Departments nationalist groups present a peculiar social problem; for instance, in several industrial centres the North African population causes difficulties. As citizens of France and the French Union, Algerians in search of work can enter France with the barest formalities. Many remain for a long time unemployed and without resources; others are employed in trades dangerous to health and limb, where, in ignorance and poverty, they accept conditions which are contrary to the law and to health regulations, and which would not be tolerated by the unions of French workers. The owners of some of these works are influential businessmen and local politicians. Other complications arise because the North Africans can often be used as a strike-breaking reserve, prepared to accept a lower wage than that officially recognized. Too often, responsibility for the North

Africans is divided between the police on one side and on the other welfare associations of worthy and a-political individuals who may be personally influential, but whose organizations have never attained the public influence of their counterparts in this country. Prefects with a North African problem, such as those in Paris, Rhône (Lyons), and Bouches-du-Rhône (Marseilles), regard it as a police problem, and not a political problem. A Prefect who goes beyond this does so under the spur of his own conscience, and he may have to challenge several strongly entrenched interests.

In other instances a racial group presents problems of a different order. In one or two Pyrenean Departments, the Spaniards who were exiled from Spain after the civil war have remained in distinct communities inside the local population. In the Ariège they have set up timber co-operatives. At one time Marxist doctrine was taught in several schools attached to these communities, and the existence of these strategically sited and politically unreliable foreign groups was a source of concern to the local Prefects. These groups had connections in places like Toulouse and some were suspected of close contact with smuggling bands and political infiltration.

Smuggling might almost be regarded as a local interest in parts of France. Almost a quarter of all the Departments have a land frontier with Belgium, Germany, Switzerland, Italy or Spain. In many cases the problem of frontier control can be safely left to the appropriate police authorities or the customs; but if it is a source of income there is the danger of corruption and interference with public services, and even if smuggling is only casual, the Prefect may sometimes be faced with the difficult problem of what to do when a well-known and influential national or foreign figure is caught *in flagrante delicto*.

To deal with local authorities and local interests, the Prefect has to exercise political and diplomatic arts; they are not peculiar to the Prefectoral Corps but are as old as the management of men. He must be a competent public speaker, able to state his thought clearly when he wishes to, and to appear to state it clearly on other occasions. He must mix with all types and conditions of men, put them at their ease, accept their confidences without either injuring them or committing himself, and have a pleasant, affable manner which is neither patronizing for the humbler men he works with, nor subservient to the men of influence. He must have a ready tongue for riposte in council chambers, and must realize that a spoken answer may not appear the same when it is printed in the newspapers as while it was being spoken. He must have a sense of the occasion and know when and when not to wear his uniform; must guess when it is opportune to provoke antagonisms between the people with whom he is dealing, and yet accept the right occasions to heal wounds, or by well-placed compliments to bolster up a damaged *amour propre*.[1] His attendance at *vins d'honneur* should be marked by conviviality but not indiscretion. He must be charitable in victory and philosophical in defeat, and he will have to learn to rejoice with Pepys in 'reckoning myself to come off with victory, because not overcome in anything, or much foiled'.[2]

His personal conduct must not give rise to gossip. The press in most areas is cautiously sympathetic to the Prefect and is certainly much less exigent about its right to prior information than is the American press. Tactfully handled the press can be a source of aid to the Prefect. Nevertheless his public position renders him vulnerable to rumour, and he must know when comment about his personal life or public actions goes beyond the point of toleration. He must then protect his name or his credit will be lost.

As regards his personal affairs he should adhere to the traditional prefectoral slogan (normally applied to politics) '*pas d'histoires*'. Clemenceau in his own way, gave them the coarser motto, '*rien dans le diocèse*'. It is fatal for a Prefect to be murdered by his mistress, as was an unfortunate Prefect of Marseilles.

[1] Ventour: *op. cit.*
[2] Diary, October 3, 1666.

Another Prefect once had to be dismissed because he loved Ronsard too well; while still a Sub Prefect he had extracted several manuscripts from the municipal archives of Vendôme, and forgot to return them.[1]

The Prefect must also know what his wife is doing: not for social or amorous reasons, but simply because an inconsequential *Mme la Préfète* who becomes involved with local clubs and social gatherings can cross the strings which the Prefect holds, and can complicate local alliances with personal and feminine issues. There are some Prefects who regard their wives' social and humanitarian activities kindly, believing that this helps their own credit in the Department; but even these agree that it is dangerous for a Prefect's wife to belong to côteries and salons.

There are a number of purely political tricks by which a Prefect can try to maintain his position. He can imply blackmail when he does not legally have the power to make his threat effective; for instance, nearly all Communes of a small Department in the east granted game licences for their domains without charge; this was a loss of revenue. The Prefect suggested putting the rights up to auction to bring in revenue, and the great majority of Communes agreed to do so. The others refused. Thereafter the Prefect deducted from the latters' applications for subventions, grants in aid, and sums from the departmental equalization fund, the amount they would have received had they agreed to lease out these hunting rights. It is doubtful whether in law he had the authority to do this, but the Communes could not know without taking the matter up to the administrative courts, and small Communes with unintelligent Mayors are more afraid of lawyers than of Prefects.

The Prefect is naturally tempted to regard the departmental capital as the most important Commune and to give it most attention. This preoccupation must be matched by his awareness that few of the departmental councillors represent it, and the remainder, from outlying cantons, are those who form public opinion, and take it back with them to their constituents. He

[1] Henry: op. cit.

P

must recognize that although the interests of the departmental capital are of importance to the whole Department and those of the cantons are not, it is better to disguise this knowledge.

The Prefect has to vary his political tactics to suit the area in which he is serving. In some his best weapon is the *délai intelligent*[1], a sense of timing as to the propitious moment to bring forward a proposal with force, and the occasion for prudent withdrawal; to know how to simulate a furious burst of energy, and when to act as if he has apparently abandoned his idea. This sense of timing is more necessary to the south of the Loire than to the north, for in the south the delay must be shorter, and more delicately timed, as the public is ingenious in attributing political motives.

Through all these tangles the Prefect must move with assurance. If he gets stomach ulcers when worried, he will not be a Prefect long. When he is urging a Mayor to build roads he must not lose sight of the Minister's instructions in favour of economy. When preparing a report for the *conseil général* he must estimate how it will sound if passed on to the Minister through the mouth of a Deputy. He may pass a convivial evening with the local federation of industries but he must not forget that Prefectures have been stormed in the absence of the Prefect.

The Prefect must bear an isolated responsibility, and is forbidden by the nature of his duties to give his entire confidence to anyone. He must meet the politician on his own ground, and match bravado with bonhomie. He must live with the appearance of ease yet always prepared for an emergency. He must double the rôles of ruthless disciplinarian and easy diplomat.

The challenge of the post is to combine thought with action. The adventurer with a flair for impetuous leadership flags under the grind of daily administration. The meditative official, who commends himself to civil service examination boards, is very rarely equipped for sudden personal action. A good Prefect is a man who sees in administration the real source of government in the country, but who rejects, as a person, the drab anonymity

[1] Ventour: op. cit.

of the normal bureaucrat. He is that rare bird in a civil service, the individualist. He, like Napoleon, would wish a visitor to his Department to say, '*Ici administre un homme de bien*'.

(5) *Public Opinion and the Prefect*

In 1950 the Prefectoral Corps celebrated its one hundred and fiftieth anniversary. During this time it has carved a place in French life, and it is surrounded by an aura which is not merely that suspicion which the French feel for their politicians, nor only the reaction they have against officials as such. It is more difficult to describe.

For some the Prefect is the object of envy, for others of distrust; some fear him, a few admire him. No Prefect can hope to end his career as a well-loved and venerable public figure. Nor can he look forward to the day when he will reach the higher ranks of his profession, in possession of great powers, admired by his colleagues and unknown to the public. The Prefect lives in the public eye, and it is a condition of his authority that he should do so.

At no stage of prefectoral history has the Corps been universally admired, respected, esteemed or ignored. The great days of the nineteenth century Prefects still, perhaps unconsciously, enhance their prestige. The excesses, pomp and authoritarianism of those times gave them a colour and status which marked them off from any other type of official, and indeed, from any other state institution. Even during their decline in the first decades of the Third Republic these attributes remained important for the public. The presence of the Prefect at local festivals, agricultural competitions, military ceremonies, fairs, inaugurations, continued to be a *sine qua non* of successful organization. Mocking tongues could, with some truth, regard the Prefect in those days as mainly a social grace for the Department, but the naïve and uneducated still saw in his uniform and presence the stamp of the sovereign Republic, one and indivisible.

With the troubles of the twentieth century a new type of Prefect had to emerge, the Prefect who could administer methodically, and yet could act with speed and assurance in the many social and political emergencies which came upon the country. This brusque assertion of authority and leadership while others remained uncertain, suddenly brought public attention upon them, and the Prefect once again came forward as the natural source of decision in his locality. They were a reserve of effective and decisive action.

Social, economic, industrial and political troubles grew during the period 1936 to 1946 more rapidly than in any previous decade of the century, and the burden on the Prefects grew accordingly. They were saddled with the task of providing what aid and protection they could for the inhabitants of their Department. The result was that they earned the hostility of those who object to administrative control as a new form of paternalism, who object to the discipline of state authority, who object to the loss of opportunity for individual enterprise and personal success. They were pointed at by the Left as the tools of repressive government, and resented by the Right for the economic control they enforced.

Some Prefects can, when challenged, point to the work they have done to benefit the country, and this is one of the reasons why politicians insist that the Corps be kept firmly under control. An active Prefect will run into trouble with the local politicians if he starts a scheme which is worth votes and fails to give the politicians the credit for it.

One of the results of the politicians' demand that the Prefectoral Corps be kept in its place is that wide sections of the French public believe that the Prefects are the Government's paid men, who foster their careers by obliging a politician, put advancement above honour, politics above honesty, and personal relations above the national interest. This is not merely the reaction of ignorant peasants or envious officials; it is held by some of the most eminent legal authorities. Before 1914 M. Jèze and M. Chardon, both highly respected jurists, described the Prefects in terms of scarcely concealed contempt, as electoral agents pure and simple, from whom no reasonable person could expect fair and impartial administration.[1]

Their comments, which had a good basis in fact when applied to the supple political Prefects of the early Third Republic, were re-echoed in 1946 by one of their most eminent professional descendants, M. Waline. He held that the Government was faced with two possible choices regarding the recruitment of Prefects; the first was 'only to place at the head of Prefectures eminent men who had been the object of rigorous selection as the result of examinations and practical tests designed to test their qualities'; the second was 'to consider that the first quality of the Prefect was political suppleness and obedience, and to content itself with people perhaps mediocre from other points of view'. M. Waline held that the governments of the Third Republic had always taken the latter course and ignored character and independence, with the result that between 1940 and 1944 'the greater part of the Republic's Prefects had without hesitation burnt the idol they had adored and zealously served the Government of Vichy'.[2]

An observer must be rather uneasy over M. Waline's point of view. To start with, it is a political Corps, and it can no more than any other branch of life escape the stamp of the politics of the day. His comments probably apply with as much force to the Foreign Service as to the Prefectoral Corps. They probably also apply equally well to senior administrators in the Ministry of Finance, except that the latter take political decisions in private while the Prefects have to accept public responsibility, and live with the population they serve.

M. Waline's view also has too much in it of popular mythology. It fails to recognize the change in the nature of prefectoral administration during the last decades of the Third Republic when there was an important growth in administrative functions, and a marked stability in personnel. And it does not recognize the real dilemma of political officials in time of war and invasion.

But this statement certainly demands attention, not only

[1] See Jèze: *Revue du droit public*, 1912, p. 272, and H. Chardon: *Le pouvoir administratif*, Paris, 1910.

[2] M. Waline: *Manuel de droit administratif*. Paris, 1946. p. 201.

because of the eminence of its author, but also because it is an argument used by other intelligent and liberal minded Frenchmen. There is a feeling that administrative powers which have a political content are not, and cannot be, equitably exercised by officials. The alternative is that they should be exercised by elected representatives of the public; this is an Anglo-Saxon point of view.

A demand for greater local liberties was inserted in the Constitution of 1946 which permitted the grant of special statutes to large towns, and of greater freedom to the *conseil général*. This is justified on valid theoretical grounds: to accept responsibility is an essential phase in developing a civic conscience. Without true responsibility local authorities will thrust off upon the Prefect the onus of unpopular decisions; their reluctance to bear unpopularity will therefore perpetuate the distrust in which local elected authorities are held by the Administration and the Government.

But there may be a close relation between the grant of powers to elected authorities and general conditions of peace and stability in a country over a long period. Should France be entering such a period the question of charters for towns, and of increased local autonomy, will again be seriously discussed. In a peaceful community the officials tend to efface themselves, at least if the community is one in which political instincts are as lively as they are in France.

The French have never known the local autonomy at one time enjoyed in this country; moreover their experience of elected bodies, including the National Assembly itself, has never given them cause for optimism. During the nineteenth century France was far more cautious about decentralization than were the British, and the apogee of local autonomy, expressed in the laws of 1871, 1881 and 1884, still left the Prefects with considerable tutelage and police powers. But whereas the growth of national services in Great Britain has led to drastic centralization, the French have preserved a steadier mean; in France powers can accumulate in the hands of the local Prefect; in Britain powers taken from local authorities pass automatically to a central authority, in default of a localized administrative service of tested competence.

There is a further point. If the demands for social action on a large scale are in some degree to be satisfied, as they have been in this country and as they may one day be in France, the power of the Administration either locally or at the centre will grow. The French may well consider that today the result of abolishing or even modifying the prefectoral system would be greatly to increase not the powers of local elected bodies, nor their local servants, but, as in this country, those of the Ministries. They may well find on consideration that a strong and active Prefectoral Corps is the best way of retaining the zest in local affairs and the virility of local government to which they have been accustomed. The damage inflicted by a few brash, inexperienced or time-serving members of the Prefectoral Corps is likely to be less than that caused by the high-level mediocrity of a distant bureaucratic aristocracy in the capital.

The essence of the French attitude to the Prefectoral Corps is that they endow its members with the vices they themselves possess, and demand from it the virtues that they, as a civic entity, lack. They know that what is lacking in French life is a social conscience and a high standard of political morality. The Prefects are expected to supply these qualities. If they fail to provide this special kind of leadership (and some do) they are branded as incompetent and perhaps dishonest. If they succeed they become the object of personal animosity, for the Frenchman, like others, does not really like the qualities which he knows he lacks.

There is often little understanding of the rôle of authority, and little discrimination between the characters and aims of different Prefects. An eminent Prefect, who has a distinguished resistance record and was deported by the Germans, spoke of the post-war years in these terms: 'C'est pendant les périodes troublées que la masse prit conscience de l'existence des préfets, qui furent dès lors rendus responsable de toutes les difficultés et gênes de leurs administrés. Pris littéralement à la gorge par les nécessités immédiates, nous avons passé de dures années à chercher du verre et des tuiles pour la reconstruction, à approvisioner en farine nos boulangeries, et à collecter, au risque de la pire des impopularités, des denrées pour nos villes.'[1] It conjures up a depressing picture of public lack of balance and discrimination.

And this is shown in many ways. The best scholar in the Corps notes how the public turns to the Prefect 'as formerly one went to the soothsayers'[2]. When a problem appears to be almost insoluble it is taken to the Prefect to resolve, and if he fails to find an answer, or if he resolves it in a way contrary to the aims or interests of the solicitor, 'public vindictiveness denounces the Prefect for inertia or incapacity'.

If the Prefect is efficient or courageous in times of trouble (and not all Prefects are) he is still repaid with public dislike and cordial distrust when peace returns. The real extent of his authority and power are known only to a few. For the remainder the Prefect is believed to have a mysterious reserve of power and influence which can come from no holy source. If he acts rapidly and with decision to overcome a crisis, the extent of his personal effort is unknown to the public which, lacking precise knowledge, prefers to imagine that he has called his hidden powers into play: the ear of powerful politicians, secret service funds, a conscience or two he has bought, inside information of the most confidential kind. He is credited with these mysterious powers when in reality he is using his personal qualities and his experience of men and things.

This pattern of social conduct is not unknown to sociologists. It is the escape from responsibility, the primitive but very real need in a society for a tangible and personal figuration of its difficulties. The Prefect has this personal responsibility projected upon him by the public.

To an observer the Prefectoral Corps at work does not con-

[1] M. Paira: op. cit.

[2] R. Bonnaud-Delamare: *Les pouvoirs du Préfet*. *Revue administrative*, January, 1950.

form to the popular myth of authoritarianism, ruthlessness, manipulation of secret forces, arcane knowledge, and political slipperiness. In real life the balance is much more subtle, the colours are less vivid, the atmosphere is less romantic, there is not that daemonic quality which is the essence of popular myths. An observer might think that the Prefectoral Corps is a body of men of which the French could, with one or two reasonable reservations, be justifiably proud. But, if they were, they would lose one of their country's favourite scapegoats.

Appendix A

ADMINISTRATIVE SERVICES IN EACH DEPARTMENT BY MINISTRY

PRESIDENCY OF THE COUNCIL:
French Radio and Television
Licence office

MINISTRY OF ECONOMIC AFFAIRS:
Economic research service
Research section

MINISTRY OF AGRICULTURE:
Water and Forestry Conservation
Veterinary service
Directorate of Agricultural services
Agricultural technical college
Enforcement office of agricultural laws

MINISTRY OF EX-SERVICEMEN AND WAR VICTIMS:
Office for ex-servicemen

MINISTRY OF NATIONAL EDUCATION:
Departmental Archives
Educational administrative authority

MINISTRY OF FINANCE:
Trésorerie générale
Directorate of Direct Taxation
Directorate of Indirect Taxation
Directorate of state property and land registration

MINISTRY OF THE INTERIOR:
Prefecture
Fire service inspectorate
Police services

MINISTRY OF POSTS AND TELEGRAPHS:
Directorate of postal services

MINISTRY OF RECONSTRUCTION AND HOUSING:
59 departmental or interdepartmental ministerial representatives

MINISTRY OF PUBLIC HEALTH AND POPULATION:
Directorate of Public Health
Directorate of Population

MINISTRY OF LABOUR AND SOCIAL SECURITY:
Directorate of Labour and Employment

MINISTRY OF PUBLIC WORKS AND TRANSPORT:
Highways and Bridges department

Appendix B

REGIONAL AREAS OF ADMINISTRATION BY MINISTRY

PRESIDENCY OF THE COUNCIL:
FRENCH RADIO AND TELEVISION:
    1 Regional directorate for Paris.
    9 Regional directorates: Lille, Nancy, Strasburg, Lyons, Marseilles, Toulouse, Bordeaux, Limoges, Rennes.

MINISTRY OF ECONOMIC AFFAIRS:
NATIONAL INSTITUTE OF STATISTICS AND ECONOMIC STUDIES:
    18 Regional Directorates: Bordeaux, Clermont-Ferrand, Dijon, Lille, Limoges, Lyons, Marseilles, Montpellier, Nancy, Nantes, Orleans, Paris, Poitiers, Rheims, Rennes, Rouen, Strasburg, Toulouse.

MINISTRY OF AGRICULTURE:
WATER AND FORESTRY CONSERVATION:
    41 Conservancy Boards: Lille, Rouen, Compiègne, Mézières, Bar-le-Duc, Nancy, Metz, Strasburg, Alençon, Paris, Rennes, Le Mans, Orleans, Troyes, Chaumont, Epinal, Colmar, Dijon, Vésoul, Besançon, Lons-le-Saunier, Niort, Limoges, Bourges, Lyons, Annécy, Clermont-Ferrand, Valence, Grenoble, Chambéry, Gap, Bordeaux, Pau, Toulouse, Carcassone, Montpellier, Nîmes, Aix-en-Provence, Digne, Nice, Ajaccio.

RURAL ENGINEERING:
    61 administrative areas.

INSPECTORATE GENERAL OF AGRICULTURE:
    11 inspecting areas.

AGRICULTURAL PRODUCTION:
    5 areas for stud farms.
    12 areas of the service for the protection of plant life: Angers, Beaune, Bordeaux, Clermont-Ferrand, Lyons, Marseilles, Montpellier, Paris, Rheims, Rennes, Strasburg, Toulouse.

AGRICULTURAL EDUCATION:
(i) Higher education:
    National Agronomic Institute at Paris.
    3 National Schools of Agriculture:
        Grignon, Rennes, Montpellier.
    National School of Agricultural Economics at Rennes.

National School of Horticulture at Versailles.
National School of Agricultural Industry at Paris.
(ii) Lower education:
9 regional Schools of Agriculture.
18 Schools of Agriculture.
14 specialized schools.

ENFORCEMENT OF AGRICULTURAL LAWS:
16 enforcement offices: Bordeaux, Clermont-Ferrand, Dijon, Lille, Limoges, Lyons, Marseilles, Montpellier, Nancy, Nantes, Orleans, Paris, Rennes, Rouen, Strasburg, Toulouse.

REPRESSION OF FRAUDS:
12 regional divisions.

NATIONAL OFFICE OF CEREAL PRODUCTION:
13 regional offices: Bordeaux, Clermont-Ferrand, Dijon, Lille, Lyons, Marseilles, Nancy, Nantes, Orleans, Paris, Poitiers, Rouen, Toulouse.

MINISTRY OF EX-SERVICEMEN AND WAR VICTIMS
21 Interdepartmental services.
20 Training centres (Rehabilitation).
12 Training centres (Appliances).

MINISTRY OF NATIONAL DEFENCE AND ARMED FORCES:
9 Military Regions: Paris, Lille, Rennes, Bordeaux, Toulouse, Metz, Dijon, Lyons, Marseilles.
3 Naval regions: Cherburg, Brest, Toulon.
4 Air Regions: Dijon, Paris, Bordeaux, Aix.

MINISTRY OF NATIONAL EDUCATION:
16 Academic regions: Paris, Aix-en-Provence, Besançon, Bordeaux, Caen, Clermont-Ferrand, Dijon, Grenoble, Lille, Lyons, Montpellier, Nancy, Poitiers, Rennes, Strasburg, Toulouse.

MINISTRY OF FINANCE:
CUSTOMS:
28 areas of investigation.
TOBACCO MONOPOLY:
20 Tobacco manufacturing plants.
7 Match producing plants.
9 Directorates of tobacco production.
LABORATORIES:
13 regional laboratories.

MINISTRY OF INDUSTRY AND POWER:
MINERALOGY:
14 regions: Bordeaux, Clermont-Ferrand, Dijon, Douai, Lyons, Marseilles, Metz, Montpellier, Nantes, Paris, Rouen, Saint-Quentin, Strasburg, Toulouse.
ELECTRICITY:
6 regional areas: Paris, Dijon, Nantes, Limoges, Toulouse, Grenoble.
WEIGHTS AND MEASURES:
10 regional areas: Paris, Dijon, Rouen, Lille, Nancy, Lyons, Marseilles, Toulouse, Bordeaux, Nantes.
10 REGIONAL REPRESENTATIVES OF MINISTRY:
Bordeaux, Lille, Limoges, Lyons, Marseilles, Nancy, Nantes, Rouen, Strasburg, Paris.

MINISTRY OF THE INTERIOR:
9 ADMINISTRATIVE REGIONS (IGAME):
Paris, Lille, Rennes, Bordeaux, Metz, Toulouse, Dijon, Lyons, Marseilles.
POLICE:
6 regions of the DST.
17 regions of Judicial Police.

MINISTRY OF JUSTICE:
COURTS:
27 Cours d'Appel: Agen, Aix, Amiens, Angers, Bastia, Besançon, Bordeaux, Bourges, Caen, Chambéry, Colmar, Dijon, Douai, Grenoble, Limoges, Lyons, Montpellier, Nancy, Nîmes, Orleans, Paris, Pau, Poitiers, Rennes, Riom, Rouen, Toulouse.
PRISONS:
9 prison regions: Bordeaux, Dijon, Lille, Lyons, Marseilles, Paris, Rennes, Strasburg, Toulouse.

MINISTRY OF POSTS AND TELEGRAPHS:
POSTAL SERVICES:
17 regional directorates: Bordeaux, Chalons-sur-Marne, Clermont-Ferrand, Dijon, Lille, Lyons, Marseilles, Montpellier, Nancy, Nantes, Orleans, Paris, Poitiers, Rennes, Rouen, Strasburg, Toulouse.
TELECOMMUNICATIONS:
17 regional directorates (as above).
POSTAL CHEQUES:
18 Accounting centres: as above plus Bastia.

MINISTRY OF RECONSTRUCTION AND HOUSING:
- 59 interdepartmental or departmental ministerial representatives.

MINISTRY OF PUBLIC HEALTH AND POPULATION:
PUBLIC HEALTH:
- 16 regions of public health: Paris, Bordeaux, Clermont-Ferrand, Dijon, Lille, Limoges, Lyons, Marseilles, Montpellier, Nancy, Nantes, Orleans, Rennes, Rouen, Strasbourg, Toulouse.

WELFARE:
- 14 National Welfare Institutes.

MINISTRY OF LABOUR AND SOCIAL SECURITY:
LABOUR:
- 14 divisional inspectorates of Labour and Employment: Dijon, Nancy, Lille, Nantes, Bordeaux, Toulouse, Montpellier, Marseilles, Lyons, Limoges, Strasbourg, plus 3 in Paris.

SOCIAL SECURITY:
- 16 regional directorates: Bordeaux, Clermont-Ferrand, Dijon, Lille, Limoges, Lyons, Marseilles, Montpellier, Nancy, Nantes, Orleans, Paris, Rennes, Rouen, Strasbourg, Toulouse.
- 16 regional Funds for Family Allowances: as above.

MINISTRY OF PUBLIC WORKS AND TRANSPORT:
HIGHWAYS AND BRIDGES:
- 27 inspecting areas.

NAVIGATION:
- 10 regional directorates: Paris, Compiègne, Lille, Rouen, Nancy, Nevers, Lyons, Nantes, Toulouse, Strasbourg.
- 59 chartering bureaux and exchanges.

MINISTRY OF MERCANTILE MARINE:
- 5 directorates of Naval Fleet Reserve: Le Havre, Saint-Servan, Nantes, Bordeaux, Marseilles.

BIBLIOGRAPHY

I have not attempted to prepare a complete bibliography, as so much has already been done by M. Doueil, whose book includes an exhaustive list of press and review articles about prefectoral and local administration published in the last decade, and by M. Henry, who gives an interesting bibliography of memoirs and biographies of nineteenth century Prefects. It may, however, be of some service to note the particulars of works which I have used and which are not included in these earlier bibliographies. I exclude only well-known text-books in the field of administrative law such as those of Duguit, Jèze, and Waline. These are indispensable for reference, and in addition a good deal can be learnt from them in discerning the changing attitudes of well-informed men towards the Prefectoral Corps over a long period of time.

Periodicals

L'ANNÉE POLITIQUE: *Revue chronologique des principaux faits politiques, économiques et sociaux de la France.* First published 1874–1906. Now annually since 1945. Paris, Presses Universitaires de France.

BULLETIN D'INFORMATION de l'Association du Corps préfectoral et des administrateurs civils du Ministère de l'Intérieur. Charleville, monthly.

BULLETIN OFFICIEL du Ministère de l'Intérieur. Paris, Dupont, monthly.

REVUE ADMINISTRATIVE. Paris, Sirey, 1948 onwards, bi-monthly.

REVUE DES COLLECTIVITÉS LOCALES, Paris, Les Presses de la Seine.

REVUE DU DROIT PUBLIC et de la Science Politique en France et à l'étranger. Paris, Librairie générale de Droit et de Jurisprudence. Quarterly.

LA VIE COMMUNALE ET DÉPARTEMENTALE. Paris, monthly.

Official Documents and Texts

ANNUAIRE DU CORPS PRÉFECTORAL ET DE L'ADMINISTRATION CENTRALE. Paris, Charles-Lavauzelle.

CODE ADMINISTRATIF. Paris, Dalloz, 1950.

ÉCOLE NATIONALE D'ADMINISTRATION: *Concours d'entrée et scolarité.* Paris, Imprimerie Nationale, 1950.

INSPECTION GÉNÉRALE DE L'ADMINISTRATION: *Rapport présenté par l'Inspection Générale pour l'organisation et le personnel des préfectures départementales.* Melun, 1942.

INSPECTION GÉNÉRALE DE L'ADMINISTRATION: *Rapport présenté par l'Inspection Générale. Tome I: sur la réforme des finances locales. Tome II: sur l'organisation et les effectifs des préfectures.* 1950–1.

J. LAFERRIÈRE: *Le nouveau droit public de la France. Recueil méthodique des textes constitutionnels et administratifs.* Paris, Sirey, 1941.

LOI DU 10 AOÛT, 1871: annotated by R. Bonnaud Delamare. Niort, 1950.

MINISTÈRE DE L'INTÉRIEUR: *Administration Centrale et Corps préfectoral.* Paris, 1952–3.

MINISTÈRE DE L'INTÉRIEUR: *Recrutement des chefs de cabinet de préfet.*
Boulogne-sur-Seine, 1952.
MINISTÈRE DE L'INTÉRIEUR: *Statut particulier du Corps préfectoral.* Paris, 1951.
RECUEIL DES ARRÊTS DU CONSEIL D'ÉTAT statuant au contentieux etc. Collection Lebrun et Panhard. Paris, Sirey.
STATUT GÉNÉRAL DES FONCTIONNAIRES. *Recueil des textes et documents relatifs à l'application de la loi.* Editions de la Documentation française. 1950.

Special Studies

Intendants
ARBOIS DE JUBAINVILLE d': *L'Administration des Intendants.* Paris, Champion, 1879.
FR. OLIVIER MARTIN: *Précis d'Histoire du Droit français.* Paris, Dalloz, 1945.
E. PELLETIER: *L'Intendant Mégret d'Étigny.* Toulouse, 1951.
E. PERROT: *Les institutions publiques et privées de l'Ancienne France jusqu'en 1789.* Paris, Sirey, 1935.

History
ASSOCIATION DU CORPS PRÉFECTORAL: *Les préfets dans l'Histoire. Cent cinquantennaire de la loi de pluviôse, An VIII.* Paris, 1950.
F-A. AULARD ed.: *L'Etat de la France en l'An VIII et en l'An IX.* Paris, 1897.
C. BRAIBANT: *Les préfets dans l'histoire. Cahiers français d'Information, No. 158.* June 1950.
E. DEJEAN: *Un préfet sous le Consulat, Jacques Claude Beugnot.* Paris, Plon, 1907.
J. GODECHOT: *Les Institutions de la France sous la Révolution et l'Empire.* Paris, 1951.
G. HAUSSMANN: *Mémoires.* 3 volumes. Paris, 1892.
P. HENRY: *Histoire des Préfets.* Paris, Nouvelles Editions Latines, 1950.
R. MILLET: *La France provinciale: vie sociale, moeurs administratives.* Paris, 1888.
J. REGNIER: *Les Préfets du Consulat et de l'Empire.* Paris, Ficker, 1913.
THE AUTHOR OF 'THE MEMBER FOR PARIS': *French pictures in English chalk.* London, Smith, Elder, 1876.

Administration
E. ALQUIER: *Le pouvoir de substitution du préfet au maire. Étude historique et critique de droit administratif.* Thesis, Toulouse, 1906.
J. BARADAT: *L'organisation d'une préfecture.* Thesis, Toulouse, 1907.
A. BONHOMME: *Fonctionnaires et agents des préfectures.* Thesis, Toulouse, 1943.
R. BONNAUD DELAMARE: *Attributions juridiques des préfets et sous-préfets.* Monte Carlo, Editions du Livre, 1951.

H. CHARDON: *L'Administration de la France*. Paris, Perrin, 1908.
J. DELBOUSQUET: *De l'organisation des administrations centrales des divers Ministères, des droits et des devoirs des employés*. Paris, Hingray, 1843.
P. DOUEIL: *L'Administration locale à l'épreuve de la guerre, 1939–49*. Paris, Sirey, 1950.
G. DUFOUR: *L'Administration française en 1883*. Paris, Chevalier-Marescq, 1883.
J. GANDOUIN: *La constitution et la réforme de l'organisation départementale et communale*. Thesis, Paris, 1950.
G. LE BRETON: *Du pouvoir règlementaire des préfets*. Thesis, Paris, 1900.
LOMBARD: *Le rôle financier du Préfet*. Thesis, Paris, 1937.
R. NESTOR: *Le contrôle du préfet sur l'administration communale*. Paris, Les Presses Modernes, 1931.
J. ROY: *L'administration intercommunale: le problème des petites communes*. Thesis, Bordeaux, 1944.
M. TRIAND: *Le statut du personnel des préfectures*. Thesis, Poitiers, 1947.

Police

P. CHEMINEAU: *Étude de l'organisation administrative de la police en France*. Thesis, Toulouse, 1944.
G. DILHAC: *Les pouvoirs de police judiciaires d'instruction préparatoire des préfets. Article 10 du Code d'Instruction Criminelle*. Thesis, Rennes, 1937.
M. ENGLINGER: *L'organisation de la police administrative dans les villes à police d'État*. Thesis, Strasburg, 1938.
P. LANTECAZE: *Les pouvoirs de police judiciaire des préfets. Article 10 du Code d'Instruction Criminelle*. Thesis, Bordeaux, 1938.
J. MARIZIS: *Les pouvoirs judiciaires des préfets et l'Article 10 du Code d'Instruction Criminelle*. Thesis, Paris, 1913–14.
H. ROTH: *L'organisation de la police d'État en France*. Thesis, Lyons, 1943.

Regions

J. BANCAL: *Origine et avenir des circonscriptions administratives de la France*. Paris, Sirey, 1945.
M. BRUN: *Départements et Régions*. Paris, Presses Modernes, 1939.
F-L. CLOSON: *La région, cadre d'un gouvernement moderne*. Paris, Berger-Levrault, 1947.
M-H. FABRE: *Les pouvoirs du commissaire régional de la République. Étude théorique et pratique de l'Ordonnance du 10 janvier 1944*. Annales, Faculté de Droit, Aix. 1944.
P. GAY: *Le préfet régional*. Paris, Sirey, 1942.
J. LEGRAND: *Les essais d'administration régionale*. Thesis, Paris, 1950.
H. ROQUELPO: *Régions et préfectures régionales*. Thesis, Paris, 1944.

Sub Prefects

A. ALFRED: *La réforme administrative et les secrétaires généraux de préfecture.* Nancy, Berger-Levrault, 1908.

E. ARNAUD: *Le rôle du sous-préfet dans une democratie.* Paris, Berger-Levrault, 1907.

A. BLUZET: *Les attributions des sous-préfets.* Thesis, Paris, 1927.

P. GUERRINI: *Origines et pouvoirs du secrétaire général de prefecture.* Thesis, Lyons, 1938.

V. HOUSSAYE: *Sous-préfets et sous-préfectures: Institution et moeurs administratives.* Paris, Dupont, 1874.

P. RIX: *Le secrétaire général de préfecture.* Thesis, Toulouse, 1938.

M. SIBRA: *La sous-préfecture.* Montauban, 1911.

P. VACQUIER: *La suppression des sous-préfets.* Thesis, Paris, 1922.

INDEX

Administrateurs civils, 62–4, 79, 81, 82, 91, 92, 94
Administrative system, 66–8, 74, 83–5, 121, 122, 124–8, 130–2, 141
Algeria, 41, 42, 95
Alsace-Lorraine, 48, 49, 221–2
Andorra, 149
Army, 30, 31, 38, 42, 51–2, 68, 137, 179–80, 207–8
Arrondissement, 12, 19, 21, 42, 48, 74, 91, 94–103, 106, 108–10, 119, 124

Basques, 222
Baylot, Jean, 155–6, 187
Belfort, 48
Bloc national, 53
Bonaparte, Lucien, 19, 23, 26
Bourgeois, 112
Budget, communal, 104–11
Budget, departmental, 45, 214–7
Bureaux, of Prefecture, 20, 74, 83–5, 121, 122, 123, 124–32

Cabinet, of Minister, 204
Cabinet, of Prefect, 83, 84, chapter III passim, 123, 132
Cambacérès, 18, 23
Cambon, Paul, 42, 49
Cambon, Jules, 42, 53
Carey, 25
Cartel des gauches, 53
Casimir Périer, 35
Castellane, 31
Centres Administratifs et techniques interdépartementaux (CATI), 138–43

Centres administratifs interdépartementaux de police (CAIP), 137, 138
Chaptal, 22
Chef de cabinet, 75, chapter III passim, 92, 123, 132
Chiappe, Angelo, 54
Church and State relations, 29, 51, 160–1, 197, 207–8, 210–11
Clemenceau, Georges, 50–2, 224
Code d'Instruction Criminelle, 184–6
Comité central d'enquête sur le coût et le rendement des services publiques, 172
Commissaires, of the Revolution, 16
Commissaires de la République, 1848, 32
Commissaires de la République, 1919, 48
Commissaires de la République, 1944, 58, 60, 61, 136
Commissaires de police, 88, 116, 134, 177, 178, 180
Commissaires généraux de police, 26
Commission départementale, 214, 216–7
Commission départementale des opérations immobilières, 192
Commissions mixtes, 38
Commission syndicale, 104
Committee of Public Safety, 16
Communes, 19, 72, 74, 98–101, 104–5, 106, 107, 109, 110, 114, 208–13, 225–6
Communications, 122–3, 129–30, 177, 184
Compagnies républicaines de sécurité, 136, 137, 139, 142–3, 179, 180
Conseil d'arrondissement, 20, 103

Conseil départemental de l'enseignement primaire, 192
Conseil de préfecture, 20, 21, 22, 115
Conseil d'Etat, 67, 81, 184, 187, 188
Conseil général, 20–1, 27, 44, 45, 56, 72, 124, 165, 201, 209, 212–7
Conseil général, chairman of, 174–7
Conseil municipal, 19, 45, 103, 105, 107–12, 115, 116, 188, 208
Constituent Assembly, 1789, 13–5
Constituent Assembly, 1848, 41
Constitution, 1946, 62, 67, 69, 72, 164, 174–6, 230
Contrôleur général de police, 139, 142
Cossé-Brissac, 31
Cour des Comptes, 67, 81

Daunou, 18, 22
De Fourtou, 39
De Gaulle, 58, 60
Departments, 14–5, 19, 25, 29, 42, 47, 48–50, 68, 72, 74, 95–6, 147–8, 161, 174–7, 209, 212–7
Deputies and Senators, 35, 44, 49–51, 53–4, 98, 100, 149, 157–161, 200–6, 208, 212–3
Dieu, 42
Directeur du cabinet, 75, 91, 94–5, 97
Directory, 16
District, 14, 15
Divisions, of a prefecture, 74, 83, 121, 122, 123, 124–32
Dufaure, 39

Ecole libre des sciences politiques, 63, 77
Ecole nationale d'administration, 63, 79–83
Electoral practices, 33, 34–6, 44, 114–5, 204, 206

Federalism, 14
Ferry, Jules, 42
Fouché, 16, 19
Freemasonry, 160–1
Fromant, 34

Gambetta, 12
Garde champêtre, 73, 104, 134, 190
Garde mobile, 135, 136, 142–3, 180
Gendarmerie, 135, 137, 179, 180
Généralité, 12
Groupes mobiles de réserve, 136

Haag, Paul, 155, 186–8
Haussmann, 40–1, 43, 102
Honours, 86–7

Inspecteur d'académie, 68, 166
Inspecteur du génie rural, 93, 110, 170
Inspecteurs des ponts et chaussées, 68
Inspecteur général de l'administration, 81, 83, 124–7, 143, 172
Inspecteur général de l'administration en mission extraordinaire, 61–2, 127, 137, 140–3, 146, 160, 179–80, 186
Instituteurs, 37, 46, 47, 110, 166
Instructions, to Prefects, 26, 27, 35, 36, 56, 187, 198
Intendants, ancien régime, 11–3, 17, 22
Intendant for economic affairs, 57–8
Intendant of police, 57, 135–6

Jessaint, 43
Judicial police, 134, 135, 136, 138–9
Junot, 30

Lamoignon de Basville, 13 (FN)
La Terme, 41
Lebrun, 18, 23
Ledru Rollin, 32

INDEX

Letter of Service, of the IGAME, 61–2, 180
Lépine, 148
Liberation, 58–64, 153–4

Mairie, 102, 108, 112
Mayors, 19, 28, 37, 45, 56, 98, 100, 102, 103, 106, 107, 109–12, 115, 116, 124, 134–5, 173, 188–91, 210, 211
Marseilles, 180, 186
Mégret d'Etigny, 13 (FN)
Méchin, 25
Minister for Algeria, 42
Minister of the Interior, 19, 30, 35, 39, 50–3, 61, 69–70, 91, 142–3, 159–61, 167, 174, 196, 198, 200, 204
Ministry of Agriculture, 70, 167, 170, 181
Ministerial services, 47, 56, 57, 66, 67, 68, 166 seq., Appendices A and B
Ministry of Defence, 68
Ministry of Education, 68, 70, 182, 192
Ministry of Finance, 68
Ministry of Industry and Commerce, 181, 182
Ministry of the Interior, 19, 42, 44, 68, 80, 81, 82, 89, 117, 160–1, 170, 182, 192
Ministry of Labour, 70, 182
Ministry of Police, 19
Ministry of Public Health, 171, 181, 182
Ministry of Public Works, 68, 70, 181, 182
Moch, Jules, 61
Molé, 25, 31
Moulin, Jean, 56

Napoleon I, 16, 17–32
Napoleon III, 37, 38
Nice, 41, 42
North Africans, 222–3

Officials, general, 37, 42, 43, 46, 47, 56, 62, 63, 69, 72–5, 151, 166–73, 181, 204, 206–8, 230–1
Officials, of the prefecture, 20, 73, 101, 102, 122, 123–32
Ordinances, 181–3, 188–9
Overseas territories, 41, 70, 74, 95–6, 145–6, 204

Paris, 39–40, 94–5, 134, 155–6, 180, 187, 223
Percepteur, 93, 110, 114
Persigny, 35
Pétain, 55
Poincaré, 98, 104
Police, 12, 19, 28, 36–8, 50, 56, 57, 61–2, 74, 115–6, 133–43, 177–81, 185, 188–90
Political attitudes, 32, 35, 54–7, 61, 98–101, 112, 116, 119, 128–9, 157–8, 161–2, 173, 175, 196–8, 200–6, 210–11, 219, 228–233
Prefect, age of, 24–5, 96–7, 146–7
appointment as, 23–4, 50–3, 58–60, 63–4, 151, 163
and the army, 30–1, 38, 51–2, 179–80, 207–8
and the Church, 29, 51, 160–1, 207–8
and the Communes, 28, 37, 45–6, 56, 72, 107, 109, 111, 115, 188–91, 208–13, 225
and the Department, 20–1, 44–6, 72, 174–7, 213–9
and elections, 33–9, 45, 204–6
and the Judiciary, 183–8
opposition to, 22, 62, 227–33

and other officials, 33, 37, 47–8, 69–71, 72–3, 165–73, 206–8
outside France, 29–30, 41–2, 48–9, 145, 163
and politics, 27–8, 33–9, 43–6, 49–54, 55, 57, 152, 163, 198–206, 223–6
posts of, 24, 26, 144–8
powers of, 20–3, 44–8, 54–5, 60–1, 67–74, 107, 115, 116–20, 133–5, 163 seq., 177 seq.
and Prefecture, 20, 47–8, 74, 122 seq.
and press, 36–7, 119, 139, 224
rights of, 75, 149–51
status of, 30, 69–72, 144–51, 163–5
(See also under *Commissaires de la République*, IGAME, Ministries, Police, Region)
Prefect of Police, 26, 138, 145, 146, 148, 149, 153–4, 160, 180
Prefect of the Seine, 29, 41, 145, 146, 149, 153, 154, 160
Prefecture, 20, 29, 47, 74, 83–6, 121–32
Press, 36–7, 119, 139, 224
Pressure groups, 217–23
Railways, 68, 89
Rambuteau, 39–40
Recueil des actes administratifs, 177
Recteur de l'Académie, 68
Regionalism, 57–8, 135–6, 167. (See also IGAME)

Renseignements généraux, 89, 135, 136, 139, 179, 205
Reports, 88, 117–8, 119
Resistance, 56, 58–60, 153
Roederer, 21

Savoy, 41, 42
Secretary General of Police, 62, 96, 133–43, 178
Secretary General of the Prefecture, 20, 23, 25, 75, 83, 94–5, 121–33
Senators, see Deputies
Siéyès, 14, 18
State Advocate, 184, 185
State of siege, 180
Statute of the Prefectoral Corps, 63–4, 79, 92–3, 151–2
Sub délégués, 12, 22
Sub Prefects, 12, 19–20, 23, 25, 29, 32, 34, 35, 41, 43, 60, 62, 63, 74, 75, 82, 83, Chapter IV passim, 146, 147, 190, 191, 205
Sûreté Nationale, 61, 68, 135–9, 203
Surveillance du territoire, 138, 170

Talleyrand, 13 (FN), 23
Thouret, 14
Tobacco monopoly, 68
Tour du Pin, de la, 31
Trésorier payeur général, 68, 114, 171
Tribunate, discussions in, 21–2
Tutelage, 71, 72, 103–11, 124, 188–91, 193, 215

Waline, 229–30

GEORGE ALLEN & UNWIN LTD
London: 40 Museum Street, W.C.1

*Auckland: Haddon Hall, City Road
Sydney, N.S.W.: Bradbury House, 55 York Street
Cape Town: 58–60 Long Street
Bombay: 15 Graham Road, Ballard Estate, Bombay 1
Calcutta: 17 Chittaranjan Avenue, Calcutta 13
New Delhi: 13–14 Ajmere Gate Extension, New Delhi 1
Karachi: Haroon Chambers, South Napier Road, Karachi 2
Toronto: 91 Wellington Street West
Sao Paulo: Avenida 9 de Julho 11388–Ap. 51*

Introduction to French Local Government

BRIAN CHAPMAN   *Demy* 8vo   18s. *net*

'A valuable contribution to the literature of his subject.... The reader with an interest in the subject will find that his facts are skilfully concise.' *Liverpool Daily Post*

'Mr Chapman has produced an admirable, clear and readable study. The structure of the "Communes" and "Départements" and the functions of the Mayor, Councils and Prefects are lucidly explained.' *Time & Tide*

'The first post-war study of his subject in either English or French.' *The Economist*

Great Cities of the World

Edited by WILLIAM A. ROBSON   *Sm. Roy.* 8vo   About 50s net

In a series of comparable studies, by experts from the cities dealt with, a full picture is given of the organization and government of many of the great cities of the world. Social, political and administrative problems are examined and an attempt is made to show how far they are similar and what general conclusions can be drawn. The problems associated with the over-spilling of population, with planning, and with the relative force of the 'democratic' element as compared with the 'efficiency' element in administration are of very widespread interest and are therefore fully discussed. The cities dealt with are Amsterdam, Bombay, Buenos Aires, Calcutta, Chicago, Copenhagen, London, Los Angeles, Manchester, Montreal, Moscow, New York, Paris, Rio de Janeiro, Rome, Stockholm, Sydney, Toronto, Wellington, and Zürich.

GEORGE ALLEN AND UNWIN LTD